REGIONS IN CENTRAL EUROPE

Central European Studies
Charles W. Ingrao, General Editor

Regions in Central Europe
The Legacy of History

SVEN TÄGIL *editor*
KRISTIAN GERNER
TOM GULLBERG
RUNE JOHANSSON
LISBETH LINDEBORG
FREDRIK LINDSTRÖM
HANS-ÅKE PERSSON

Purdue University Press
West Lafayette, Indiana

This work has been sponsored by the Erik Philip-Sörensen Foundation and the Swedish Council for Research in the Humanities and Social Sciences (HFSR).
Translated from the Swedish by Jasmine Aimaq
Maps drawn by Tomas Tägil
Assistant Editor: Fredrik Lindström

First U.S. edition 1999
Copyright © 1999 by Sven Tägil. All rights reserved.
Published under license from C. Hurst & Co. (Publishers) Ltd., London
This edition available only in the United States and Canada.
Printed in Malaysia

03 02 01 00 99   5 4 3 2 1

Library of Congress Cataloging-in-Publication Data
Regions in Central Europe/edited by Sven Tägil. —
 1st U.S. ed.
   p. cm.—(Central European studies)
 Includes bibliographical references (p.) and index.
 ISBN 1-55753-185-4. —ISBN 1-55753-186-2 (pbk.)
 1. Europe, Central—History. 2. Regionalism—Europe, Central.
 I. Tägil, Sven. II. Series.
 DAW1038.R44 1999
 943 —dc21   99-31902
                                                        CIP

CONTENTS

Editor's Preface	page xi
The Co-Authors	xvi

PART ONE

The Impact of Imagination: History, Territoriality and Perceived Affinity RUNE JOHANSSON 1

Territoriality and the Possession of Territory	1
The Region as Function and Feeling	4
Identities as Constructions and 'Reality'	7
Territoriality, Ethnicity and Nationality	11
Identities in Early History	17
Modernisation and Identity Construction	21
Territoriality and Identity: Conclusion	26

PART TWO

The Roots of Identity: Territoriality in Early Central European History SVEN TÄGIL 30

Romans and Germanic Peoples	32
People and Territory in the Ancient Germanic World	36
Central Power and the Stem in Feudal Society	37
The Stem Duchies	41
– Saxony	41
– Thuringia	42
– Franconia	43
– Swabia	43
– Frisia	43
The Border Area between France and Germany	44

Germanic Peoples and Slavs	46
– Bavaria	48
– The Magyars	48
The Stem Duchies in the German integration process	48
The medieval legacy?	50

Regional Deep Structures in the German Cultural
Space   LISBETH LINDEBORG   53

Introduction	53
Defining the German Cultural Space	59
From Germanic Tribes to German Bundesländer and Regions: A Historical Overview	62
From 1933 to 1945	80
Federalism and Regionalisation in Germany after 1945	82
Regions in West Germany	85
Regions in East Germany	93
German Regions on the Eve of the 21st Century: the Significance of Deep Structures for Regional Development	97
Regional Diversity: Baden-Württemberg	99
– Württemberg	101
– Baden	105
– Baden-Württemberg	110

PART THREE

Region, Cultural Identity and Politics in the Late
Habsburg Monarchy   FREDRIK LINDSTRÖM   115

Region and Cultural Identity in a Long-Term Perspective	117
– Bohemia and Moravia	118
– Hungary and Transylvania	120
– Austrian Integration and De-integration	122
Place and Cultural Identity in the Nineteenth Century	124
– Bohemia and Moravia	124
– Hungary and Transylvania	128
The Region and National Space	129
– Bohemia and Moravia	130
– Hungary and Transylvania	137
Conclusions	144

The Primacy of the Nation and Regional Identity:
Carinthia, Burgenland and State-Formation after the
Dissolution of the Dynastic System   TOM GULLBERG   147

   Introduction   147
   The Historical Region as an Analytical Instrument   151
   Carinthia: From Duchy to Bundesland   154
   The Tradition of Independence   157
   The National Histories   158
   The Political Dilemma of the Slovene National Identity   162
   From Comitate to Bundesland: Burgenland   165
   The Austrification of Western Hungary   170
   An Austrian Necessity   173
   Regional Identities and the Nation-State   175

PART FOUR

Regions in Central Europe under Communism:
A Palimpsest   KRISTIAN GERNER   178

   The Concept of Region   178
   Parameters for Regions in Central Europe   183
   The Soviet Imprint   186
   Historical Parameters   188
   Traces in the Palimpsest   190
      – Transylvania   191
      – Moravia-Silesia   197
      – Silesia   200
      – The Vilna area   203
      – Carpatho-Ruthenia   204
      – The Kaliningrad Oblast   205
   Conclusions   207

Viadrina to the Oder–Neisse Line: Historical Evolution
and Regional Cooperation   HANS-ÅKE PERSSON   211

   The Region as Project   212
   – The West European Model   214
   The River System in the Borderland during the Age of
      Nationalism   216
   The Borderland and the Resurrected Polish State   220

– *Silesia: a Historical Region* 221
War, Migration and Territorial Revisions 225
– *Soviet Security Policy, Poland's Western Boundary and
  Ethnic Cleansing* 228
*The Oder Region, Pax Sovietica and the 'Peace-Frontier':
  the First Post-war Transformation Process* 231
– *Ethno-demographic Changes and the Settlers* 233
– *Expelled Persons, Integration into the German States
  and the Dream of 'die alte Heimat' East of the Boundary* 237
– *The Construction of Socialist Society in the Border Area* 241
– *Regional Cooperation in the Borderland* 244
*The Collapse of Communism and West European
  Integration: the Second Post-war Transformation Phase* 247
– *Deutsch-polnischer Grenzraum: a Post-Communist
  Modernisation Project* 248
The Borderland: Past, Present and Future 252

Index 259

MAPS

Central Europe, end of 1990s	x
The Empire of Charlemagne, 814	35
Germany at the beginning of the 10th century	40
Germany, 1991	55
South Western Germany, 1815-1945	100
The Austro-Hungarian Empire, 1867-1918	114
Linguistic Groups in the Austro-Hungarian Empire, 1900	124
The Republic of Austria	152
Ethnic Minorities of Carinthia and Burgenland	166
Eastern Central Europe	191
Territories ceded to Poland and the USSR after 1945	232
The 'Euroregion' along the Polish-German border	250

EDITOR'S PREFACE

Today's European Union (EU) can be described as a far-reaching project designed to transform the continent. Peace, coordination and cohesion are to supersede Europe's traditional characteristics of discord and division. Throughout history, however, efforts to integrate the continent have all ultimately capitulated to the forces of dissolution. During the Middle Ages the empire of Charlemagne, the Ottonian German realm and the papal endeavours to establish supremacy over the western Christian world each met the same fate. During the sixteenth century the House of Habsburg appears to have had the possibility of crystallising a central power with control over much of Europe. However, already by the end of that century it was evident that disintegration had again prevailed.

Subsequent attempts to restructure and unify the continent by force have also failed. At the beginning of the nineteenth century, Napoleon Bonaparte's plans to consolidate Europe under the rule of France were thwarted due to popular resistance, combined with the surge of national movements in many parts of the continent. The Nazi vision of a united Europe, embodied by Hitler and founded on extreme ideological and racial principles, was also shattered, after bringing unparallelled suffering to the peoples it sought to enslave.

Thus, while particularist tendencies have emerged in diverse forms throughout history, they have invariably proved more potent than the integrative forces. Multiplicity and fragmentation make up the dominant pattern of European history. Hitherto the EU has appeared more successful in several respects. After the relatively sluggish pace of integration in the first postwar decades, the European community on the threshold of the twenty-first century is confronted with a number of organisational and political questions that must be resolved. The debate on the future of Europe involves three main alternative visions, each with its own advocates and supporters. In simplified terms these may be labelled the United

States of Europe, the Europe of the States, and the Europe of the Regions.

The first notion presupposes that the integration process will progress and the supranational structure be strengthened at the expense of the nation-state, as an ever greater number of spheres of authority are transferred to the supranational apparatus. Those who adhere to the second model, the Europe of the States, maintain that the EU is composed of traditional territorial states that will largely continue to lead the development. The EU will thus be a league of sovereign states. The third vision, the Europe of the Regions, conceives of the region as both a traditional base and a springboard for individual involvement and activity. As the state appears ever more remote and thus unable to solve local problems, the region emerges as an increasingly attractive forum. In certain parts of Europe, particularly areas characterised by a distinct historical tradition and cultural affinity, regional identity poses a challenge to the cohesion of the state and in some cases threatens its very existence. The three alternatives highlight different trends that are all discernible in today's Europe. But to what degree are they mutually exclusive? Are combinations and intermediate forms more likely than the realisation of only one of these models? In a historical perspective it is more fruitful to view the three tendencies as concurrent, interwoven phenomena, where the continuous movement between integration and disintegration has steadily generated new forms of territorial organisation and identity.

The most prominent of these tendencies in modern European history has been the rise and consolidation of the traditional territorial state. The development of a politically united Europe – the United States of Europe as discussed above – thus faces a powerful counterforce in the established dominance of the traditional territorial state. In the strain between these two discrepant forces the third alternative, the Europe of the Regions, has gained ground. Indeed, 'region' is employed as a catchword by the advocates of each of the three alternatives, albeit in different contexts and with different objectives. A regional dynamic has thus been kindled in a Europe where the contours of the future are still undefined. The political consequences of this accelerating dynamic are difficult to determine, but in contributing to the spatial rearrangement of Europe, actors at various levels are employing the concept of region as an instrument. The process may well be of lasting importance to both cultural and territorial identities and forms of organisation. This development would not be dissimilar to the pattern of recurrent transformations of such forms and identities so manifest in European history.

The focus of this book is on Central Europe. Although this term is not clearly defined or homogeneously applied, it is generally recognised that the areas included in Germany and the former Habsburg monarchy form a core area in this region. The precise demarcation of Central Europe from the rest of the continent varies, depending on the choice of criteria – geographical, political, economic or cultural – as well as the period under consideration. Since the present book has a long-term historical perspective, it is impossible to delimit the area according to static boundaries, given the significant variations in centres of gravity, communication patterns and networks over time.

In a historical context Central Europe can be thought of both as a region of its own and as a conglomerate of smaller shifting regional units and networks. The contributions in this book concentrate on the emergence and evolution of this pattern, and highlight different parts of this ever-changing Central Europe in various periods. They share an approach that brings *region* to the fore. This concept has proved valuable to investigations of the spatial transformation of Europe in history.

There is no universally accepted definition of *region*, and the concept had been employed differently by different scholars. However, a sort of lowest common denominator is that *region* presupposes a territorial basis, within which human activities take place. In theory regions can vary significantly in size, but in practice the term is reserved for an intermediate level that lies above the local community yet below the state. The categorisation itself is rather conventional, and does not qualitatively distinguish between a macroregion such as Europe, the traditional territorial states and regions of smaller size.

The delimitation of *region* downward and inward, from the local community, is subjective, but a certain minimum size is necessary for institutionalisation, and is likewise considered a condition for the emergence of regional identity. In certain instances it may be warranted also to discuss microregions, a concept employed by Lisbeth Lindeborg in her chapter on Germany. *Region* as used in this book pertains to different types of territorial entities that have longer or shorter histories. A few have experienced periods of some form of statehood, but all are better analysed on the basis of the more open concept of region.

The theoretical implications of the use of this term are discussed in greater detail in the chapter by Rune Johansson, who concentrates on the broad complex of problems linked to the concepts of region and territorial identity. The empirical chapters deal with different aspects of regional development in Central Europe ranging in time from the appearance of the German 'stem' duchies in the early Middle Ages to the cross-border cooperation project in the Oder area today. The geographical span encompasses substantial parts of the region, from Baden-Württemberg in the West to Transylvania, Carpatho-Ruthenia and the present-day Kaliningrad enclave in the East. Moreover, the authors all highlight the complex of problems associated with identity and cultural aspects.

The first of these articles, by Sven Tägil, discusses the emergence of historical regions in Europe rooted in the Age of Migrations. Name-forms such as Saxony, Bavaria and Lotharingia suggest regions with traditions dating back as much as a millennium. The question is thus why certain historical regions evolved into nation-states, while others did not. Lisbeth Lindeborg likewise focuses on Germany. Her point of departure is the present-day regionalisation process, but the analysis stretches back to the earliest German history and the appearance of the territorial principalities and up to the postwar evolution of federal Germany. She demonstrates the pervasive importance of regional deep structures, both in relation to the overarching federal level and within the regions. The concrete consequences of this phenomenon are exemplified in an investigation of one of today's prominent German regions, Baden-Württemberg.

The former Habsburg empire forms the basis for two separate studies, by Fredrik Lindström and Tom Gullberg. Lindström discusses the significance of historically institutionalised regions to the construction of culturally and territorially defined communities, in the context of mounting political struggles generated by the nationalities problem in the Habsburg realm toward the end of the nineteenth century; the specific case-studies are the regions of Bohemia, Moravia, Transylvania and to a lesser extent Hungary. Gullberg investigates the dissolution of the Habsburg monarchy around the conclusion of the First World War, and the nation-states that emerged as a result, most notably the Austrian republic. During this period the concept of the nation-state dominated the restructuring of political space, yet Gullberg illustrates the intricate web of problems involved in identification at the regional level.

Kristian Gerner discusses the virtually non-existent preconditions for local and regional development in Central and Eastern Europe during the Soviet era. The revisions of state borders and the extensive population transfers invariably took place without consultation with those most affected. Indeed, the Communist system of governance did not allow for local or regional initiatives of any kind. As the system collapsed in 1989, the national governments in the former Soviet satellites entered an adjustment period ridden with problems, not least concerning the development and relations at the regional level. Various types of regions, with varying lifespans, were then revived.

In the concluding chapter Hans-Åke Persson presents *'Oderraum'* the current cross-border project between Germany and Poland, initiated after the signing of a friendship treaty in 1991, in order to bring about collaboration in an area that historically has been both cohesive and marked by sharp divergence. Despite good intentions, the implementation of the scheme has met serious obstacles. Developments in *Oderraum* reveal that historical experiences and identities that history has fostered can obstruct a project that was thought to have good chances of success both economically and politically.

These studies of the development and constitution of Central Europe's spatial organisation illustrate different attempts at establishing identity-structures. Some structures have a long continuity, others are comparatively new. In some cases the identity has grown progressively from below and from within, while in others external forces and decisions from above have determined the territorial organisation. To understand how ethnoterritorial identities arise as well as their potential impact, it is necessary to consult the historical record. This collection thus contributes to the understanding of some of the major trends in today's Europe.

Lund, Sweden SVEN TÄGIL
Spring 1999

THE CO-AUTHORS

Kristian Gerner, born 1942. Ph.D. in History, 1984. Professor of East European Culture and History, University of Uppsala. Among his publications in English are *The Soviet Union and Central Europe in the Postwar Era* (1985) and (with Stefan Hedlund) *The Baltic States and the End of the Soviet Empire* (1993;1997).

Tom Gullberg, born 1965. MA (Licencié-ès-Lettres), University College of Åbo, Turku, Finland. Has studied national self-determination with emphasis on the restructuring of Central Europe after the First World War.

Rune Johansson, born 1943. Ph.D. Professor of Ethnicity Studies at the University of Linköping. His research has largely focused on ethnic and national problems in Europe. Among his publications in English are *Studying Boundary Conflicts: A theoretical framework* (co-author, 1977), *Regions in Upheaval* (co-author, 1984) and *Small State in Boundary Conflict* (1988).

Lisbeth Lindeborg, Marburg. BA, University of Lund. Has written extensively on European regional issues. Currently working on Ph.D. thesis at the University of Frankfurt am Main: 'Die Bedeutung der Versammlung der Regionen Europas für die Entwicklung eines Europas der Regionen'.

Fredrik Lindström, born 1965. Research associate at the Department of History, University of Lund. Has studied political and cultural problems in the late Habsburg Monarchy. Currently working on a book entitled *The Politics of Austrian Identity*.

Hans-Åke Persson, born 1948. Ph.D. (Lund). Currently Assistant Professor, University College of Malmö, Sweden.

Sven Tägil, born 1930. Professor emeritus of Empirical Conflict Research at the Council for Research in the Humanities and Social Sciences, University of Lund. Ph.D. in History 1962. Has published *Deutschland und die deutsche Minderheit in Nordschleswig* (1970) and *Vers un avenir meilleur?* (Mémoires du Monde, 15, 1995). Editor and co-author of *Studying Boundary Conflicts* (1977), *Regions in Upheaval* (1984), *Ethnicity and Nation-Building in the Nordic World* (1995).

PART ONE

THE IMPACT OF IMAGINATION
HISTORY, TERRITORIALITY AND PERCEIVED AFFINITY

Rune Johansson

Territoriality and the Possession of Territory

A territory is an area, large or small, a fragment of the earth's surface, and the quest to control or possess it has always been a central characteristic of human behaviour. At the deepest level, land and some form of command over an area of it have been necessary for survival, and thus territorial conflict has been a persistent feature in human history from time immemorial. Rivalry over the right to gather, hunt and fish in a certain territory was undoubtedly present in the prehistory of the human race. The eventual transition to agrarian society engendered a need for land, both for cultivation and for the maintenance of pasture animals. This fuelled competition and strife not only over the land itself but over how it was to be utilised. The biblical tale of the quarrel between Cain the shepherd and Abel the farmer mirrors a human reality that has been repeated innumerable times.

Conflicts over land and territory occur at the individual level, manifested in everyday disputes over abuttals and the 'actual' boundaries of one's property. Societies have likewise required land and territory for their evolution. The modern state is in fact founded on the principle of control over a specific territory and full sovereignty within a given area. Accordingly, the dominant position of the state in international politics has contributed to the strict territorial division of the world throughout the last centuries.[1]

---

[1] See discussion in Jean Gottmann, *The Significance of Territory*, Charlottesville, VA, 1973, and James Mayall, *Nationalism and International Society* (Cambridge, 1990).

Given the importance of territorial control, it is not surprising that states compete for power over a certain area. Such antagonism is as frequent between states as between individuals, as past and contemporary history amply demonstrate.

Neither at the social nor at the individual level can all territorial claims be attributed to a basic need for survival – or to the maximisation principle which presumes that one consistently strives to occupy as much territory as possible. Not all territorial acquisitions are necessarily considered worth struggling for. A first step towards a more focused analysis is to stipulate that the possession of a certain area gives a state, a group or an individual a certain value. In the context of states, this is commonly analysed in terms of material gains such as a strategically desirable boundary, greater natural or human resources, or an improved communications structure.[2] Such analyses correlate to a view of international relations inspired by the Realist school and the anarchy model, and characteristic of the entire geopolitical tradition that has been central to international politics, not least in the early twentieth century. However, even if territorial conflicts are interpreted in terms of value conflicts, this should not be limited to the power or strength of states, or the need to acquire a material power-base.[3] Not all activity, individual or social, can be reduced to material terms, and the analysis must therefore be broadened.

Several theories broach the question of why individuals and states act as they do in territorial contexts, and the concept of territoriality is particularly interesting within this framework. Territoriality is defined as a special relationship between an individual or a group and a given area. A very general explanation related to sociobiology highlights man's inherent need to 'mark his territory',[4] but this is far too sweeping to be applicable to specific cases, since it does not necessarily explain why a certain area is

---

[2] A general discussion on causes behind boundary- and territorial conflicts figures in Sven Tägil (ed.), *Studying Boundary Conflicts*, Stockholm, 1977. For the debate concerning certain specific cases, see Hans E. Peterson, *Power and International Order* (Lund, 1964).

[3] On territory as a base for power, cf. Rune Johansson, *Världens gränser* (Stockholm, 1988).

[4] See for instance Torsten Malmberg, *Human Territoriality*, The Hague, 1980. Cf. Steven Grosby,'Territoriality: the transcendental, primordial feature of modern societies', *Nations and Nationalism,* vol. 1, pt. 2 (1995).

seen as especially relevant or desirable, while another is apparently less so. Given this consideration, there may be more justification for relating territoriality to goal-oriented human behavior.[5] Yet territoriality is a complex phenomenon, and the role of the historical process in binding together people and place must also be recognised.[6]

All individuals perceive that they exist in a special relationship to a given area or to certain localities, and thus feel a particular affinity with such an area. This is internalised in the person's belief system, and the place may thus become a part of that individual's self-understanding. The process fulfils an important psychological function, giving an individual a sense of being anchored and having roots. Often, though not always, we experience such a 'sense of place'[7] in connection with our birthplace, and we may also have such feelings for our home community – however this is defined. The significance of localism is evident in various contexts, from sport to local politics. However, the development of an affinity with a territory or place has other dimensions too. Affinity with a state can involve the belief that a given region is an indispensable component of the state territory as history amply testifies. For example, developments in the 1990s in former Yugoslavia provide the example of Serbian attachment to Kosovo.

Feelings of territorial affinity and belonging can be of great significance in the political sphere in bringing about a particular policy and mobilising the population in favour. In addition, such sentiments may also serve to confer political legitimacy on a particular regime or a particular political structure.[8] The principal focus of this chapter is precisely on these feelings of affinity and identity: how they emerge and evolve, and how they relate to other identities of primarily ethnic or national character. An important element will be the question of which territories appear to be associated with such feelings of affinity. We open by discussing a prominent concept in this context – that of 'region'. Despite its

---

[5] Robert D. Sack, *Human Territoriality: Its Theory and History* (Cambridge, 1986).

[6] See Alan Pred, 'Place as a historically contingent process', *Assoc. of American Geographers Annals* 74 (1984).

[7] This conceptualisation is discussed in E.C. Relph, *Place and Placelessness* London, 1976.

[8] On legitimacy, see Edward Lehmann, *Political Society* (New York, 1977).

vague character, 'region' has been explored more comprehensively and with more theoretical rigour than other relevant concepts, such as 'place'.

The Region as Function and Feeling

What is a region? The concept has been applied in different ways in various disciplines.[9] A basic definition forming a sort of lowest common denominator is that it is a territory or an area in some way demarcated or at least spatially defined. There may be divergent views on how the territory has acquired its spatial definition or demarcation and on its role or function. Some scholars have tended to regard territory as the overarching concept and region as a smaller area, e.g. a province or district.[10] Although this approach invokes a 'commonsense' understanding of the concept of region, it does not apply universally: in political analysis, regions – and in some contexts macroregions – often comprise large geographical expanses. Thus we speak of regional great powers in, for example, the Middle East or Western Europe. In this perspective Central Europe constitutes a region as does the area covered by the European Union. What factors distinguish this type of region?

A region is generally understood to be marked by some internal similarities, cohesion or affinity which differentiate it from the outside world. The internal cohesion that makes a region can vary in form and be linked to political as well as cultural or economic aspects. Political-administrative divisions can to some extent engender regions, insofar as they can entail greater or lesser congruence within them, e.g. concerning taxes or social services. The residents of such a region do not necessarily feel a special affinity or identity with it and with its other inhabitants, although they may indeed do so. Historical administrative divisions such as the Swedish administrative provinces and the Habsburg '*Kreise*' or '*Bezirke*' have generally not fostered particular feelings

---

[9] See Paul Claval, 'From Michel to Braudel: Personality, Identity and Organisation in France' in Hooson (ed.), *Geography and National Identity*, Oxford, 1987. Cf. also Johansson, Rönnquist and Tägil, 'Territorialstaten i kris? Integration och upsplittring i Europa' in Tägil (ed.), *Europa – historiens återkomst* (Hedemora, 1998).

[10] Gunnar Törnquist, *Sverige i nätverkens Europa*, p.13 (Malmö, 1993).

of affinity.[11] The evolution of such feelings, which depends on a number of factors, is elaborated below. To illustrate the process thoroughly, it is necessary to investigate several empirical cases of the conditions around the development of identification, e.g. in the relatively recent German *Bundesländer*. The current trend towards regional reorganisation in many countries makes this relevant.

The economic aspects are important, because a specific economic structure can provide the basis for a region. This view has a long tradition in economic and economic-geographical contexts, and is quite prevalent today, e.g. with the growth areas of the EU, the so-called 'bananas'. Patterns of economic interaction and transaction have often been said to define regions, particularly in the analysis of trading and market areas.[12] However, it is common today to distinguish between regions and networks. The latter, which are charted on maps as points and lines, are less clearly demarcated and often extend across borders.[13]

Neither networks nor economic regions are generally associated with feelings of affinity and identification; hence factors other than economic realities are critical to the evolution of these feelings.[14] For instance, attempts, particularly in Germany, to invoke an affinity with the Hanseatic economic structure founded in the Middle Ages have met with little success among the populations concerned. Like administrative structures, economic regions and networks are essentially functional entities. However, in the presence of other dimensions, there is nothing to prevent functional regions from relating also to dimensions such as perceived affinity and identification, and it is likely that the regions comprising such dimensions were primarily functional at some stage. Meanwhile, territorial identities have become increasingly significant in recent

---

[11] See for instance the discussion in Peter Aronsson, *Regionernas roll i Sveriges historia*, Stockholm, 1995; also Eva Österberg, 'Tradition och konstruktion. Svenska regioner i historiskt perspectiv' in Blomberg and Lindqvist (eds), *Den regionala särarten* (Lund, 1994).

[12] W. Christaller, *Central Places in Southern Germany* (Englewood Cliffs, NY), 1966. See also the discussion in Tägil et al., *op. cit.*, 1977.

[13] See for instance Törnquist, *op. cit.*

[14] See the discussion in S. Rokkan and D. Urwin, *Economy, Territory, Identity: Politics of West European Peripheries*, London, 1983.

years despite, or perhaps because of the increased functional orientation both within the states and within the EU.[15] Yet identification is not directly linked to function; hence at what point, and under what circumstances, does the region become a basis for territorial identification?[16]

Various scholars have insisted that territorial affinity and identity must be taken into consideration.[17] However, only a limited number of thorough analyses exist. One such is the Finnish geographer Anssi Paasi's study of regions and identity, which builds partly on the ideas of Anthony Giddens in its discussion of the identification connected to the Finnish, now largely non-functional provinces.[18] The key concept in Paasi's analysis is institutionalisation, linked to the emergence of 'standardised, quite permanent modes of behaviour which are controlled by expectations connected with various roles'. Institutionalisation thus relates to common definitions of culture as based on patterns of thought and behaviour.[19] These patterns are in some sense value-guided, and Paasi's notion of institutionalisation involves the development of special 'structures of expectation', i.e. modes of organising knowledge and utilising it for interpreting new information. According to Paasi, institutionalisation entails four stages that need not follow each other in any particular order. These involve the acquisition of territorial shape and form, conceptual or symbolic content, and a specific place or role in a contemplated regional or territorial system. Paasi has outlined several important features in the evolution of regional consciousness by highlighting the process and striving to join territory and culture in a broad sense. However, neither Paasi nor others who have studied the issue succeed in satisfactorily defining the way regional consciousness is developed, its precise

---

[15] See, e.g., Sidney Tarrow, 'Introduction' in S. Tarrow, P. Katzenstein and L. Graziano, *Territorial Politics in the Industrial Nations* (New York 1978), also Johansson, Rönnquist and Tägil, *op. cit.*, 1993, p.26.

[16] Cf. S. Tägil (ed.), *Regions in Upheaval* (Stockholm, 1984).

[17] David Knight, 'Identity and Territory: Geographical Perspectives on Nationalism and Regionalism', *Assoc. of American Geographers Annals* 72 (1982).

[18] Anssi Paasi, 'The institutionalisation of regions....', *Fennia*, 164:1 (1986). Also Johansson, Rönnquist and Tägil, *op. cit.*, p.26.

[19] Rune Johansson, *Kulturella beroenden*, Lund, 1976.

content and the nature of its relationship to other forms of consciousness and identification.

Identities as Constructions and 'Reality'

Regional consciousness is a phenomenon that is as difficult to grasp as it is to describe. Writers have used various conceptions such as 'semiosphere' and '*Lebenswelt*', but most of the pertinent literature accepts 'identity' as a central notion in this context.[20] Yet although this concept is frequently used, it often appears quite obscure. One problem is that the critical distinction between what may be labelled the 'essentialist' and the 'constructivist' angles is commonly overlooked.[21] The essentialist angle presumes that identity is tangible and manifest, and also fundamental for the individual. Identity is broadly understood as primordial and therefore constant.[22] A common identity implies that individuals of different generations resemble each other in various ways that are evident both to themselves and to the external environment. This is a common element within a group and allegedly remains consistent over time.

As for the regional context, an essentialist perspective was developed early, e.g. by the French geographer Paul Vidal de la Blache, who proceeded from the idea that geographic conditions, such as natural environment, resulted in the evolution of clearly defined identities.[23] In principle, this implies that tangibly distinct national identity should exist within the parameters of the state territory, and by extension maybe also what could be called a 'national character'. The notion of such national identities has been quite popular among both older and contemporary historians, e.g. in Henri Pirenne's argument that external circumstances have

---

[20] Cf. the discussion on identity in A. Lange and C. Westin, *Etnisk diskriminering och social identitet* (Stockholm, 1981), pp. 179-224.

[21] P. Jackson and J. Penrose, 'Placing "race" and "nation"' in Jackson and Penrose (eds), *Constructions of Race, Place and Nation* (London, 1993).

[22] For a classic example of an essentialist view see Edward Shils, 'Primordial, personal, sacred and civil ties', *Br. J. of Sociology*, 1957.

[23] See M.-C. Robic, 'National Identity in Vidal's *Tableau de la Géographie de la France*' in D. Hooson (ed.), *Geography and National Identity* (Oxford, 1994).

fostered a wider Belgian identity not contingent upon the differences between Walloons and Flemings.[24]

In a regional context, those who espouse the essentialist angle may believe that identity is reflected in both the behaviour and thinking of the individual. In other words, Bavarians and Tyroleans act in a certain way because this is in the 'nature' of the group. As in Paasi's study, however, behaviour can also be linked to roles and expectations regarding roles. This implies that individuals behave in a certain way because it is expected both by themselves and by the society around them.[25] The question whether territorially delineated groups share specific cultural features and have a specific, culturally-defined identity has been much debated, with discussions of the extent to which such identities are distinguishable in everyday behaviour,[26] and to which identity determines the behaviour of individuals. Although identities clearly do not entail some sort of predetermined behaviour, they do appear to involve a 'repertoire' of habits, thought-patterns and values that manifestly influence people.[27] The problem lies in determining just how the identity has arisen and exactly what it involves.

In so far as one rejects the view that identities are primordial and somehow fixed once and for all, one must presume that an identity emerges at some point and thereupon acquires some form of content.[28] It is common here to invoke historical growth, and 'historical region' is often considered synonymous with 'identity-related region'.[29] This requires closer analysis of the factors that may influence the development of identity and of the way such a process occurs. Whether they go back far in time or are of

[24] See for instance Claval, 'From Michel to Braudel', *op. cit.* On Pirenne and Belgian identity, see R. Johansson, *Small State in Boundary Conflict* (Stockholm, 1988).

[25] See Paasi, *op. cit.* Paasi distinguishes between 'regional identity' and 'identity of the region'. The latter relates to characteristics ascribed to the region as such, and the regional inhabitants as a collective.

[26] See Michael Billig, *Banal Nationalism* (London, 1995).

[27] Ann Swidler, 'Culture in Action: Symbols and Strategies', *Amer. Sociological Rev.*, 5 (1986).

[28] Cf. Rune Johansson, 'Nationer och nationalism. Teoretiska och empiriska aspekter' in S. Tägil (ed.), *Den problematiska etniciteten* (Lund, 1993).

[29] Cf. for instance S. Tägil, 'De historiska regionernas egenart' in S. Tägil, H.-Å. Persson and S. Ståhl (eds), *Närhet och nätverk, op. cit.*, 1994.

more recent origin, historical ties and cohabitation do not of themselves foster the rise of a common identity. Nonetheless there is a strong inclination, not least among the actors in territorial strife, to refer to historical bonds and roots in a certain region in arguing that the region belongs to, or should be controlled by, one or the other party. As in the former Yugoslavia, both parties in a conflict can use history as a weapon.

A constructivist perspective may be valuable in investigating which elements are included in identity as well as the way identities arise. An important aspect of this approach is well captured in Benedict Anderson's phrase 'imagined communities'.[30] The point of departure is that the sense of cohesion is limited to individuals who are in direct contact with each other, and that a true community in history could therefore not be extended beyond the village. Yet it is possible to construct communities within much larger frameworks, such as regions and nations, and thus induce people to identify with these communities. One could argue that the village too did not necessarily serve as a basis for community and perceived sense of affinity. However, Anderson's essential point is valuable in that it underlines that community and identity may need to be constructed, and are thus not immediately given or an inevitable product of the course of history. A correlation can be traced between this approach and the research conducted into the 'invention of traditions'. Despite criticisms concerning the exact age of different traditions, this research has revealed that much of what we experience as traditional characteristics, e.g. of a region, has in fact quite recently been 'invented' for various purposes.[31]

Thus the constructivist approach suggests that identities are phenomena that have been created and are therefore malleable. Regional and national identities are not constant, but change according to the content one wishes to ascribe to the identity at a given point in time.[32] The same individual can embody several

---

[30] Benedict Anderson, *Imagined Communities: Reflections on the Origin and Spread of Nationalism* (London, 1993).

[31] E. Hobsbawm and T. Ranger (eds), *The Invention of Tradition* (Cambridge, 1983).

[32] Cf. for instance B. Ehn, J. Frykman and O. Löfgren, *Försvenskningen av Sverige* (Stockholm, 1993).

different identities at once: it is fully possible to be Nuremberger, Bavarian and German at the same time. In the constructivist perspective, this fact is often taken as evidence of the flexibility of identities, suggesting that, depending on circumstances, they may play a smaller role, be interchanged or be abandoned altogether.

However, against the background of the actual development of territorial conflicts, it is important to note the tenacity of identity, the sluggishness that characterises the process of identity. The fact that identities are constructed does not mean that they are easily revised:[33] once they have taken hold, they tend to be more durable than has commonly been assumed, e.g. in traditional Marxist and Liberal political science theories. They are preserved through such means as myths, legends and symbols long after the course of events is presumed to have led to '*Entzäuberung*' or 'disenchantment' in the Weberian sense. In Poland, for instance, different national myths have survived and been important over long periods of time.[34] Identities may be latent insofar as they need not influence people's behaviour, but in certain circumstances they can be stirred and effect intensive identification with political consequences.[35]

The constructivist angle thus illuminates relevant aspects in the development of identity, although it yields no more than the essentialist approach regarding precisely which factors characterise an identity. According to the view presented here, a social identity is primarily based on an affinity or mutual connection of which an individual is more or less aware, and less on manifest behaviour. However, behaviour may well be important in this context, particularly if the role-expectations within or outside the group presuppose behaviour of a certain kind, as in fundamentalist religious identities. How social context and the external environment define a group plays crucial roles in the evolution and perpetuation of identities. It serves to demarcate boundaries for the social position and status of the group's members.[36] Individuals need not be

---

[33] See the discussion in Jackson and Penrose, 'Placing "race" and "nation"', *op. cit.*, 1993.

[34] B. Plewa Törnquist, *The Wheel of Polish Fortune* (Lund, 1993).

[35] See for instance Tägil (ed.), *Regions in Upheaval*, and Johansson, 'Nationer och nationalism'.

[36] See Fredrick Barth, 'Les groupes ethniques et leur frontières' in P. Poutignat and J. Streiff-Fénart, *Théories de l'ethnicité* (Paris, 1995).

aware of these demarcations until a particular situation brings them to the surface. A notorious example of this type of situation was Hitler's rise to power, which so tragically revealed the precarious position of Germany's Jews.

In conclusion, neither the essentialist nor the constructivist approaches satisfactorily resolve the question of how, and in what circumstances, identities are engendered and maintained. A principal issue here is the way territorial or regional identities relate to other social identities.

Territoriality, Ethnicity and Nationality

A series of different identities may exist parallel to the regional one. For example, class and gender may both be highly relevant to shaping an individual's views and sense of belonging. Regional, ethnic and national identification are commonly viewed as gender-neutral, but in reality they often involve the perpetuation of traditional gender structures.[37] It is only quite recently that this reality has been recognised and has triggered objections, but the debates on the relationship between class, region and ethnicity have a far longer history. The traditional Marxist claim that the worker has no mother-country to identify with has in principle applied also to the native community and regional affiliation. But in reality workers have often felt affinity with their home regions, and the result may have been cross-pressure and diminished mobilisation either in one dimension or in both. The theoretical apprehension of regional identification has not prevented workers from being regionally mobilised over economic or social demands on the central government; this inclination has presumably been strongest where diverse identities have been fused. Class, territoriality and ethnicity may not be incongruous, insofar as a given region may have a class structure that is quite homogeneous, while diverging ethnically from the remaining state territory.[38]

Religious identity may also be relevant here. Religion and religious affiliations can be associated with regions in various ways and intrinsic religious aspects can play a central role in the

---

[37] Floya Anthias and Nira Yuval Davies (eds), *Woman-Nation-State*, London, 1989.

[38] See the discussion in Johansson, Rönnquist and Tägil, 'Territorialstaten i kris?', *op. cit.*, and the literature referred to there.

establishment and demarcation of a region, and may contribute to a region having a particular character. Such a process can occur within the state, with more or less impact depending on the prevailing views in society, but there are religiously defined regions that comprise several states. The division of Europe into Western Christianity and Orthodoxy provides one such example.[39]

Nationality and ethnicity, however, are the phenomena of most interest where regional identities are concerned. Regional, national and ethnic identities all relate to territorial divisions and to the way the world is arranged territorially. Congruence and compatibility among different identities or, on the other hand, conflict are thus of particular interest here.

However, both nationality and ethnicity are highly complex matters. The concepts 'nationality' and 'nation' are linked to the state, whether this state has already been constructed or is merely contemplated.[40] A nation is thus a group of people who, through their identity, relate to a certain state. A rough distinction can be made between two different types of nations and nation-formations. The first is based on the state as such and its political system, and hence all its citizens are included in the nation regardless of cultural particularities. The development of such a nation requires that an over-arching national identity be constructed and diffused among the population, as occurred in the multicultural society of late nineteenth-century France.[41] The process shares essential characteristics with the formation of regional identities, and a territorial nation-formation can be said to lead to a state-nation, or 'civic' nation.[42]

---

[39] See for instance R. Johansson, 'Idéer om Europa – Europa som idé' in S. Tägil (ed.), *Europa-historiens återkomst, op. cit.*, and the discussion in K. Gerner, S. Hedlund and N. Sundström, *Hjärnridån. Det europeiska projektet och det gåtfulla Ryssland* (Stockholm, 1995).

[40] On nations and nationalism see R. Johansson, 'Nationer och nationalism', op. cit. Compare with James G. Kellas, *The Politics of Nationalism and Ethnicity*, London, 1993.

[41] Eugen Weber, *Peasants into Frenchmen: The Modernization of Rural France, 1878-1914* (Stanford, 1976). Cf. R. Johansson, ' "La France sera la France" –stat, nation, region och Europa i den franska utvecklingen' in S. Tägil (ed.), *Europa – historiens återkomst, op. cit.*

[42] Liah Greenfeld, *Nationalism: Five Roads to Modernity*, Cambridge, MA, 1992.

In contrast to the constitution of regional identities, however, nation-building within the framework of the state always has distinct political implications. It is crucial to the state that its citizens have an identity that links them to that state and gives them some sense of affinity with it since this identity may be the basis for loyalty to the state and furthermore confer legitimacy on the elite. This became especially important in connection with modernisation. In this process the traditional frames of reference for identity were removed and the need arose to integrate industrialisation's labouring masses into a national context. Certain efforts to constitute state-nations have been more or less successful: for example France and the immigrant countries of Australia and the United States appear to have integrated the majority of the population, though not its totality, into the state-nation. But alongside these comparatively fortunate cases are failed attempts at state-nation formation in both older and more recent history. In this the Habsburg monarchy can be seen as resembling the later Soviet Union and Yugoslavia.

The reasons why nation-building fails vary. The nation is not fundamentally incompatible with regional identities, which can be allowed to exist as politically innocuous bonds to people's native communities, and may in fact be encouraged and exploited by the leaders of the state. During the nation-building of the late nineteenth century, a sort of contest emerged between states that prided themselves on their different local cultures which were understood as particularly authentic and as models for the nation in question and its characteristics. The Swedish nation-building process provides one such example: an imagined or constructed Dalecarlia become a symbolic model for the whole of Sweden.[43] The exploitation of regional, politically neutralised cultures was also a feature of Soviet politics, in accordance with what commentators termed 'indigenisation'.[44]

Problems arise when different principles and different modes

---

[43] On the general features in this development, see O. Löfgren, 'Materializing the Nation in Sweden and America', *Ethnos*, 3-4 (1993). See also B. Sundin, 'Upptäckten av hembygden. Om konstruktionen av regionala identiter' in Blomberg and Lindquist (eds), *Den regionala särarten* (Lund, 1994) and P. Aronsson, *Regionernas roll i Sveriges historia, op. cit.*, 1995.

[44] On 'indigenisation' see John Coakley, 'The Resolution of Ethnic Conflict', *International Political Science Review*, 13, 1 (1992).

of handling nation-building meet and come into conflict. The state or civic nation was discussed above. What has been described as a culture-nation, today more usually named an ethnonation, represents another main category. In essence this form of nation consists of people who are distinguished by specific ethnic features. According to the nineteenth-century notion of *'ein Volk, ein Staat'*, each separate people has the right to its own state. This has been the basis for the principle of national self-determination, which was of major influence in international politics in the late nineteenth century, has influenced the revisions of the map of Europe, and continues to play a key role in today's Central and Eastern Europe.[45] The ethnonational way of thinking is based on the belief that the nation has discernible ethnic characteristics and is bound for various reasons to a given territory. However, ethnicity is not nearly as clear-cut a phenomenon as nationalists or certain analysts would have us believe. An overview of how the concept is used and interpreted in different contexts has shown large variations, and concludes that ethnicity essentially consists of what individuals choose to include in it.[46]

Such subjective categorisations naturally impede the use of ethnicity as a valuable term in analyses of political development. Accordingly, there have been attempts to determine what 'actually' and objectively forms the core of ethnicity. It is common in this context to discuss shared culture and perceived common descent[47] but as was mentioned earlier, it is often difficult to identify tangible, objectively manifest cultural distinctions among diverse groups and areas. In nineteenth-century Europe, cultural differences may have been based on class rather than ethnicity. Cultural variations that arose between different ethnic groups were largely the result of deliberate construction – a parallel is the attempt in the 1990s to create a Bosnian identity. Common descent, also a somewhat complicated instrument for demarcating ethnic groups, is generally accepted by analysts as a crucial criterion for ethnicity, and recurs in almost all argumentation by the ethnic groups themselves. In

---

[45] See for instance Ø. Østerud, *Hva er nasjonalisme?* (Oslo, 1994) and J. Mayall, *Nationalism and International Society* (Cambridge, 1990).

[46] W.W. Isajiw, 'Definitions of Ethnicity', *Ethnicity*, 1, 2 (1974).

[47] See for instance N. Glazer and D.P. Moynihan, 'Introduction' to *Ethnicity: Theory and Experience* (Cambridge, MA, 1975).

its most essential form, kinship and ancestry come within genetic parameters. Nazi ideology was not alone in espousing this line of thought. Since, in theory, this definition impedes assimilation, it may ultimately be translated into ethnic cleansing and genocide, particularly if the identity is defined in terms of '*Blut and Boden*', i.e. both territory and genetic descent.[48]

In reality, given the extensive migrations and the blending of peoples throughout history, common descent must to some extent be based on constructions. The quest to establish more tangible, objective criteria for group affiliation may partly explain why various ethnic groups have sought to link identity to factors such as a common language different from that spoken by the surrounding population, or a common and distinctive religious affiliation. A number of possible 'ethnic markers' exist, including race (which, however, is linked to descent) and socioeconomic structure, which can become relevant in instances where the ethnic group is defined in accordance with its principal occupation, as with the Samis (Lapps).[49] There is also reason to believe that such distinctions were already made earlier in human history if not to demarcate ethnic groups in the modern sense, then to define so-called 'ethnies', prototypes for today's ethnic and ethnonational groups.[50]

However, these 'markers' also involve a series of problems. Language is not a factor that is simply there to begin with. It is largely created for various purposes. For instance, Ljudevit Gaj's construction of the Serbo-Croatian written language was intended to form a basis for Yugoslavian 'thinking'.[51] The Romantic national tradition of Herder and others attached great importance to language as the expression of the *Volksgeist*, and in Central Europe as in other areas, efforts have been made to forge specific languages on the basis of different dialects, as was the case in Slovakia.[52]

---

[48] See Coakley, 'The Resolution of Ethnic Conflict', *op. cit.* (n. 44 above) 1992.

[49] See the discussion in S. Tägil (ed.), *Regions in Upheaval: Ethnic Conflict and Political Mobilization* (Stockholm, 1984).

[50] On the concept of '*ethnie*' see Anthony D. Smith, *National Identity* (Harmondsworth, 1993).

[51] On Gaj's language reforms, see K. Nyström, 'Regional Identity and Ethnic Conflict: Croatia's Dilemma' in Tägil (ed.), *Regions in Upheaval, op. cit.*

[52] On language in ethnic and national contexts, see J. Blommaert and J.

However, this does not imply that all languages are linked to an ethnic identity. In short, language as such is neither a necessary nor a sufficient foundation for ethnicity.[53]

Religion as an ethnic marker has received increasing attention in recent years, but it also involves analytical problems since segments of a given group do not truly adhere to the beliefs with which they are associated, or actively practice the religion.[54] Moreover, a diverging religion or religious orientation is not necessarily associated with any particular ethnic identity. As ethnic markers and grounds for ethnonational affiliation, both religion and language are mainly constructed '*ex post facto*' after a sense of identity has already grown up among at least certain portions of the group. It is against this background that one must understand Ernest Gellner's thesis that nationalists shape the nation, rather than *vice versa*.[55]

The same is true of history as an ethnic marker. History plays a crucial role in all ethnic identities, but this is a constructed history distinct from history as an academic discipline.[56] This type of history, which highlights certain aspects and interprets them within an ethnic and national framework, also plays an essential part in the creation of ethnic groups, demarcated by subjective feelings of cohesion and solidarity rather than any objective criteria. Ethnicity can be said – according to the discussion in this chapter – to acquire criteria that are more precisely delimited, e.g. a constructed language and a specific interpretation of history. However, it must be emphasised that a basic subjective element underlines the formation of ethnic and national groups.[57] Because ethnicity has a subjective nature it is not therefore less significant or less 'real'. According to Thomas's theorem, a phenomenon is

---

Verschueren, 'The Role of Language in European Nationalist Ideologies' in C. Schäffner and A.L Wenden (eds), *Language and Peace* (Aldershot, 1995).

[53] See the discussion in Ernest Gellner, *Nations and Nationalism* (Oxford, 1983).

[54] See the discussion in Rune Johansson, 'Varieties of Conflict Development: Ethnic Development...in Belgium, Finland and Switzerland' in S. Tägil (ed.), *Regions in Upheaval, op. cit.*

[55] Gellner, *op. cit.*

[56] See K.-G. Karlsson, 'Historiens samband med livet. Om historiens bruk, missbruk och ickebruk i Sovjetunionen och Sverige', *Historiedidaktik i Norden*, 4 (Kalmar, 1990).

[57] Eric Hobsbawm, *Nations and Nationalism since 1789* (Cambridge, 1994).

real if its consequences are real, and the relevance of ethnic and ethnonational identification as mobilising forces in political history is undeniable, not least in the creation of new states.

For ethnic identity to become significant to the territorial configuration of the world, it is first necessary for an active identification with the group and its interests to be developed. Under different circumstances, such as pressure from the state or perceived economic, cultural and political deprivation, an ethnic group can rise up against the constitutional conditions and demand self-rule or independence.[58] An ethnic group can exact some form of non-territorial cultural autonomy, particularly if its habitat is geographically diffuse; this proved important to the internal debate in the Habsburg monarchy.[59] However, claims generally pertain to a territory that is in some way demarcated: they may be said to define an ethnonational group, but the very selection of a certain territory and its boundaries is meaningful in itself. The territory or region in question is inseparable from the group's identity and worldview and represents its permanent 'homeland', even if the group is in fact a minority within the area, e.g. the Serbs in Kosovo and the Germans in Bohemia before the First World War.[60] In the political sphere, ethnic and regional identity are often bound together, with political consequences.[61] However, to comprehend the underlying mechanisms, we must discuss the construction and reproduction of identities in history.

Identities in Early History

Identities are understood here as variable phenomena receptive to the influence of outside developments and of deliberate actions

[58] See S. Tägil, 'Ethnoregionalism as a Problem in Conflict Theory', *op. cit.*, and R. Johansson, 'Nationer och nationalism', *op. cit.*; also Tägil, 'The conditions for Ethno-Regional Conflict' in Tägil (ed.), *Regions in Upheaval, op. cit.*

[59] Uri Ra'anan, 'Ethnic Conflict:...' in Ra'anan, *Ethnic Resurgence in Modern Democratic States* (Oxford, 1980).

[60] On the role of territory in national perception, see for instance Grosby 1995. See also the discussion in Anthony Smith, *National Identity, op. cit*, and John Breuilly, *Nationalism and the State* (Manchester, 1985).

[61] For empirical examples of the link between ethnic and regional identity and the development of political demands, see the various articles in S. Tägil (ed.), *Regions in Upheaval, op. cit.*

by a diversity of actors. This is essentially true of all identities, not least those that relate to ethnicity, nationality and regionalism. In connecting regionalism and ethnicity, it is crucial to establish a context which includes the region as an integrated element in the individual's belief system. In regional settings, the development can engender what has been called topophilia, or attachment to a context, where the physical locality is one element, as are durability and constancy in the locality, affinity between the person and local nature, and a living cultural code that is particular to the sense of place and preserves it.[62] From the angle which concerns us here not all of these factors need to be present to make up a regional identity. However, as we see below, historical development and deliberate political steering result in several of them figuring in the identity and being integrated into it.

Invoking the territory which one group inhabits as a basis for distinction from other groups goes back to ancient times. An early definition of the concept of 'people' and 'nation' by Isidorus of Seville in the seventh century stipulated that national belonging was determined by subjective considerations, ancestry and also by the place of residence.[63] In medieval universities the area from which one was descended long remained the basis for classifying nations. Moreover, within different regions in Antiquity and the Middle Ages, not least the semi-sovereign entities engendered by feudalisation, the uniqueness of the region and its inhabitants was underlined. For instance, pilgrims to Santiago de Compostella were instructed on how they should behave in different areas. Crystallising the particularity of a region, and imparting to it a special value could be achieved by ascribing common descent to the inhabitants, e.g. rooted in Antiquity or in the heroes of Biblical narratives.[64]

[62] See J. Asplund, *Tid, rum, individ och kollektiv* (Stockholm, 1983). See also E. Österberg, 'Tradition och konstruktion' in *Den regionala särärten, op. cit.*

[63] B. Zientara, ' "Populus-Gens-Natio". Einige Probleme aus dem Bereich der ethnischen Terminologie des frühen Mittelalters' in Otto Dann (ed.), *Nationalismus in vorindustrieller Zeit* (Munich, 1986). In several chapters of that volume, territoriality and group-formation in the Middle Ages and later are discussed. See also A.D. Smith, *The Ethnic Origins of Nations* (Oxford, 1986), and Susan Reynolds, *Kingdoms and Communities in Western Europe 900-1300* (Oxford, 1984).

[64] On various myths of descent, see Denis Hay, *Europe: the Emergence of an Idea* (Edinburgh, 1957). See also Rune Johansson, 'Nationer och nationalism', *op. cit.*

It appears that already during the Middle Ages there were tendencies towards the constitution of regions and the development of some type of regional identity. But it is more difficult to estimate to what degree regional and national thinking had penetrated the belief systems of the population at large. There appear to have existed relatively evolved identities that disappeared, or decreased in relevance, due to subsequent political developments and the fact that no one perpetuated the regional tradition. Such instances are found in the history of France, e.g. for regions such as Champagne and Poitou, and in parts of the German domain. In the late Middle Ages the consolidation of state power led to a reduction in the political leeway possessed by the region. However, this process took a long time to complete, proceeded at different speeds in different areas, and had not ended by the time of the French Revolution.[65]

As we noted earlier, a common history does not necessarily foster regional identity, and an identity can furthermore change. Identities that have at some point been institutionalised can become dissipated over time, but they have generally proved enduring. Regional identities that have been established, even in embryonic form, have been more likely to survive if certain factors were present. Geographical position has played a role in this where regions have been a periphery relatively little affected by the central power and periodically outside its control.[66] Generally, however, the central authority's ability to implement measures that advance centralisation is always critical in regional development. At the same time, the central power's ability to act is influenced by the situation in both the international and the domestic arena, and by the political and economic conditions. A weakened central government can give regions the opportunity to acquire and retain special privileges and rights in the political, administrative and judicial realms.

[65] See for instance Charles Tilly, *Coercion, Capital and European States, AD 990-1990* (Cambridge, MA, 1990); also Gottmann, *The Significance of Territory, op. cit.* On France, see Rune Johansson, 'La France sera la France', *op. cit.*

[66] See the discussion on the relation between the centre and various types of peripheries in Stein Rokkan and Derek Urwin, 'Introduction: Centres and Peripheries in Western Europe' in Rokkan and Urwin (eds), *The Politics of Territorial Identity* (London, 1982). See also same authors, *Economy, Territory, Identity, op. cit.*

The preservation of regional rights as a basis for the future development of identity has always required that there were people in the region with both the interest and the political ability to safeguard these rights. The history of Europe from the close of the Middle Ages to the French Revolution is riddled with conflicts between the centralised state power and regional ambitions, with a different outcome in different countries. Both within and outside the Habsburg empire, regional special privileges were at various times guarded by the nobility and the political classes, particularly in Bohemia, Hungary, Transylvania and Croatia. Despite aggression from the centre, the regional elites were long able to preserve their rights and in addition to construct a myth of liberty around these privileges.[67] This was made possible by the vulnerable position of the Habsburg domain, e.g. *vis-à-vis* the Ottoman empire, as well as its marked diversities in geography and culture. Developments in other countries, e.g. France and Sweden, resulted in diminished regional influence. The collapse of Sweden's great power status made the opposition of the Baltic nobility irrelevant. Regional differences existed, as did a certain interest in regional history, but the Swedish central power was generally successful in its striving for integration, including some of the provinces newly acquired in the seventeenth century.[68]

The German Holy Roman Empire exemplifies yet another evolution, through the development of virtually independent principalities after the Peace of Westphalia of 1648. It is difficult to discover if an identity was forged within the framework of these principalities, and to what extent such an identity might have been diffused. This would depend on the size and integration of the entity.[69] The embryos of Prussian, Hanoverian and Bavarian identities appear in this context, but they did not necessarily reach

---

[67] See Fredrik Lindström 'Region och kulturell identitet. Ett kaleidoskopiskt perspektiv på det habsburgska Centraleuropas historia före 1990', unpubl. ms., Dept. of History, Lund University, 1995. On the Croatian special rights see K. Nyström, 'Regional identity and Ethnic conflict', *op. cit.*

[68] Harald Gustafsson, 'Conglomerates or Unitary States? Integration Processes in Early Modern Denmark-Norway and Sweden' in T. Fröschl (ed.), *Föderationsmodelle und Unionstrukturen* (Vienna, 1994). See also P. Aronsson, *Regionernas roll...*, *op cit.*

[69] See H.-Å. Persson, ' "Soweit die deutsche Zunge klingt". Statslösningar och identiteter i den tyska historien' in S. Tägil (ed.), *Europa – historiens återkomst*, *op. cit.*, 1998, and the literature referred to there.

the broad strata of society, and may also have been balanced by a general German identity among intellectuals as well as by traditional feelings of affinity, as among Swabians, within the framework of the German '*Stämme*'.

Modernisation and Identity Construction

The nineteenth and twentieth centuries have brought profound changes for the evolution of identity. According to the modernist perspective prevalent in much research and represented by, for example, Ernest Gellner and Eric Hobsbawm,[70] modern identities presuppose an essential structural transformation in industrialisation, urbanisation and literacy, which reorient traditional society toward greater geographical and social mobility. Without adhering to this approach entirely, one may observe that the development of society has forged new conditions for the creation and diffusion of various identities among the population. It has become possible to influence and mobilise the masses. Indeed, the principal difference between earlier and more recent identity-development is quantitative rather than qualitative. History suggests that corresponding identities existed in some form before modernisation, and that these have served as bases for identities to evolve later. Like Anthony D. Smith's '*ethnies*', Hobsbawm's notion of 'protonation' relates to historical identities and the need to explain the later development of nationalism.

Much of the academic discussion on modern identities has been focused on ethnonations and ethnonational separatism within multinational states. However, the process of modernisation also influenced the more or less successful attempts to construct statenations within an existing state territory,[71] and likewise played a role in constructing regional identities. During the nineteenth and early twentieth centuries there was a greater focus on the regional dimension, and this included identity-formation on the

---

[70] Gellner, *Nations and Nationalism, op. cit.*, and Hobsbawm, *Nations and Nationalism since 1789, op. cit.* See also R. Johansson, 'Nationer och nationalism', *op. cit.*, and J.P. Arnason, 'Nationalism, Globalization and Modernity', *Theory, Culture and Society*, 7, 1990.

[71] See for instance Anthony H. Birch, *Nationalism and National Integration*, 1989. See also Breuilly, *Nationalism and the State, op. cit.*

basis of pre-existing elements. Efforts were made to discern a sustaining element or a *mythomoteur* as a foundation for identity.[72] The element in question could consist of former regional institutions and special privileges, although these were sometimes reinterpreted and given a wider scope. Another element could be what was called historical tradition; this could have a very flimsy basis, and often involved new dimensions due to modern interpretation of historical phenomena. However, history and tradition were not the only elements included in the construction of regional identity. Reference was made to the territory itself and its nature, and often presented in ideal-typical form.[73] Probably such constructions still largely determine people's relation to a region, and thus bring about a connection between them and the territory.

Which individuals sought to highlight the regional dimension? As noted earlier, regional identity did not automatically contradict the state's quest to secure control and forge a national identity. The state could construct models for national development by emphasising appropriate regional characteristics. This does not imply that those who promoted the region were directed by the state authority, although they were often from the upper strata of society;[74] their involvement presumably stemmed from affection for their native community, and may be understood as the search for roots and the desire to return to one's origins, a phenomenon that took hold from the Enlightenment onwards.[75] Independently of intentions, however, the results could be such as to sustain state and society.

This does not mean that regional identities as such were, or became, politically irrelevant outside the context of state-building and the connection to national notions. Consider the identification

[72] On the concept of '*mythomoteur*' see Anthony D. Smith, *The Ethnic Origins of Nations, op.cit.*, and John Armstrong, *Nations before Nationalism* (Chapel Hill, NC, 1982).

[73] See David Lowenthal, 'European and English Landscapes as National Symbols' in David Hooson (ed.), *op. cit.*

[74] See for instance P. Aronsson, *Regionernas roll....*, *op. cit.*; also B. Sundin, 'Upptäckten av hembygden....' in *Den regionala särarten, op. cit.*, and Gunnar Broberg, 'När svenskarna uppfann Sverige' in G. Broberg, U. Wikander and K. Åmark (eds), *Tänka, tycka, tro. Historia underifrån* (Stockholm, 1993).

[75] See for instance Cornelia Navarri, 'The Origins of the Nation State' in L. Tivey (ed.), *The Nation State: The Formation of Modern Politics* (Oxford, 1981).

The Impact of Imagination

with Schleswig-Holstein – '*ob ewig ungedeelt*' – that was significant to Danish-German developments in nineteenth century. A clearly evolved, politically meaningful but multiethnic regional identity also existed in other places, e.g. Transylvania.[76] But it is clear that regionalism and regional identity acquired a particular political role in conjunction with, or in relation to, the construction of ethnic identities. During the nineteenth century there were various groups which combined ethnic and regional claims, not least in Central Europe.

Broadly, the development appears to have had various stages.[77] In the first a few intellectuals constructed a belief in the ethnic uniqueness and character of a group. This notion was crystallised and became the basis for a political movement in the second phase, while the third phase involved increased support and mass mobilisation behind the ethnonational and ethno-regional demands. The earliest and most ardent backing generally came from intellectual and middle-class circles (rarely the upper middle class); thus the ethnic movement was an element in the newly-established *bürgerliche Öffentlichkeit*. Its success among the working class came later, and the peasantry was the last class which was absorbed into this mobilisation.

This is necessarily a simplified and generalised picture of a complex phenomenon that in reality showed variations, and depended on factors such as the group's resources and the activities of the state government.[78] Actions within the group and the internal process that generated the construction of identities were also important. The intellectuals in the first phase played a key role in demarcating the group, developing markers for group affiliation, and giving content to the identity. They would endeavour to create a common language on the basis of different dialects, which were themselves selected out of ethnopolitical considerations. Serbo-Croatian was earlier mentioned as an example. Likewise,

---

[76] On Schleswig-Holstein, cf. S. Tägil, 'De historiska regionernas egenart', *op. cit*. Transylvania is discussed in Lindström, 'Region och kulturell identitet', *op. cit*.

[77] Miroslav Hroch, *Social Preconditions of National Revival in Europe* (Cambridge, 1985).

[78] See for instance S. Tägil, 'The Conditions for Ethno-Regional conflict', *op. cit*.

Slovak dialects that were comparatively close to Czech were used as a foundation for the Slovak written language.

Although language was a significant element in the construction of ethnic identities, it could not stand alone. History was reinterpreted and rewritten in ethnic terms and this entailed not only highlighting certain aspects but also 'forgetting' others, in a way that was already pointed out by Ernest Renan in the 1880s.[79] Myths were collected from popular balladry and merged with a factual though somewhat rearranged history. Historic battles such as Kortrijk 1311, Kosovo Polje 1389 and the Boyne 1690 were given great prominence and became components of the Flemish, Serbian and Irish Protestant belief systems. Territorial dimensions were also emphasised and integrated with the group's past and future, so that the group would be understood as having a historic claim over a given area. In numerous instances, it was possible to proceed from an already existing regional identity and provide it with ethnic overtones. This in turn set up friction with other groups who inhabited the region, and served to fracture regional unity. Bohemia is one of many examples of this.[80]

The first phase in the evolution of ethnic or ethnonational groups generally did not include demands for self-rule or independence for the group or region. Neither the Czech Frantisek Palacký (1798-1876) nor the Finn J.W. Snellman (1806-81) sought to shatter the empire he lived in, but wished only to obtain for his own people equal status in the multinational structure. In reality, it took time for demands for change in the existing state structure to evolve and gain widespread support.[81] The ethnonationally-based revisions of the map of Europe stipulated in the treaties after the First World War came earlier than had been expected by the affected groups, and outstripped popular support.[82]

[79] Ernest Renan, *Qu'est-ce qu'une nation? et autres essais politiques* (ed. Joël Roman), Paris, 1992. See also Ernest Gellner, 'Nationalism and the two forms of cohesion in complex societies' in *Culture, Identity and Politics* (Cambridge, 1987).

[80] For Bohemia see Lindström, 'Region och kulturell identitet', *op. cit.*, and the literature referred to there.

[81] The development of the Flemish movement provides one example. See R. Johansson, 'Varieties of Conflict Development', *op. cit.*

[82] The peace after the First World War is discussed in Tom Gullberg, 'Nation och gräns', unpubl. MA thesis, Åbo Akademi, 1994. See also Tägil *et al.*, *Studying Boundary Conflicts, op. cit.*

But the general trend was towards greater ethnonational and ethnoregional demands, and this entailed conflicts with the government as well as with other groups. The situation could become particularly critical in cases where the surrounding states made claims on the area in question.[83] Territorial demands were not necessarily inspired by ethnonational considerations, but were nevertheless often internally and externally justified by the argument that the region was a part of the ethnonationally-defined state territory. It was on such grounds that both Serbia and Bulgaria made claims to Macedonia.

In the quest for power, different elites strove to secure support for their policies and to increase mobilisation. This continuous propaganda could bring about changes in identity and its *mythomoteur*, given changes in the group leadership and objectives.[84] However, a principal aim was to reach out to the broadest possible cross-section of the population. Socially this required efforts to strengthen the identification of groups that before had been relatively unaffected. There was also a geographical dimension in the mobilisation efforts, since attempts were made to involve peripheral areas. This was the case particularly with border areas, which have often been characterised by a low degree of ethnoterritorial identification and a high degree of indifference among the inhabitants.[85] The striving to preserve and reproduce identities and fuel popular mobilisation were generally successful, especially when violent conflicts and full-scale war created martyrs and reinforced cohesion and identification.[86] Current events in Central and Eastern Europe are dramatically affected by surviving nationalism and ethnoterritorial identification, showing the tenacity of identities once constructed and established. They can indeed endure for much

---

[83] See for instance Myron Weiner, 'The Macedonian Syndrome', *World Politics*, 1972.

[84] The discussion of Poland's territorial identity and extension provides one example. See Jozeph Babicz, 'Two Geopolitical concepts of Poland' in D. Hooson (ed.), *Geography and National Identity, op. cit*, 1994; also B. Plewa Törnquist, *The Wheel of Polish Fortune, op. cit.*

[85] Two examples of this are Eupen-Malmédy on the Belgian-German border and Schleswig. See Kim Salomon, *Konflikt i graenseland* (Copenhagen, 1989), and Johansson, *Small State..., op.cit.*

[86] See Anthony D. Smith, 'Wars and Ethnicity:.....', *Ethnic and Racial Studies*, 4 (1981).

longer than outside observers had tended to believe, particularly when traditional territorial conflicts have been revived. The process of conflict itself influences identification, and impels people to adopt a position based on simplified notions of 'us' versus 'them'.[87]

Territoriality and Identity: Conclusion

Our discussion has centred on territory and territoriality as political factors, and particularly highlighted the emergence of territorial identities and territorial identifications. Identity-formation has been approached largely from constructivist angle, which does not imply that identities are easily altered or politically irrelevant. On the contrary, they are normally incorporated into the individual's 'perceived reality' affecting individual behaviour and playing a key role in situations of conflict.[88]

The connection between ethnicity and territoriality has been emphasised, but territorial identities have more than ethnic significance, in conjunction with both the emergence of state-nations (civic nations) and of regional identities that are not specifically ethnic. There is evidence that the latter form of identity may become more relevant in the future as it plays a crucial political role, e.g. in the mobilisation behind Lega Nord in Italy in the 1990s.[89] When studying concrete instances, it may be difficult to see whether an identity is ethnically defined or not, since ethnicity is itself vague as a concept. In certain cases efforts have been made to tie together the ethnic and regional dimensions by means of constructions. Historical examples include Bohemia, but today we too are witnessing attempts to forge ethnoregional identities. Tendencies towards such a development are apparent in Moravia, for instance, and in the Swedish context efforts have been made to denote the southern province of Scania as an ethnically distinct region and the Scanians as an ethnonation.

---

[87] See the discussion on conflict development in Liesbet Hooghe, 'Nationalist Movements and Social Factors' in J. Coakley (ed.), *The Social Origins of Nationalist Movements* (London, 1992).

[88] See O. Löfgren, 'Materialising the Nation in Sweden and America', *Ethnos* 3-4 (1993).

[89] See Robert Putnam, *Government and Politics in Italy* (Cambridge, MA, 1995).

The possible growth in the importance of regional identity may be linked to current efforts at decentralisation and regionalisation, a trend apparent in various areas and endorsed by the European Union Commission. 'Europe of the Regions' may thus be a vision of the future although the ability of the present states to influence the course of events should be borne in mind.[90] Some of the regions, e.g. Bavaria, are rooted in a previously developed regional identity, and others, Flanders, Wallonia and Scotland, have a tradition of linking territoriality and ethnicity, and of ethnoregionally defined conflict.

However, many of the regions in today's Europe lack such a background and are essentially functional. The continuing political institutionalisation of regions in terms of 'meso-government'[91] could in the long run form a basis for identity-formation. Yet historical experience shows that this involves a long process that has not been experienced in all historical regions or all territorially demarcated peoples and languages.[92] Today's media structure might offer new possibilities for a relatively rapid development of identity, and there is an evident need in our society today for a sense of roots and belonging. It has been claimed that this is reflected in a postmodernist trend toward 'tribalism', which could be manifested in phenomena like gang activity as well as the assertion of regional and ethnic identities.[93] There may be some validity to this argument, but the question is whether in the future newly-created identities will show the constancy necessary to acquire true political relevance.

Various ethnoregional demands were made during the 'ethnic revival' in Western Europe in the 1970s.[94] In some instances these demands were just one element in an enduring conflict

---

[90] See the discussion in Johansson, Rönnquist and Tägil, 'Territorialstaten i kris?...', op. cit.

[91] See for instance L.J. Sharpe (ed.), *The Rise of Meso-Government in Europe* (London, 1995).

[92] See E. Gellner, *Nations and Nationalism*, op. cit., 1983, and A.D. Smith, *National Identity*, op. cit. 1995. On peoples and languages in Europe, see Thomas Lundén, *Språkens landskap i Europa* (Lund, 1993).

[93] See for instance Jonathan Friedman, *Cultural Identity and Global Process* (London, 1994).

[94] Rokkan and Urwin (eds), *The Politics of Territorial Identity*, op. cit., and S. Tägil (ed.), *Regions in Upheaval*, op. cit., 1984.

between the state apparatus and the ethnoterritorial group that later acquired more distinctive overtones of ethnonationalism. In some cases, the example from other regions resulted in a sort of 'emulation effect' combined with the 'small is beautiful' aura of the day. In such instances the notion of territoriality and regional demands have appeared unable to achieve long-term relevance despite substantial coverage by the mass media. Although identities can be constructed, they are not formed overnight and are difficult to manipulate according to passing situations.

Our discussion has not suggested that an extensive regionalisation of Europe is likely, particularly if regional identity is to be the basis for such a development. However, there is reason to believe that regional and ethnoregional identities will continue to be important in Europe over the next decades. This applies mainly to regions where the identity has previously been institutionalised. Identity can then become the prevalent discourse and largely form the individual's 'space of experience' and 'horizon of expectation'.[95]

This suggests that, contrary to what has been maintained since the time of Giuseppe Mazzini,[96] increased regionalisation will presumably not serve as a guarantee for peace. Often within the framework of identity lies the notion of special privileges for the individual's own group, accompanied by a perception (whatever its accuracy) of earlier maltreatment by other groups. Each group recalls its own martyrs and historical injustices, and these memories can often come to the surface in situations that trigger feelings of subordination and discrimination. It is in vain that academics and the outside world deny the relevance of such feelings. Identity and the sense of affinity among disparate individuals is a construction, that can affect behaviour in various circumstances, irrespective of reality.

This does not imply the inevitability of territorial conflict. Federalisation represents one way of solving related problems, and it has been suggested in discussions concerning the EU's subsidiarity principle. The Swiss canton system is often mentioned as model worthy of emulation. However, while federalisation and decentralisation can avert or mitigate conflict, they are not infallible. The

---

[95] For the conceptualisation see Reinhard Koselleck, *Futures Past: On the Semantics of Historical Time* (Cambridge, MA, 1985).

[96] See the discussion in R. Johansson, 'Nationer och nationalism', *op. cit.*

Swiss system is rooted in a long tradition and solidly institutionalised. Where federalisation has been adopted late and as a consequence of ethnoregional and national conflict, as in Belgium, a solution has proved elusive.[97] The European map will perhaps be revised again. New states may emerge, preferably through peaceful means, as in the former Czechoslovakia. However, the fact that no region has a homogeneous population is a complicating factor which may fuel future conflicts within both the regions and the prospective new states.

---

[97] R. Johansson, 'Varieties of Conflict Development', *op. cit.*

PART TWO

THE ROOTS OF IDENTITY
TERRITORIALITY IN EARLY CENTRAL EUROPEAN HISTORY

Sven Tägil

The idea of the nation-state has occupied a central position in the evolution of the European states. This is true of both the states formed during nineteenth and twentieth centuries according to the principle of self-determination, and the territorial states whose nation-and state-building processes date further back into history. In both cases, notions of common descent, with roots frequently traced back to the dawn of European history, and a long cultural continuity have been key components in identity formation. The nation-state has often been understood as the self-evident final phase in this development, the ideal scenario being that of absolute consonance between the people and the territory, between the nation and the state.

However, the reality has not been quite so straightforward. Many groups have found it impossible to crystallise a state of their own, despite satisfying the criteria for a nation-state: ethnic and cultural homogeneity, a distinct language, and a contiguous territory that the group has inhabited for several generations. As is true of states, such historically grown regions differ from each other. Awareness of the population's distinctiveness may vary in strength both over time and among the members of the population, as too can the political willingness to assert this distinctiveness. External factors such as dynastic, political, religious or economic conditions have in certain instances prevented a historical region from achieving the status of independent state.

Ethno-territorial developments took a singular course within the Central European area. In Francia the foundations for a certain stability and continuity had already been laid before the age of migrations had ended. By contrast, Central Europe was divided among ethnic groups that long preserved their identities, but were unable to politicise them and thus embark on the nation-building process that was slowly developing in much of Europe.

The ethno-territorial evolution in this area was already distinctive in the early Middle Ages. Indeed, the realities of this period proved highly significant to subsequent developments and continue to be relevant today. The Germanic tribes, territorial configurations, the organisation of society, and legal and political realities have all influenced the direction of ethnoterritorial development. As often in history, integration and disintegration were the two main contending alternatives. In Germany's case, the later so-called Holy Roman Empire of the German Nation – the realm founded by Otto the Great in the tenth century (he was crowned Emperor by the Pope in 962) and formally abolished by Napoleon only in 1806 – exemplified integration, while disintegration was reflected in a mosaic of some 1800 more or less sovereign areas that had come to comprise the Empire by the end of the Middle Ages. It is difficult to give a coherent picture of the emergence of this myriad of kingdoms, duchies, margravates, palatine countships, countships and other secular principalities, ecclesiastical entities, such as bishoprics, autonomous dioceses and abbeys, and free imperial cities and knights. However, it is still possible to distinguish certain principal features in Central Europe's ethno-territorial development.

Our focus here is primarily on the emergence and permanence of historical regions. Elements of continuity and a sluggish pace of change figure alongside the more rapidly changing, constantly shifting configurations in Central Europe's lengthy history. In certain instances, present-day regional structures reflect ancient divisions and identities. In others, little more than the name of the ethno-territorial entity has survived and the borders and social structures of the area have been totally altered.

In the following sections we discuss the German stem duchies of the early Middle Ages which have kept a remarkable titular continuity: Saxony, Frisia, Lotharingia (Lorraine) and Bavaria, for example, are historically evolved regions with traditions that go back over 1,000 years. These names endure today both in administrative and political divisions and in the consciousness and culture of the people. In the current debate on the integration and development of the European Community historical regions have a significant place, particularly those classified as nations yet which never achieved statehood.

Romans and Germanic Peoples

Central Europe first appears in recorded history at the dawn of the first Christian millennium. By this time, the area north of the Alps had begun to be absorbed into the Roman cultural sphere through trade and peaceful contact as well as through warfare and conquest.

The heart of the Roman Empire lay in southern Europe. The Mediterranean was its hub and principal means of communication. The inner and northern portions of Europe were of less interest to the Romans, and physical geographic considerations impeded further penetration northwards. In prehistoric times, a number of Celtic peoples inhabited the area that is today southern and western Germany, Switzerland and eastern France. There were Celts also in Bohemia, Moravia and Lusatia as well as in northern Italy ('*Gallia Cisalpina*') and the Celtic domain has been called by some archaeologists 'the first Europe'. The area long functioned as a buffer-zone between northern Europe, largely inhabited by Germanic peoples, and the Roman Empire in the south. However, the Celts were successively marginalised, and what remained of the once predominant people ultimately faded into the eastern and western peripheries.

The Romans extended their influence northward across the continent and under Julius Caesar crystallised their control over the Celtic areas in Gaul (*c.* 50 BC). The Romans now came into direct contact also with the Germanic peoples. The devastating defeat of the Roman general Varus by the Cheruskian chief Arminius in the Teutoburger Forest in AD 9 gave the first signal of the northern menace. During this time the Romans strove to establish a fortified boundary to the Germanic world, a frontier that would span some 500 km. of the Rhine and Danube as well as the land between them. Wooden palisades were erected later to be replaced with ramparts and stone walls; especially vulnerable sites were given watchtowers and citadels. The defences were complemented with strategic roads. Since Britain had been incorporated into the Roman province system, a *limes*-structure was also built there as a defence against the Celtic peoples who inhabited the island's remoter parts.

Pressure against these *limes* (boundaries) successively escalated, however, and in several places the Germanic tribes were able to break through Celtic settlements and penetrate Roman territory. They were highly mobile during this time, and new settlements often entailed new loyalties and revised tribal identities. Germanic tribes that merged with others included the Alemanns, who settled in the area between the Rhine and the Danube; the Frisians by the North Sea coast; the Saxons in the lowlands by the Elbe; and the Thuringians south of this area. The Roman tactic consisted of establishing, where possible, friendly relations with the Germanic tribes; indeed, many of the latter moved into the Roman Empire as farmers or warriors. Under the Empire entire tribes settled in the border areas, where they were granted land in return for acting as military defenders of the border.

By the dawn of the Middle Ages, the entire Germanic world was breaking apart and experiencing profound change. The mass migrations *(Völkerwanderungen)* involved the extensive movement of people throughout Europe, mainly from north to south – from areas that had suffered climatic deterioration and famine, to wealthier and more fertile lands. Several groups travelled long distances and founded new, primitive state-formations in various parts of the decomposing Roman Empire. For example, the Visigoths initially conquered Rome and vast sections of Italy, but ultimately settled in Spain, founding a kingdom there. The Vandals moved further still, ending up in North Africa, the richest province of the Roman Empire. Amid this turbulence the Roman Empire finally collapsed. The imperial power survived, but by the late fifth century it survived only as an eastern state based in Constantinople with Western and Central Europe well out of reach.

The migrations likewise brought upheavals to Central Europe. Germanic peoples migrating south abandoned many areas of the continent up to the Baltic Sea, areas that would later be populated by the newly arrived Slavs. The boundary between the Slavic and the Germanic settlements stretched from the Elbe to the Danube, although Slavic peoples also penetrated the Balkans further south.

Earlier research generally distinguished between two main types of states engendered by the *Völkerwanderungen*: those invaded by armies and those settled by people. However, this categorisation is no longer accepted as unequivocal. Those invaded by armies were established in Roman areas and, as already mentioned, the Germanic peoples constituted a sort of hired defence force against potential intruders. The Roman bureaucracy often remained, but the Germanic chief wielded the decisive power in these provinces. The Germanics were nevertheless exposed to the influence of the far more pervasive Roman culture, and Germanic properties such as language and other cultural manifestations vanished within only a few generations. Neither the Ostrogoths, the Visigoths, the Vandals, nor the Lombards left behind an enduring cultural legacy that can be described as specifically Germanic. Ethnically a fusion had taken place, and the distinct tribes in the area would gradually acquire a purely mythical character.

In Central Europe the outcome of the migrations was different. Areas conquered by peoples were the most common type of settlement, and this implied that the Germanic culture could assert itself more thoroughly. The Roman governing and administrative officials were replaced with Germanics. This pattern was especially prominent in the originally Celtic area of Gaul. In the early fifth century, Germanic Franks, Burgundians and Alemanns had migrated to Gaul, abandoning their original settlements east of the Rhine. Among these groups, the Franks – a collective label for a number of tribes – were the most dynamic. They conquered areas around what is now Paris from the last Roman governor, defeated several other Germanic peoples, including Alemanns and Burgundians, and in the sixth century established a state that was relatively stable by the standards of the time under their Merovingian kings.

Over the following centuries the Frankish empire continued to expand south to the Pyrenees and beyond. A number of Germanic areas in the north and east were incorporated in the eighth century, such as the Frisian settlements by the North Sea coast, the Saxons as far as the Elbe, and the Bavarians in present-day Bavaria. The Lombard kingdom in what is now Italy included Rome and also ended up as part of the Frankish empire. The majority of these conquests were achieved through warfare under Charlemagne (768–814). Wars of conquest were not waged exclusively against the Germanic peoples, but also against Arabs, Berbers, Avars and Slavs. In order to protect and preserve the Frankish empire, special

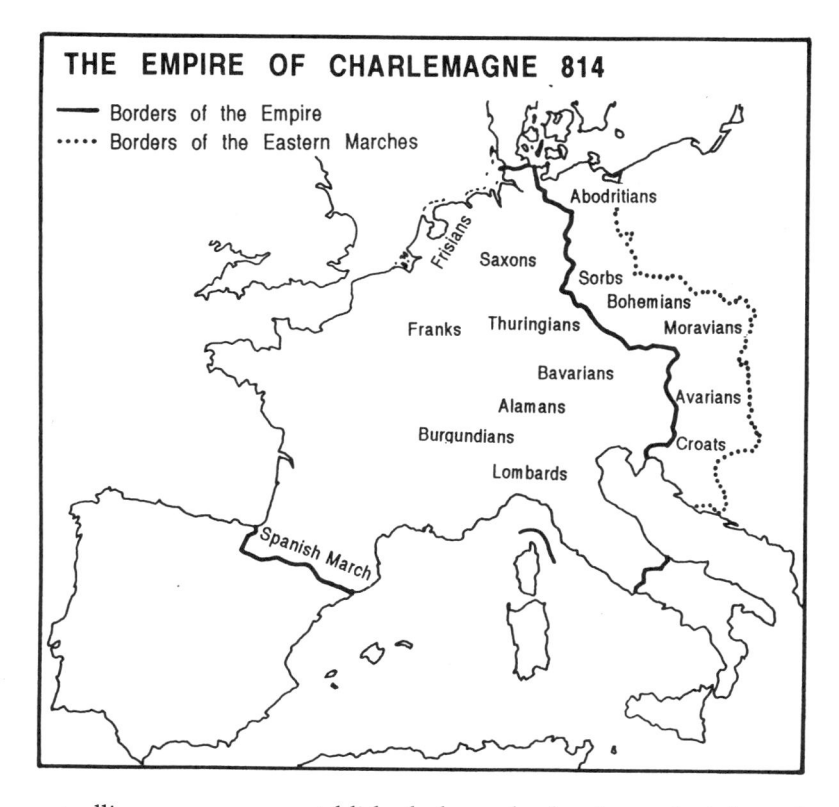

THE EMPIRE OF CHARLEMAGNE 814
— Borders of the Empire
····· Borders of the Eastern Marches

Abodritians
Frisians
Saxons
Sorbs
Bohemians
Franks
Thuringians
Moravians
Bavarians
Alamans
Avarians
Burgundians
Croats
Lombards
Spanish March

patrolling areas were established along the borders, administered by margraves answering directly to the Emperor.

The state-formation that was the Carolingian Frankish empire did not rest on stable institutions, and after Charlemagne's death it was repeatedly partitioned according to dynastic principles. In 843 the sons of Louis the Pious – Charles, Lothar and Louis – divided the old Frankish domain into three kingdoms. Charles became ruler of its western half comprising Neustria, Aquitania, Septimania, Gascony, Navarre and Hispanic March; Louis was allotted the eastern portion of the empire, stretching from present-day northern Germany to the Alps; and Lothar obtained the land in the middle. The Carolingian empire had been largely based on Charlemagne's personal power and could not withstand the numerous dynastic shifts that followed his death. It survived as no more than an enduring illusion of a peaceful European community within the Western Christian world. The political and cultural distinctions between 'French' and 'German', which would later prove so critical, were established at this time. The German language prevailed in the Germanic zones north of the Rhine and Danube, while various Romance languages based on Latin evolved in the south.

People and Territory in the Ancient Germanic World

Knowledge of the emergence of ethnic primary groups in Central European prehistory remains fragmentary. It is unclear at what point related primary groups merged into tribes, but the process was apparently punctuated by both convergence and separation, integration and dissolution. Such processes take a long time to complete, and, where the emergence of the Germanic areas are concerned, it is no exaggeration to estimate a 1,000-year transitional period, from the Iron Age to the middle of the first millennium.

The most ancient ethnic groups ('tribes') were based on ancestry, kinship and marital bonds. Internal cohesion was necessitated both by the need to ensure secure living conditions in peacetime and by the importance of coordinating defences in wartime. Alongside purely biological factors, the emergence of a specific identity within such groups had been fostered by the need for common legal norms and devotion to a shared cult, linked to certain sites visited by the group members. From these primal communities arose more evolved forms of shared experiences, or communities of tradition. However, a long time would need to elapse before the cultural process had progressed to the point where the identity could be invoked for political mobilisation.

Already in the earliest tribes leaders and elites played critical roles. Chiefs carried out important duties as leaders in wartime, and as the performers of cult functions in peacetime: sacred tasks appear to have been a central responsibility of ancient kings. The altered conditions brought about by the major *Völkerwanderungen* of the fifth and sixth centuries led to new tasks for the tribal leaders. Cult functions became less important, while the ability to direct military initiatives successfully became the priority. Despite significant differences between areas invaded by armies and those settled by peoples, great importance was attached in both to forceful leadership. The armies of the *Völkerwanderungen* period often consisted of several tribes, and the tribal popular assembly was replaced by a military assembly in which warriors were the principal actors. The relationship between the leader and his subjects, which was critical during the *Völkerwanderungen*, also became a central component in the hierarchy of medieval feudal society.

The tribes of the late *Völkerwanderungen* consisted of several closely related peoples and were numerically far stronger than previous entities. These populations are sometimes called 'stems' or 'great tribes'. The turbulence of this period meant that the parameters of the tribal settlements changed, in some cases through expansion, in others through the possession of new areas with no prior connection to the original area. As settlements became more permanent, the foundations for territorially-bound identities were laid.

The authority of the ancient tribal chief was always tied to his group rather than to any specific territory. This was true also in the migrant states such as those of the Visigoths in Italy and Spain, and of the Vandals in North Africa. The king would designate himself as '*Rex Visigothorum*' or '*Rex Vandalorum*', that is, the king of a people rather than of state or territory.

Central Power and the Stem in Feudal Society

The division of the Carolingian empire yielded two separate kingdoms: the West Frankish realm, which ultimately evolved into France, and Eastern Francia, which developed into Germany. A principal cause of the Carolingian empire's decline was the shortage of officials and administrators to secure the interests of the central power in the provinces. The dissolution of this poorly-developed state power enabled the dukes (leaders of the stems) to propagate their own power. At no time in the Carolingian era did these dukes abandon their traditional popular power-bases.

The title 'duke' – *hertich* or *hertoch* in Middle-Low German – had originally been applied only to the tribe's temporarily appointed leader in wartime. In his work of *c.* AD 100 on the Germanic peoples, Tacitus distinguished between *rex* (a king who performed tasks pertaining to the sacred realm) and *dux* (a military leader in war). The latter title had been used by Germanic peoples in this latter sense already during the later Roman period.

The duke was originally elected from among the leading strata of the stem but the position later became hereditary. He could thus represent the king in a given region, but his power was not exclusive: there were also often hereditary countships directly subordinate to the king. The duke's power was based largely on the strength of his military resources and when there was no war his primary responsibility was ensuring that the legal norms of the land were upheld. The dukes were also confronted with rival contenders other than the counts (*comites*), principally from the Church and the expanding feudal aristocracy. As a result, they relied increasingly on the estates and property of their own kin, and in many regions their fortresses and defensive structures also became fiscal and administrative centres. This development implied that the territory itself now acquired far greater importance than the ancient tribal communities.

In the early Middle Ages, Germanic tribal society underwent transformations linked to the rise of the feudal system, a form of social organisation rooted both in Germanic and late Roman tradition. One of its basic elements was the mutual loyalty between lord and vassal (its precursor was the relationship between chief and warrior, duke and army, in Germanic tradition). The system was hierarchical. In the so-called feudal pyramid the lord was followed by vassals and under-vassals. The vassal was not an official as the Roman governor had been: he had commended himself to the lord by an oath of loyalty or fealty and committed himself to preserving the lord's interests. In return, the lord gave the vassal not only physical protection but also land, called a *beneficium* or fief. If the vassal's service was terminated, the fief returned to the lord.

This hierarchical structure not only provided a base for security and peace, but also entailed decentralisation, which prevented the development of a strong, all-encompassing central power. In feudal society control over the fief was a critical issue: those who conferred the fief wanted to preserve their right to reclaim it, and thus to prevent such landholdings from becoming hereditary. The inheritance question was part of the reason why the right to clerical investiture became decisive in the struggle for power over the Empire.

In East Francia, the central power had been virtually nullified on the dissolution of the Carolingian empire. The German king/emperor had only nominal power, although in accordance with feudal norms he formally retained the formal headship of the entire empire. A certain friction was thus inherent in the relationship between lord and vassal. In France, this tension was resolved to the benefit of the royal authority, but in Germany it resulted in amplified power for the vassals.

The dukes progressively became the most important intermediaries between the king on the one hand and the nobility and Church. Tribal particularism and the escalating power of the nobility combined to erode the state authority which the king represented. In this process, a number of the older tribes obtained renewed importance as organisational entities, and this applies particularly to the five great stems: the Franks, Bavarians, Swabians, Saxons and Thuringians.

The idea of an overarching European imperial power, which Charlemagne had sought to realise within the framework of his Western Christian empire, endured in the eastern portion of the domain. One of the stem dukes was elected king in this area and at first had little authority outside his own duchy. The first appointment brought a Frankish duke to power, but for the next two centuries the Saxons held the throne within their ruling house. The Saxon duke Otto was elected German king at a ceremony in Aachen, once the residence of Charlemagne, and in 962 he was crowned emperor, a clear indication that he intended to perpetuate and revive the Carolingian tradition.

The remaining dukes had played important roles in this context, and this was symbolically reflected when they literally placed the new king on the throne and hailed him as their overlord. In the ensuing religious ceremony Otto was crowned wearing Frankish dress, at the high altar in Charlemagne's basilica by the archbishops of Mainz and Cologne. Both the kingly coronation in Aachen and the imperial coronation in Rome marked a continuity from both the Roman Empire and from Charlemagne's.

Later in the Middle Ages, Otto's creation was officially entitled the Holy Roman Empire of the German Nation, a name which itself deserves some attention. The Roman Empire had been a multiethnic state based on citizenship, rather than on language and ethnicity. The phrase 'holy empire' ('*sacrum imperium*') related to the realm of Western Christianity, reminiscent of Charlemagne's equivalent claim regarding his Carolingian empire. Finally, ('German nation') the third element of the title which evolved far

GERMANY AT THE BEGINNING OF THE 10TH CENTURY

- March of the Billungs
- Nordmark
- Frisia
- Saxony
- Lusatia
- Thuringia
- Meissen
- Lorraine
- Franconia
- Bohemia
- Moravia
- Swabia
- Bavaria
- Ostmark
- Burgundy
- Carinthia

later, involves an ethnic designation, although it is difficult to appraise the precise implications of the term during this period.

The original significance of '*deutsch*' (the German word for 'German') invokes the connotations of 'nation'. Its root lies in the Germanic word *theoda* meaning 'people' like the Latin word *natio* and the Greek *ethnos*. '*Theodisce*' was employed during Charlemagne's time to designate the spoken language, as opposed to Latin, the written language. Thus, by the tenth century 'German' had evolved from denoting only a language to embrace also those who spoke it: *diutisc*. The Latin form of the term, *Regnum teutonicorum*, appears at this time, 'Teutonic' representing a collective label for the East Frankish tribes.

The name given the German empire was of great symbolic importance. However, it had little real meaning for the majority of the population, and it was long before a German identity emerged. Tribal loyalties continued to be significant, though somewhat eroded through the feudal system, which engendered a new type of relationship between feudal lords and their subordinates, through dynastic transactions, wars and territorial conquests.

The Stem Duchies

During the High Middle Ages there was a strain in the German realm between the imperial authority's efforts to expand the central power, and particularist claims made primarily by the stem duchies and thus posing a threat to the central power. The royal centre struggled to counteract the power of the dukes through feudal strategies: vassals were tied directly to the king, and special officials, known as counts palatine, were appointed specifically to safeguard royal possessions. The Catholic Church also played a role in this context: the secular nobility had usurped the right to make fiefs hereditary at the expense of the German kings and because the Church was a great landowner, it became increasingly important for the German kings to be able to invest new incumbents of bishoprics and other clerical offices, so as to keep the total enfeoffment potential of the land more or less under their own control. The ensuing struggle between the emperors and the papal power over the right to issue investiture resulted in a compromise, the Concordat of Worms of 1122. The Pope retained the right to designate clerical officials and the Emperor his position as overlord of the secular feudal state.

The German stem duchies formed after the upheavals of the *Völkerwanderungen* were based on both people and territory. However, no fixed boundaries existed, and interrelated groups residing in the territory of the principal stem could be assimilated into the majority group. The territory had a core area, but its boundaries, both external and with other stem duchies, could shift.

SAXONY

The West Germanic Saxons were mentioned in the middle of the second century AD by the Alexandrian geographer Ptolemy. They resided along the lower Elbe and in Holstein at this time, but eventually expanded to the south. At this early period the Saxons incorporated several closely-related ethnic groups into their stem. Their areas of settlement were successively broadened and, after the maritime expeditions of the fifth century, came to include Britain. The Saxon core area extended from the land of the Danes in the north to present-day Hesse in the south, westward to Westphalia and eastward to Saal. The place-name Saxony dates from the fifth century. An expansion of the territory took place in the early sixth century at the expense of the Thuringian stem duchy, whose possessions were divided between the Saxons and the Franks.

Ancient Saxon history was a time of constant antagonism with the Franks. Charlemagne was ultimately able to suppress the Saxons and forcibly Christianise them. With the military defeat the ancient tribal homeland of Saxony lost its independence. However, the foundations were now laid for the important role the Saxon stem duchy would play within the East Frankish realm.

During the Carolingian period, the power of the Saxon dukes had been largely confined to their exploits in time of war. The duke was selected from among the stem's upper echelons through the drawing of lots, and functioned as military leader. This changed after the dissolution of the Carolingian empire, when a prominent aristocratic family, the Ludolfingians, established a position strong enough to claim the title permanently. It was on the resources of this dynasty that Otto founded his power, which culminated in the creation of the Holy Roman Empire in the mid-tenth century. However, the draining involvement in Italy and the expansion eastward also contributed to ultimate erosion of the position of the Saxon stem duchy. Alter a series of dynastic transactions, Saxony's political role was terminated with the fall of the Welf dynasty and Duke Henry the Lion in 1180.

THURINGIA

During the *Völkerwanderungen* the Thuringians inhabited the area between the Danube and the Elbe. An alliance of Saxons and Frankish Merovingians conquered their land, which was partitioned between the two victors: the western section was incorporated into the stem duchy of Franconia, while Thuringian Mark further east gradually lost its independent status. The character and borders of the original region of Thuringia were altered through repeated dynastic division and merging, but the name itself survived. Indeed, in today's resurrected Germany, Thuringia is equivalent to one of the *Bundesländer* in the eastern part of Germany.

FRANCONIA

The stem duchy of Franconia was the core of the German state founded after the division of Charlemagne's principalities and imperial towns. Among the princes in Franconia, the Count Palatine (Pfalzgraf) of the Rhine was to play an important political role: for instance, he sat in the electoral college that appointed the Emperor. When Franconia was conquered by Otto the Great, the duchy's independent status came to an end. By the twilight of the Middle Ages the name of Franconia was tied to the Franconian *Kreis* in the south-east of the region, and when the German empire was dissolved in 1806, it was joined to Bavaria and apportioned into three *Kreise* – upper, middle and lower Franconia.

SWABIA

Swabia, south of the Franconian stem duchy, was named after the Svebians who in the third century repressed the Celt settlers in this area, and in the fifth century founded a province in the north-western portion of the Iberian peninsula. A substantial number of Svebians nevertheless remained in the older settlement territory north of the Alps, and admitted several other Germanic groups into their own. The area was known in the Carolingian period as Alemania, a name that the West Franks would eventually apply to the entire East Frankish realm. The stem duchy of Swabia was resurrected after the disintegration of the Carolingian domain and ruled by the house of Hohenstaufen from the latter half of the eleventh century.

By the close of the medieval period, Swabia was likewise experiencing dissolution, and the area was apportioned into a great number of vassalages and autonomous towns. The name continued to figure in various contexts, for example in the Swabian League of Cities that was created to protect the status of the towns, and in administrative matters, as reflected in the designation 'the Swabian *Kreis*'.

FRISIA

At the beginning of recorded history the coastal area by the North Sea, between the Rhine and Weser, was inhabited by the West Germanic Frisians. Based in this core area, a stem community evolved under the leadership of native stem dukes during the seventh and eighth centuries. However, the Frisians were vanquished by Charlemagne. They were christianised and incorporated into the Carolingian empire in the ninth century. The role of the dukes was now abrogated, and the area was sectioned into a number of administrative areas. Following the divisions of the Frankish empire in the mid-800s, the Frisian territories would belong first to Lothar's domain and subsequently to the East Frankish German empire.

Several factors contributed to the breakup of the Frisian stem community. In the high Middle Ages, its western portion came under the influence of the Dutch counts and in the mid-fourteenth century it became an enfeoffment of the German Wittelsbach dynasty and subsequently of the Habsburgs.

The name 'Frisia' endured in the eastern portion of the original stem territory, where Frisian distinctiveness and specific legal structure were long preserved, and the feudal manorial system did not spread as on the rest of the continent. By the end of the Middle Ages, the East Frisian core area was transformed into a German imperial countship. As one of the seven united 'nether lands', the province of Frisia continued to have a significant place in the independent state of the Netherlands, which was internationally acknowledged in the Peace of Westphalia in 1648.

The Border Area Between France and Germany

In imperial Roman times, the Rhine was an enduring boundary between the Empire and the Germanic world. The two Roman provinces of Germania Superior, with Mainz as the principal town, and Germania Inferior centred on Cologne had been Romanized at an early stage. However, the entire expanse had again been Teutonised and made into a core area within the Frankish empire. At the result of the breakup of the Carolingian empire in the mid-ninth century an autonomous duchy named after Lothar II –'*Lothari regnum*' or Lotharingia – came into being along the border between the eastern and western Frankish realms. The duchy was eventually partitioned into two areas, Lower and Upper Lotharingia, but from the late Middle Ages the name 'Lotharingia' was associated only with the latter.

Lotharingia's autonomy could not be sustained in the long run given its position in the intersection of the eastern and western Frankish spheres of interest. It was brought into the East Frankish realm as its fifth stem duchy in AD 925, although Lotharingia was not, like other such duchies, a stem confederation. The area was ethnically dominated by West Franks, and the name of this new political formation was applied to both the people and the territory, in contrast to the remaining stem duchies where the stem name was decisive.

However, the status of Lotharingia did not crystallise in spite of its incorporation into the German orbit, and it long remained a bone of contention between France and Germany. Its boundaries were drawn and redrawn and the process of feudal disintegration was clearly taking place. Formally, the duchy of Lotharingia remained within the same ruling house up to its incorporation into France in the eighteenth century. However, the duke's territorial holdings were fractured, both within and outside the duchy.

Burgundy likewise occupied a critical position as a buffer between the French and German domains. After various tribulations, the Burgundians (believed to be of Scandinavian origin) finally settled in Savoy, a strategic border area between Italy and Gaul. The Burgundian kingdom was brought into the Frankish empire in the early sixth century, and the name of Burgundy was applied in various contexts in the areas west of the Alps and south to the Mediterranean coast. The Burgundian kings did not enjoy a particularly strong position, but by the late fourteenth century, marital transactions and inheritance made possible a resurrected Burgundian state-formation, legally subordinated to the German Emperor.

The southern portions of Burgundy were successively incorporated into France in the High Middle Ages. Towards the end of the Middle Ages, however, greater Burgundy, called the Great Duchy of the West, was a remarkable complex of territories that both the French monarchy and the Habsburgs laid claim to. The area comprised land in upper Burgundy, Luxemburg and the 'low countries' by the North Sea coast. Lotharingia figured as a wedge between the southern and northern parts. Moreover, a dividing line in the south separated the duchy of Burgundy (Bourgogne), administratively subordinated to France, and Franche-Comté to the east, subject to the German emperor. The border between France and the German empire thus directly traversed Burgundy.

The struggle for the Burgundian provinces was resolved in the Peace of Westphalia, whereupon the French kingdom extended its power to the areas by the Rhine. By this time, both Switzerland and the Netherlands had achieved independence. What remained of the complex of Burgundian lands was annexed by Louis XIV, and this was confirmed in the Peace of Nijmegen in 1679. In sum, the unfolding of events, ethnic and territorial divisions, the perpetual revision of boundaries, dynastic complications as well as feudal mechanisms combined to obstruct not only the development of a strong and enduring Burgundian state-formation but also the evolution of a regional identity tied to the old Burgundian kingdom.

Germanic Peoples and Slavs

During the reign of Charlemagne, the essential boundary between Germanic peoples and Slavs had stretched from the Elbe and Saal in the north to the Danube in the south. Germanic colonisation progressively pushed the border to the east, and domains were thereby established along the Baltic Sea east of the Elbe, and in the plains south of Erzgebirge and the Sudetes. In the *Völkerwanderungen*, the most northerly territory settled by Slavic tribes was by the Baltic coast between the Elbe and the Oder. This area was originally named Billunger Mark after the ruling house and was already taxed by the Franks in the Carolingian period. The population, which the Germans and northerners called 'the Wends', was progressively Germanised. The duchy of Mecklenburg was established here in the Middle Ages.

A number of smaller border regions (Uckermark, Mittelmark, Neumark) were amalgamated to form the larger region of Nordmark. The process followed the usual course. Immigrant Slavs had settled here during the *Völkerwanderungen*, after the Germanic founders of the regions had moved out. In the tenth century it was the turn of German colonists to elbow out the Slavs, who were either slaughtered, expelled or assimilated into the Germanic cultural sphere. By the mid-twelfth century the area was brought together as the margravate of Brandenburg, the core of which endured despite various dynastic transactions. The political importance of Brandenburg was accentuated with the Golden Bull

The Roots of Identity

of 1356, whereby the margrave obtained a permanent seat in the electoral college that named the Holy Roman Emperor.

The Sorbs, a Slavic people, had arrived in the borderlands south of Brandenburg during the *Völkerwanderungen*. They were also known as Lusatians, and the province of Lusatia was named after them. In contrast to the majority of Slavic settlers in the northern areas, the Sorbs conserved their Slavic language; Low Sorbian was spoken in lower Lusatia into modern times, but is now dying. However, the high Sorbian dialect spoken in upper Lusatia still exists, although its chances of survival are slim. Politically, and possibly culturally too, Lusatia became part of the German empire during the tenth century, but dynastic fluctuations caused recurrent shifts in the actual status of various parts of the region.

South-west of Lusatia, in the area designated Thuringian Mark in the High Middle Ages, another margravate named after its chief town, Meissen, was established and played a critical role in the struggle against various Slavic peoples.

A prominent position as a buffer-zone between Germanic and Slavic domains came to be occupied by Silesia, originally named after the Germanic Silingians, presumably a Vandal tribe. Slavs had moved into this area after the Germanic element had left it during the *Völkerwanderungen*. By the late tenth century, they found themselves within the established Polish domain under the Piasts, but were subsequently brought into the realm of the German empire. Silesia remained a bone of contention between the Polish, German and Bohemian interests until the area was transferred to Poland following the Second World War, with the Oder–Neisse Line as the new boundary (see below, pp. 212-58).

The encounter between Germanic and Slavic peoples cannot be understood exclusively as a struggle over territory, since it also involved a meeting of cultures. Indeed, at certain times the German and Polish kingdoms cooperated with each other in their struggle against those Slavic peoples still characterised as heathens.

The margravate of Meissen was interested not only in the territories to the east, but also in Bohemia in the south. This province had been named after the Celtic Boii, its inhabitants since the dawn of recorded history. During the *Völkerwanderungen* the area first witnessed the arrival of a Svebian stem, the Markomanians ('border-people'), followed by Slavs, who founded their own country here in the ninth century. From the middle of the tenth century Bohemia became liable to taxation under the German empire, in spite of being formally an autonomous imperial province under a king approved by the German Emperor. In the High Middle Ages, Bohemia and Moravia became important power resources in German politics, as bases for the Luxemburgian emperors in the fourteenth century and for the Habsburg dynasty from the early sixteenth.

Bavaria. During the *Völkerwanderungen* the Germanic Bavarians had forced the Celts out of the area between the Danube and the Alps. A duchy was created at an early stage within this region and was brought into Charlemagne's orbit in the late eighth century. After the division of the empire in 870, Bavaria was consolidated as a duchy and subsequently as a kingdom, first under the Welfs and then under the house of Wittelsbach. The formal rule of the latter dynasty only ended after the First World War.

Bavaria experienced territorial revisions in the Middle Ages, as did many other Central European areas. The duchy was at its largest during the tenth century, comprising territories south of the Alps including Bavarian Ostmark, Steiermark and Carinthia. In the High Middle Ages, Bavaria was reduced to the core area that still bears its name.

The Magyars. In the early tenth century the Magyars had moved into the Hungarian steppe, and from this base repeatedly made plundering expeditions deep into Central Europe. They entrenched themselves in the Slavic world and soon represented a severe threat to the East Frankish empire. Indeed, the need to coordinate defences against them was one factor leading the Germanic stem duchies to agree on the establishment of a central royal authority. Meanwhile, Magyar assaults on Bohemia were part of the reason why the Bohemian king turned to Germany for support and accepted the Emperor as overlord.

The Stem Duchies in the German Integration Process

The German Empire founded by Otto the Great around 1000 was to be based on four pillars: Germania, Gaul, Italy and the West Slavic areas. Known from the late Middle Ages as the Holy Roman Empire of the German Nation, the Empire was scarcely holy, Roman or German. Its claim to embrace Catholic Christianity

The Roots of Identity

rested on grounds even weaker than those propounded by Charlemagne. In addition, its continuity with the Roman Empire was no more than symbolic, and the substance of the phrase 'German Nation' was clearly dissimilar to what it would become in the nineteenth century. However, the composition of the German Empire is of great interest in any analysis of the preconditions for state- and nation-building throughout Central Europe. Despite similar points of departure, none of the stems in East Francia became the foundation for a stable, distinct state-formation, as the West Franks had in France. The need to coordinate defences against the Slavs and Magyars led the stem dukes to accept the creation of a central authority, although this newly-created power had only limited resources at its disposal.

Meanwhile, stem duchies were established within territories that had been institutionalised and demarcated before the *Völkerwanderungen*. This implies that the identities of the various ethnic groups were linked to the stem rather than to the territory, where the degree of continuity was less apparent. The feudal fief system later gained ground quickly in this area, which inhibited the evolution and preservation of territorial identities.

Central Europe was parcelled into a myriad of small entities perpetually subject to change due to feudal and dynastic processes, wars and treaties. These realities prevented the Emperors from strengthening a German central power, while also preventing the dukes from consolidating regionally unified power-bases. The imperial power was ultimately victorious in the struggle between Emperor and stem dukes, and Otto the Great could thus claim the entire duchy of Franconia alongside his Saxon territories, while simultaneously seeking to curtail the influence of the remaining stem dukes.

However, the territorial base of the German imperial power was not enough to consolidate an all-embracing state in medieval Central Europe. Nor did the electoral college, with its heterogeneous composition of ecclesiastical and secular princes, have a power base that could be developed sufficiently. However, this did not mean that the role of the elector lost its importance, and several of the leading ruling houses (Ascanian, Wittelsbach, Hohenzollern) attempted to increase their influence in the empire by consolidating their local territories. The independence of the territorial princes was accentuated after the abdication of the imperial power, connected with the so-called Interregnum in the mid-thirteenth century. However, before the end of the Middle Ages no single prince could single-handedly amass a territorial power base able to balance the collectivity of the other princes.

The Medieval Legacy?

The German Empire, comprising over 300 sovereign principalities and imperial cities, subsisted in name till 1806, when it was conclusively dissolved by Napoleon. The old German empire was never re-established, nor was the so-called *Rheinbund*. Instead a federative system – the German League – was organised, consisting of some forty sovereign states. Two of these states, Austria and Prussia, were stronger than the others and it was the rivalry between them that ultimately caused the disintegration of the League, the exclusion of Austria and the unification of Germany in 1871 on terms dictated by Prussia.

The constellation of states established at the Congress of Vienna in 1815 had varying origins, but dynastic matters had played a more or less decisive role in every case. No direct link to the historic territorial divisions was made in the establishment of these states, but some of the ancient place-names were preserved as in for example the kingdom of Saxony and a series of smaller principalities that included the name of Saxony: Saxe-Coburg, Saxe-Altenburg, Saxe-Meiningen and Saxe-Weimar.

A limited number of the older principalities, like Bavaria and Württemberg, continued to exist during the German League period, but most were completely new creations, with new core areas and new borders. The case of Prussia was exceptional. At the time of unification, it excluded Austria, Bohemia, Liechtenstein and Luxemburg, while annexing and taking control of the historical provinces of Schleswig, Holstein, Lauenburg, Hesse, Hannover and Frankfurt am Main. After 1871 twenty-five territorial entities existed within the framework of the newly-established Prussian empire, although their independence existed only on paper.

During the period of the Weimar Republic the number of states was further reduced, as seven small Thuringian states unified to become one, and Saxe-Coburg was transferred to Bavaria. The remaining territorial structure was essentially unaltered and survived the Nazi era. Except for such revisions as enlarging the Hamburg area and ending Lübeck's status as an autonomous Hanseatic city, few territorial changes were made. Some boundaries were redrawn, e.g. portions of Mecklenburg were joined to form one *Land*. However, such administrative adjustments were scarcely relevant compared with the shattering transformations effected by the Nazi *Gleichschaltung*, which made the division into *Länder* obsolete.

This entire territorial structure, consisting of a singular blend of older and newer and larger and smaller entities, diverse legal constitutions and varying dynastic and historical claims, was revived after the Second World War: the four victorious Allied powers were now confronted with the task of forging new administrative bodies in their zones of occupation. The resulting *Länder* division in the Federal Republic of Germany created in 1949 and the corresponding regional constructions in the German Democratic Republic reflect the difficulty of breaking from historically constructed notions. The border between the two systems was drawn without consideration for former divisions. The West German *Bundesländer* consisted of new constructions, merged older areas such as North Rhine-Westphalia and Baden-Württemberg, and regions with long historical continuity such as Schleswig-Holstein and Bavaria. In the case of Bavaria titular continuity can be traced back to the Middle Ages, and the core area remains unaltered. It is thus unique insofar as it is a historical region with a cultural, territorial and political continuity that goes back uninterruptedly further than is the case in any other present-day German region.

In essence, the *Länder* structure has persisted into present-day Germany, despite the reunification of the country in 1990. In the Eastern portion, the old GDR, the *Länder* abolished in 1952 have been re-established. One of them, Thuringia, correlates to an early medieval embryonic ethno-territoriality, and the name of Saxony figures in no less than three contemporary *Bundesländer*, namely Sachsen, Sachsen-Anhalt and Nieder-Sachsen. Few traces remain of the three oldest stem duchies in present-day Germany. Feudalism and dynastic politics had already stifled ancient ethno-territoriality before the High Middle Ages. Nationalism and state-formation in the German area of Central Europe subsequently proceeded along a singular course for centuries. The question remains whether the German historical regions will be significant in an even more integrated Europe. Deep structures are tenacious.

SELECT BIBLIOGRAPHY

Bachofer, W. and H. Fischer (eds), *Ungarn – Deutschland. Studien zu Sprache, Kultur, Geographie und Geschichte* (1983).

Baumann, H., 'Die Bedeutung des Kaiserstums für die Entstehung der deutschen Nation' in *Nationes I, Aspekte der Nationenbildung im Mittelater. Ergebnisse der Marburger Rundgespräche, 1972-75,* 1978.

———, 'Regnum Teutonicum und Rex Teutonicorum in ottonischer und salischer Zeit' (*Archiv für Kulturgeschichte* 55, 1973).

Brücher, W., and P.R. Franke (eds), *Probleme von Grenzregionen,* Faculty of Philosophy, Saarland University, 1987.

Demant, H. (ed.), *Deutschlands Grenzen in der Geschichte* (1990).

Franz, G. (ed.), *Grenzbildende Faktoren in der Geschichte* (1969).

Fritze, W.H., 'Corona Regni Bohemiæ' in L. Kuchenbuch and W. Schick, *Frühzeit zwichen Ostsee und Donau,* 1982).

Gebhardt, *Handbuch der deutschen Geschichte* (9th edn, V.A. Grundmann, vol. 1, 1970).

Hlawitschka, E., *Vom Frankenreich zur Formierung der europäischen Staaten- und Völkergemeinschaft, 840-1046* (1986).

Karp, H.J., *Grenzen in Ostmitteleuropa während des Mittelalters. Ein Beitrag zur Entstehungsgeschichte der Grenzlinie aus dem Grensaum* (1972).

Kienast, W., *Deutschland und Frankreich in der Kaiserzeit (970-1270),* 3 vols (1974-5).

Köbler, G., *Historisches Lexikon der deutschen Länder. Die deutschen Territorien vom Mittelalter bis zur Gegenwart* (1988).

Maurer, H., 'Confinium Alamannorum. Über Wesen und Bedeutung hochmittelalterlicher "Stammengrenzen" ' in *Historische Forschungen für Walter Schlesinger,* 1974.

Mitteis, H., *Der Staat des hohen Mittelalters* (1953).

Rokkan, S., and D.W. Urwin (eds), *The Politics of Territorial Identity: Studies in European Regionalism* (1982).

Schlesinger, W. (ed.), *Die deutsche Ostsiedlung des Mittelalters als Problem der europäischen Geschichte* (1975).

Schultz, H.D., 'Pax Geographica. Räumliche Konzepte für Krieg und Frieden in der geographischen Tradition' (*Geogr. Zeitschr.* 75, 1987).

Schulze, H.K., *Vom Reich der Franken zum Land der Deutschen* (1967).

Schönberger, H., 'Der römische Limes in Deutschland. Begriff und Funktionen' in Franz, 1969.

Szás, Z.M., *Die deutsche Ostgrenze. Geschichte und Gegenwart* (1961).

Thomas, H., *Zwischen Regnum und Imperium. Die Fürstentümer Bar und Lothringen zur Zeit Kaiser Karl IV* (1973).

Wendt, B.J., ' "Mitteleuropa" – Zur Kontinuität deutscher Raumpolitik in zwanzigsten Jahrhundert' in Bachofer and Fischer, 1983.

REGIONAL DEEP STRUCTURES IN THE GERMAN CULTURAL SPACE

Lisbeth Lindeborg

Introduction

Within the framework of the gradual realisation of a 'Europe of the Regions' as the third level in the European Union (EU), issues concerning ongoing or new regionalisation processes (as in Italy and Sweden), together with the establishment of federal structures (as in Belgium), are becoming increasingly important in both theory and practice.[1] This implies that the regionalisation process must be seen not only in an intraregional perspective, but also as an integral part of supranational, state and local developments.

The opening of borders within the EU has increased the need for a spatial reorganisation of Europe. Accordingly, both the EU's Directorate General for Regional Affairs (DG XVI) and Europe's stronger regions, most notably those in Germany, have begun coordinating planning strategies in which regions have a central role.[2] Moreover, parallel to the Europeanisation and regionalisation processes, there is another profound transformation, namely the structural changes and the transition from a traditional industrial society to a knowledge society with its new knowledge-based industries. In this context the region is emerging as an arena of new dignity, as new structures are required, for example small-scale networks, supporting diversification and pluralism. Thus both globalisation and regionalisation of the economy run in tandem.

Thus the region as a territorial unit to be reckoned with has received increasing attention in recent years. In certain states, such as Switzerland and Belgium and also Germany, Spain and

---

[1] Four decision levels are distinguished in the EU, namely the supranational, the nation-state, the regional and the local.

[2] The label for this planning strategy is 'Europe 2000+' and proceeds mainly from the territorial/spatial perspective.

Italy (at least in parts), regional awareness has long been the basis for claims to demarcated physical areas. Conversely, in states where regional awareness has been neglected or suppressed for the sake of forced national homogeneity (e.g. in Scandinavia), the regional dimension entails a new challenge of uncertain character.[3] Irrespective of the different regional experiences, however, political answers have to be provided to questions regarding such issues as a given region's territorial parameters, the scope of its authority, its administration and management, its economic potential, physical planning, infrastructure and cultural and educational opportunities. Each of these fields of activity includes an essential issue, namely the significance of the regional identity – the regional deep structures.

The Council of Europe and the Assembly of European Regions (AER) have defined the region as the territorial body of public law established at the level immediately below that of the state and endowed with political self-government, thus providing a categorisation reflecting the developing regional reality of Europe.[4] This definition corresponds to the first basic quality of a region as a political, administrative and functional space. Another quality encompasses the region as a cultural space where the individual has a sense of belonging and identifies with it. In some cases these two archetypes may coincide, as in Catalonia, Saxony, Alsace, Lombardy, Jura, Vorarlberg, Saarland, Wallonia, Flanders and Brittany.

A characteristic of the region as a cultural space is its dynamism, involving a wider scope of possibilities than the nation-state. While awareness within the latter is confined to a specific, closed space and therefore has to be curbed within the state borders, several levels of regional awareness can exist at the same time. Typically the regional levels are often interwoven and their territorial parameters shift as various regional functions and operations are expanded or curtailed, renewed or revised. Many of these regional contexts are rooted in older regional deep structures, often recently rediscovered. Others are based on newly-formed communities

---

[3] For an analysis of the reasons and conditions for the regionalisation process, see Lisbeth Lindeborg, *Regionfrågan i Sverige* (The regional issue in Sweden), Stockholm, 1997.

[4] Ibid.

Regional Deep Structures in the German Cultural Space 55

GERMANY 1991

with identities constructed later.[5] A person living in the south German city of Ulm, for instance, can claim to belong to the old monarchy of Württemberg, the post-war *Bundesland* Baden-Württemberg, the microregion Danube-Alb, the cross-border macroregional Danube area, and, according to the notion of functional regions, a modern science and technology region.[6]

In 'Europe of the Regions', the regions in the federal states such as Germany and Austria, and in regionalised states like Italy, serve as models for regions in decentralised states such as the Netherlands, and in the unitary ones such as Britain and Sweden.[7]

Thus, German federalism as well as the microregionalisation of the *Bundesländer* and the cross-border cooperation along the German borders have been highlighted in connection with discussions on the future of Europe. Of what relevance are the regional deep structures in those contexts? Can the phrase 'regional belonging' really be applied when speaking of the German *Bundesländer*, which are largely artificial, post-war constructions? (When using the regional definition of the Council of Europe and the AER, the *Bundesländer* constitute the German regions. But beside this regional level another current process is going on inside some of the *Bundesländer*, dividing them into smaller units and thus creating yet another administrative level between the region (*Bundesland*) and the local community (*Gemeinde*). This

---

[5] On identities as constructions and 'reality', see Rune Johansson's chapter (pp.1-30, above).

[6] According to the definition employed here, '*microregions*', which may be of varying size, exist either within the physical boundaries of a region, or are cross-border areas of two or more regions within one state. '*Macroregions*' cut across national boundaries and comprise several regions, often together with microregions, in rather loose constellations. The scholar Klaus Kunzmann, whose research focuses on the region, has provided a detailed categorization of functional regions in his report *Raumordnerische Aspekte des EG-Binnenmarktes*, for the Bundesministerium für Raumordnung, Bauwesen und Städtebau (Bonn, 1991). According to Kunzmann, functional regions are not only territorially defined, but should also be defined on the basis of their distinct tasks and competencies.

[7] See Christian Engel and Wolfgang Wessels, *Regionen in der EG* (Bonn, 1993), pp. 15-16. According to their definition, the difference between regionalised and decentralised states is that regions in the former category exercise greater political power and have a wider scope of authority. Unitary states are centrally governed entities with a 'weak' regional level.

Regional Deep Structures in the German Cultural Space 57

process is either called 'regionalisation' or 'microregionalisation'. In this chapter the latter term, microregionalisation, is used.)

Before tackling these questions, we should note that the issue of regional and microregional identity has become increasingly important in the 1980s and '90s.[8] There are several reasons for this. First, it has become evident that a sense of regional belonging invigorates the region: a strong sense of regional identity gives the local population the self-confidence it needs to make itself heard, both at the national and the European levels.[9] Being the resident of a region involves the adoption of a new role, that of '*Homo regionalis*', encompassing both rights and responsibilities. When there are several coexisting regional/microregional identities as in the case of Ulm, there is a greater number of arenas in which to act.

Second, there is a growing need to anchor oneself historically, to define one's local/regional roots in a world that is steadily changing and appears increasingly unstable. This leads to the third reason, namely, that a distinctive identity also gives the region/microregion its particular profile or image. The identity holds a kind of market value, within the framework of the region's two rather contradictory roles – as partner in a context of amplified regional cooperation, and as contender in the struggle for a more prominent position in the European and global ranking lists of regions.[10]

A fourth reason for the growing interest in the issue of regional/microregional identities has to do with the concept of a region's 'endogenous potential'. In order for that to be activated it is important for people to identify with the region where they live.[11] The process of regionalisation, which can generally be

---

[8] See Lindeborg, *Regionalt samarbete i Europa* (Stockholm, 1995), pp. 26-7 (English edition, 1999).

[9] In an interview with the author in 1991, Bruce Millan, the former EU Commissioner for regional affairs, noted that the 'strengthening of regional identity [...] serves to stimulate economic development'.

[10] See Lindeborg, *Regionalt samarbete...*, *op. cit.*, p. 439.

[11] See, for instance, Ernst Brugger, 'Die Infrastruktur im Dienste der Regionalpolitik' in Christian Hauser and Simon Huber (eds), *Hat die traditionelle Infrastrukturförderung für die periphere Regionen ausgedient?* (Basel, 1982). 'Endogenous' refers to the inherent political, cultural and social possibilities that exist within a demarcated territorial space.

described as one of emancipation and democratisation, is promoted by a sense of regional affinity. Last but not least, there is the realisation that the diversity of Europe, as represented by the regions, is in itself one of the continent's greatest resources. Thus, recognition of the significance of regional belonging has generated investigations into and rediscoveries of often long-forgotten and neglected regional deep structures, as well as the forging of new identities.[12]

The pervasiveness of regional deep structures within the context of regional development was demonstrated in Germany in May 1996 by a popular referendum on the merging of Berlin with the region of Brandenburg. Although this consolidation was rational and economically sound, the people of Brandenburg voted against it. Given the centuries-old distinction between the identities of the hectic city of Berlin and their tranquil region the Brandenburgers voted according to their emotional imperatives. Also, more recent structural differences contributed to the outcome of the referendum. For many residents of Brandenburg, Berlin symbolises both East German centralism and West German arrogance, and the two are considered equally repugnant.[13]

Against this background, which emphasises the current processes of (micro)regionalisation and significance of regional identity, our main object here is to test the hypothesis that the existence of deep structures, whether uninterrupted over the course of time or rediscovered recently, is of decisive importance to the course of regionalisation and regional development.[14] This investigation is limited to the German cultural space, and within that context the above hypothesis leads to two further questions: first, in what form has a historically and culturally formed regional awareness persisted in the German cultural space? And secondly, how important are the regional deep structures within the context of

---

[12] One example is provided by Europe's largest region, Nordrhein-Westfalen (North Rhine-Westphalia). While seeking to create a specific 'we-feeling' in this region, an active rediscovery of the deep structures in its microregions is currently taking place. See pp. 90-2 below.

[13] This was revealed in statements made to the press and on television during the election campaign and after.

[14] The term 'regionalisation process' is used in this chapter to denote the region-building process. The phrase 'regional development' refers to the interior development of any regional territory, independent of its political power.

(micro)regionalisation processes and regional development in the post-war Federal Republic?

Defining the German Cultural Space

> Einzig die Dichter wussten noch,
> was deutsch zu nennen sich lohne.
> Sie hätten die deutsche Sprache als
> letztes Band geknüpft. Sie seien das
> andere, das wahrhaftige Deutschland.
> (Günter Grass)[15]

> So weit die deutsche Zunge klingt,
> Und Gott im Himmel Lieder singt,
> Das soll es sein....
> (Ernst Moritz Arndt)[16]

> Es ist undeutsch, bloss deutsch zu sein.
> (Friedrich Meinecke)[17]

The quotations above suggest the complexities involved in concepts such as 'the German question', 'the land in the middle', '*Sonderweg*', '*die verspätete Nation*', '*das schwierige Vaterland*' and '*Deutschtum*' (Germanness). They imply a lack of congruence between people-state-territory-language, and that the German *Kulturnation* does not coincide with the German nation-state.[18]

Although the poet Walther von der Vogelweide used the terms '*thiudisk*', '*tütsch*' and '*teutonicus*' (German) as early as c. 1200, to

---

[15] Translation: 'Only the poets can know what it is worthwhile calling German. They would tie the German language together as a final ribbon. They would be the other, the true Germany.' Günter Grass, *Das Treffen in Telge* (Reinbek, 1981), p.90.

[16] 'So widely is the German tongue heard, that even God in his heaven sings German songs. Thus it will be...' Ernst Moritz Arndt, 'Geist der Zeit', [1808] *Ausgewählte Werke*, ed. H. Meissner and R. Geerds (Leipzig, 1909), vol. XI, p.177.

[17] Translation: 'It is un-German to be merely German.' See Klaus Vieweg, 'Es ist undeutsch bloss deutsch zu sein. Zur Aktualität des universalistischen Denkens bei Hegel' in P. Braitling and W. Reese-Schäfer (eds), *Universalismus, Nationalismus und die neue Einheit der Deutschen* (Frankfurt am Main, 1991).

[18] See, for instance, Helmut Plessner, *Die verspätete Nation* (Frankfurt am Main, 1974); Helga Grebing, *Der deutsche Sonderweg in Europa, 1806-1945. Eine Kritik* (Stuttgart, 1986); Werner Weidenfeld, *Nachdenken über Deutschland* (Cologne, 1985).

describe a formation where linguistic-cultural roots were indistinguishable from political ones, his conception did not correspond to the reality of the time, nor would it have for long afterwards.[19] The prevailing political structures were as poorly adapted to linguistic boundaries as the language was to the political dividing lines. For example, the eleventh-century border between the West Frankish/French and the East Frankish/German empires did not correspond to that between the Germanic and Romance languages: substantial Romance-language areas existed in the duchy of Lorraine; West Frankish Flanders was largely German-speaking; and in the east the German political domain extended into Slavic-language areas.

The German historian Werner Conze labels this phenomenon *'Die Doppelsinnigkeit deutscher Geschichte'* (The ambiguity of German history), referring to the separate evolution of a cultural history on the one hand and a political history on the other.[20] The longing to consolidate language and culture-areas into a politically unified territory has always existed alongside a strong element of political particularism. However, this ambition was not realised till 1871, although there had been opportunities to achieve it earlier. For instance, in 1635, a particularly militarily rewarding year for the German emperor, it would have been possible to unify the principalities and the duchies under a single monarch, but such opportunities were invariably missed, partly because the French monarchy much preferred Germany divided rather than unified and partly because, since the Middle Ages, tribal identities, which were firmly anchored in a thoroughly implemented feudal system and in strong local communities, had impeded the evolution of an overarching sense of national German cohesion. Such tribalism enabled external forces to obstruct unification of the German states more easily.

It was only around 1800 that a significant degree of German national awareness became apparent.[21] This development posed a

---

[19] See Werner Conze, 'Einheit und Vielfalt in der deutschen Geschichte' in W. Conze and W. Hentschel (eds), *Ploetz Deutsche Geschichte* (Freiburg, 1979), p.10.

[20] Ibid.

[21] The Napoleonic wars were a significant factor in liberating a German sense of national affinity.

number of questions. Who was to be counted as German? Was language to be the criterion? Not everyone who spoke German wished to be German; this was true of the Swiss Germans and portions of the population of Alsace. Should inhabitants of a German state – the Czechs in eastern Bohemia, the Italians in South Tyrol and the Poles in Prussia – all be defined as Germans?

In the early nineteenth century, the poet and historian Ernst Moritz Arndt suggested that language be established as a criterion for national belonging. His proposal, whereby Germany would stretch 'from the North Sea to the Carpathians, from the Baltic Sea to the Alps, and from the Vistula to the Scheldt', can be understood as an expression of patriotic euphoria rather than a realistic plan.[22] Other proposals implying a 'Great German' (*grossdeutsch*) solution and likewise proceeding from the notion of a German *Kulturnation* were subsequently laid forth.[23]

When the 'Little German' (*kleindeutsch*) solution was implemented in 1871 in connection with the unification of Germany, it incorporated the German national minorities in certain border areas, but substantial parts of the German populations outside the core area were excluded. The German *Kulturnation* would for ever remain far larger than the German nation-state, and the distinction between *Volksdeutsche* and *Reichsdeutsche* thus emerged.[24] The territorial boundaries of Germany, which have repeatedly shifted over time, e.g. in Alsace, the Saar, and Oder–Neisse, have not corresponded to the larger German language and cultural space that continues to preserve its identity. In addition to Austria, Switzerland and Liechtenstein, the German language and cultural space comprises a minority in Belgium, enclaves in Poland (Silesia), the Volga Germans in Russia, those in northern Italy's Alto Adige or South Tyrol, a tiny minority in southern Jutland, and a few other groups.

While today's reunified German state has 80 million inhabitants, the German-language population runs to at least 100 million. For

---

[22] See Harald Schmidt, 'Fremde Heimat' in Helmut Berding (ed.), *Nationale Bewusstsein und kollektive Identität* (Frankfurt, 1994), pp.394-443.

[23] Ibid.

[24] *Reichsdeutsche* were citizens of the German state, and generally resided within its boundaries. *Volksdeutsche* were ethnic Germans who lived outside of the state itself and were not citizens of the German state.

instance, the evolution of territorially anchored Austrian and German-Swiss identities has not obliterated the sense of affinity between the peoples in various parts of the language area, as has been reflected in intensive cross-border cooperation activities. Similarly, Austria's rapid federalisation after the Second World War was certainly influenced by the examples of federalisation in southern Germany (Baden-Württemberg and Bavaria).

The untroubled relationship in the present between Austria and Germany is also due to Austria's deliberate efforts to distance itself from Germany after the Second World War. Thus, the myth of a 'German-Austrian people' was dismantled by invoking the ancient heritage of the Central European tribes – Bavarians, Alemanns, Franks and Danube-Swabians. With his statement in Bonn in 1975 that the first Austrians were not a Germanic but a Celtic people, the Austrian Chancellor of the time, Bruno Kreisky, accentuated Austria's detachment from Germany. The regional diversity in Austria, he emphasised, resulted from the intermixing of the Austrians with Hungarians, Slavs, Huns and Turkic peoples.[25]

The discrepancy between the German *Kulturnation* and the German nation-state has been described by Günther Nenning:

Never, except for a short-lived catastrophe, was Germany unitaristic, let alone a centralistic nation-state; it was a historically matured boundless realm of minds. A colourful bundle of tribes, dialects, small states. Common content: language, culture. Common source of conflict: the nation-state as a dream. The nation-state as a reality meant nightmare.[26]

From Germanic tribes to German Bundesländer and regions: a historical overview

'Seen in a long-term perspective, it seems an open question...whether the existence of quite a number of German states in the middle of Europe would not correspond to European normality – if there ever was something which could be called normality.'[27]

---

[25] See Fritz Stüber, 'Wie Deutsch ist Österreich heute noch?', *Deutsche Annalen. Jahrbuch des Nationalgeschehens* (1976), pp.138-49.

[26] Günther Nenning, *Grenzenlos Deutsch* (Munich, 1988), pp.15 and 21.

[27] Wolfgang Mommsen, 'Weder Leugnen noch Vergessen befreit von der Vergangenheit', in Serie Piper, Bd 816: *Historikerstreit* (Munich, 1987), p.318.

Regional Deep Structures in the German Cultural Space 63

To what extent did geographic-topographic, political and cultural circumstances contribute to *Kleinstaaterei*, and later to regionalisation within the German cultural area? And to what extent have early regional deep structures survived?

The *Sib* or family clan, along with a certain degree of domestic organisation and judicial structure, stood at the core of the medieval German tribes, which included the Franks, Alemanns (later known as the Swabians), Bavarians, Saxons, Frisians and Thuringians. However, with the exception of the Bavarians these tribes lacked a unifying internal structure and administrative order. Power was exercised locally, through various leagues and groups of families.

In AD 500 the Frankish royal authority was able to consolidate the Frankish tribes into a 'state'-formation, but as the power of the monarchy intermittently waned, the various tribes gained the upper hand once more. This changed during the rule of the Carolingian dynasty. Under Charlemagne (768-814), the Frankish realm reached its greatest extent. After 814, as noted in a previous chapter, his three sons divided the empire among themselves, with Louis obtaining the eastern part, the embryo of what was to become Germany.[28] Various tribes or 'stems' were incorporated into the Carolingian state-formation, and this proved crucial both to the evolution of the 'state' and to developments concerning the 'stems'.

To monitor the activities of both the sub-tribes (*Teilstämme*) and the incorporated Alemanns, Bavarians and others, their leaders were assigned certain 'state' functions within the Frankish empire. The 'institutions' that were set up to that end were called 'duchies', the head of the tribe being a 'duke'. The duchies were responsible mainly for acting as intermediaries between the royal authority and the stem. Another function was vaguely described as 'maintaining peace'.[29]

The boundaries between the various functions and spheres of authority of the royal power, the stems, the duchies and so on were diffuse. This was further complicated by the presence of other contenders, such as the ecclesiastical officials – the bishops

---

[28] The year 936 is generally accepted as marking the birth of the German empire. In August of that year, dukes, counts and other nobles gathered at Aachen for the coronation of Otto I as King of Germany. Otto became Emperor in 962.

[29] See Sven Tägil's essay in this volume (pp.30-52).

and abbots. In the absence of a central authority, the kings delegated certain administrative functions to the Church, whose interests did not always coincide with those of the royal power. The medieval German state was dualistic, with its state functions divided between kingly or imperial power, which was elected and thus not based on territorial origins, and tribal peoples, the nobility and the Church.[30] In sum, the domestic arena in medieval Germany was generally fragmented and anarchic.[31]

The cultural and political realities that paved the way for *Kleinstaaterei* and regionalisation can thus be traced back to the early Middle Ages. A strong local affiliation in conjunction with *Sibs* and *Teilstämme*, and with the focus on small, relatively independent entities, survived over time. However, the desire to consolidate the smaller entities into a larger federal unit evolved alongside the continuous process of particularisation. Indeed, such endeavours became ever more prominent over the centuries, as was noted by Otto von Gierke (1841-1921) in his voluminous standard work on German *Genossenschaftsrecht* ('*Genossenschaft*' refers to fraternity, union and, later, cooperative federation). Gierke's work presents the history of the German people as a history of *Genossenschaft*.[32]

A phenomenon directly related to early local affinity, which promoted further particularisation, was the *Heimatstadt*. Small towns of between 1000 and 10,000 inhabitants called *Heimatstädte* evolved in the German core area in the period from the Peace of Westphalia in 1648 to the unification of Germany in 1871.[33] Despite variations among them, they operated on a similar basis: a narrow view of life, anachronistic institutions, resistance to modern developments,

---

[30] This meant that not only state functions but statehood itself were divided.

[31] See Theodor Mayer, 'Die Ausbildung der Grundlagen des modernen deutschen Staates im Hohen Mittelalter', in Hellmut Kämpf (ed.), *Herrschaft und Staat im Mittelalter* (Darmstadt, 1964), p.293.

[32] Otto von Gierke, *Das deutsche Genossenschaftsrecht*, 4 vols, Berlin, 1896-1914.

[33] See Wilhelm H. Riehl, *Die Naturgeschichte des Volkes als Grundlage einer deutschen Sozialpolitik* (Leipzig, 1935). Riehl, an ethnologist, wrote of an 'individualised Germany' and of the 'varied encyclopedia of our society'.

strong individual identification with the home community, and exclusive interaction within families, kin and associations.[34]

The *Heimat* itself is likewise concerned with an identity rooted in the local/(micro)regional community. The Swiss educationalist Johann Heinrich Pestalozzi (1746-1827) was among the first to develop a *Heimat* theory based on man's immediate physical space.[35] The theme has subsequently been dealt with by sociologists and ethnologists as well as philosophers and poets. In the aftermath of the Second World War the *Heimat* concept was discredited and acquired highly negative connotations. *Heimat* was seen as a manifestation of the German people's problematic relationship to nation and native community which had led to disaster; it evoked memories of Nazi Germany's '*Blut und Boden*' mythology.[36] In the early 1930s Kurt Tucholsky noted: 'When it comes to patriotism, we are outdone by everyone; when it comes to affection for the *Heimat*, we outdo everyone.'[37]

Only in 1980s did the concept of *Heimat* come to lose some of its negative content: affection for one's native community was not a repugnant phenomenon *per se*. Narratives of high quality were presented, both in film and literature. For instance, Edgar Reitz produced an epic film called *Heimat*, with manifestly Leftist overtones. Such productions served to 'decontaminate' the concept, and a veritable *Heimat* renaissance was launched.[38] This development signalled a longing for pre-modern, easily comprehensible structures, and the sense of security that can only come from possessing a full grasp of one's immediate surroundings – '*Geborgenheit im*

[34] See Mack Walker, *German Home Towns: Community, State and General Estate, 1648-1871* (London, 1971), p.174.

[35] See Johann H. Pestalozzi, *Die Abendstunde eines Einsiedlers* (1780).

[36] The Nazis did not understand '*Blut und Boden*'/*Heimat* as regional pluralism, and instead used the phrase as a slogan against asphalt and an absence of roots, against urban life and tolerant cosmopolitanism, in other words a lifestyle attributed to the Jews. See, for instance, Kurt Stavenhagen, *Heimat als Grundlage menschlicher Existenz* (Göttingen, 1939), pp.10-12.

[37] Kurt Tucholsky, 'Heimat', *Gesammelte Werke*. Bd III: 1929-1932, pp.312-14.

[38] The *Heimat* in question in Reitz's film is Hunsrück in Rheinland-Pfalz, where, prior to 1989, the American nuclear missiles were stationed. This gave rise to the phrase '*Militärheimat Hunsrück*' an ironic reference to the film, but one which indicates that the term *Heimat* has shed its association with the Nazis and can now be used freely.

Selbstverständlichen' (security in what we take for granted).[39] In addition, the *Heimat* museums which had since 1918 been used for political purposes have become much more popular over the past decades.[40]

While the *Heimat* renaissance can be understood as an extension of the German particularist tradition, it also draws from the force of post-war regionalism, the environmental movement, the 'small is beautiful' trend, and growing interest in local and regional history. Thus, particularisation, *Kleinstaaterei* and (micro) regionalisation are peculiar to the German cultural space, which bears a dense network of deep (micro)regional boundary lines. This is a recurrent theme in both domestic and international research.[41] However, there are few studies dealing with the evolution in specific territories, where more recent regional contexts, e.g. (functional and other) microregions and cross-border regions, are the point of departure.

We now return to the Middle Ages. The transfer of various 'state' functions to the newly-appointed 'stem' institutions – the 'duchies' – conferred a political legitimacy on the tribe and its territorial successors (principalities, countships, small states etc.) The decentralisation and institutionalisation of state operations such as the judicial system, peace keeping, founding of cities, customs and the monetary system instilled a sense of self-confidence in the stems' successors. Then, as now, certain functions shifted between state and regional institutions and were not rigidly confined to either level. Thus the political legitimation of the medieval 'stem' duchies evolved as a tradition that is today manifested by the *Bundesländer*.[42]

The *Sibs*, 'stems' and duchies were not the only factors behind the early development of *Kleinstaaterei*: the distinctive German

[39] See Christian Graf von Krockow, *Die Reise nach Pommern* (Stuttgart, 1985), p.153.

[40] Several cultural surveys produced in the past few decades indicate that the *Heimat* museums are the most popular museums in Germany.

[41] See, for instance, Celia Applegate, *A Nation of Provincials: The German Idea of Heimat* (Berkeley, CA, 1990).

[42] German federalism is dealt with below, pp.82 ff.

evolution within the parameters of feudalism is also relevant here. Like the other European states, Germany had a class of specialised soldiers who served the kingly/imperial/princely authorities, and were rewarded for their military services with enfeoffment. This vassal system, or *Lehnswesen*, was based on mutual loyalty. The king/prince offered the vassal a gift of land (the fief), and protection, in return for absolute loyalty and obedience. In the medieval chronicle *Sachsenspiegel* this system was concisely summed up as '*Das Lehen ist der Lohn des Ritters*' (The fief is the knight's reward).

Since the feudal system was practised at every level, in Germany feudalisation soon encompassed the entire empire. The German feudal state, having a separate judicial system, was not subject to general laws, which meant it would develop in a distinct direction of its own. In addition, enfeoffment became hereditary. It was decided that the entire fief would be bequeathed to one single heir, but this rule was ignored: when the vassal died, the fief was often apportioned among several heirs. Hence, the law of the right to property took precedence over the law concerning the fief.

In the early thirteenth century, the first indications occurred of a transition away from the 'anarchy' described above, and towards a decentralised structure more extensively organised. This development took place under the Staufer Emperor, Frederick II. In the law of *Confoederatio cum principibus ecclesiasticis* (1220) land was granted to the ecclesiastical princes at the expense of the imperial cities. A subsequent law, the '*Statutum in favorem principum*' of 1231-2, stipulated that the secular small princes (often called *Landesherren*) would likewise be granted additional land to the detriment of the crown.[43] Frederick adopted such measures because of compelling political considerations, and the laws thus did not indicate that the possible advantages of federalism had suddenly been recognised. The Emperor, after all, depended heavily on the support of the minor princes, and this reality lay at the root of the new legislation. The decisions of 1220 and 1231-2 nevertheless proved decisive for developments in Germany. From this time, *Landesherrschaft* would be part of the structural foundation of the state. In contrast to most other European powers, where the founding of

---

[43] The introduction of these laws entailed no tangible loss for the Crown, since they essentially formalised a state of affairs that had long been in place.

the state produced more centralised structures, German state-building began in the small states.

The boundaries between the small principalities continuously shifted due to feudal transactions, marriages, divisions of joint property, quarrels and outright warfare, with the result that the number of principalities steadily grew. By the time of the French Revolution, no fewer than 1,790 independent, and mainly small, 'states' existed.[44] The internal divisions caused several powerful cities to emerge, and these in turn paved the way for leagues of cities, such as the Hansa.

In 1495 Emperor Maximilian I convened a 'parliament' at Worms and series of reforms followed, with the aim of transforming Germany into a unified area of peace and law. The consolidation of a *Reichstag* (imperial diet), the establishment of a central court of justice and the introduction of an imperial tax were the first firm foundations for a federally structured constitution.[45] The development was further affirmed by the division of the Empire into ten so-called 'imperial circles' (*Reichskreise*), in accordance with a decision of the parliament in Cologne in 1512. These were Austria, Burgundy, Kurrhein, Franconia, Bavaria, Swabia, Oberrhein, Obersachsen, Niederrhein-Westfalen and Niedersachsen.[46] Their primary function was to ensure internal peace (*Landesfrieden*), and organise the defense of the state. At a later *Reichstag* in Worms in 1521, a decision was taken to implement a more efficacious imperial tax (*Wormser Reichsmatrikel*), but all other measures aimed at promoting the further consolidation of joint interests, e.g. the introduction of a uniform customs area, foundered.[47]

In addition, for much of the sixteenth century constitutional development was hampered by recurrent warfare between Protestant and Catholic princes. Once a religious truce had been achieved at Augsburg in 1555, the reforms could proceed. A *Reichskreistag* that would meet regularly was set up, a uniform monetary system

---

[44] See Deutscher Bundestag, Referat Öffentlichkeitsarbeit (ed.), *Fragen an die deutsche Geschichte* (Bonn, 1988), p.27.

[45] It was also during this imperial diet in Worms that the so-called Eternal Peace (*Ewiger Landfrieden*) was decreed.

[46] With the exception of Kurrhein and Austria, all these districts exist today as regions, microregions or cross-border regions.

[47] This imperial diet is best known for its Edict against Luther.

was introduced and the Imperial Chancellery and Imperial Court Council were reinforced.[48]

What were the repercussions of sixteenth-century religious warfare on the identity of the various tribes and principalities in both the western and eastern German cultural area? In the Middle Ages tribes had to some extent fused with one another in the eastern areas that formed the boundary to the Slavic tribes. These parts were a long distance from the western core of the empire, which contained the traditional seat of the imperial power as well as the empire's ecclesiastical and cultural centre. The eastern portions were thus alienated from the major nuclei of the empire.

Regional differences were crystallised by the Protestant influence in the east. The 'settler' regions in this area lacked traditions of their own, and were thus fertile ground for Luther's teachings and for the development of a *Landeskirche*.[49] While the denominational boundaries in the west were fluid and often overlapped, tribal, state and religious borders broadly coincided in the east. The denominational boundaries between regions and microregions have in essence remained into modern times. Present-day Bavaria is overwhelmingly Catholic, while the five *Bundesländer* that belonged to the former GDR are predominantly Protestant. (In 1995-6, Bavaria found itself in conflict with the remaining *Bundesländer* over issues pertaining to its denominational affiliation.[50]) A significant Catholic microregion, Rheinland, exists within Protestant Nordrhein-Westfalen. Among German Protestants, including those who do not actively practise their religion, one encounters a definite unwillingness to move to Catholic regions, and vice versa.

The Peace of Westphalia of 1648 is a milestone in European history. For Germany it entailed a perpetuation of *Kleinstaaterei*.

---

[48] In 1555 an 'Imperial Chamber of Delegates' was adopted, as a higher authority than the *Reichskreistag*, that gave the ten districts the possibility of joining the imperial power in its efforts to secure national peace.

[49] The *Landeskirche* continues to play an important role, particularly in predominantly Protestant *Bundesländer*.

[50] The problem concerned the Bavarian tradition of displaying crosses in schools: did an institution of public education have the authority to refuse to display the cross in its buildings?

Although the Emperor Frederick II had succeeded in consolidating the Estates under a joint imperial military authority (in Prague, in 1635), this was upset by the Peace of Westphalia, whereby it was decided that the Estates should regain their right to enter into military alliances with one another and with foreign powers. The authority of the imperial power in military and foreign affairs was thus curtailed.[51] In the German Empire after 1648 small-state particularism and localism, strongly anchored in a tribal historical tradition, were asserted and promoted in political committees, ecclesiastical *curia* of communions and the public arena. One spoke of a *Landesherrschaft* as a community of power, shared interests and a common destiny. To the extent that individual statehood existed, it was directed by a powerful administration and embraced an equally prominent ecclesiastical hierarchy (*Landeskirche*), which in its turn was the result of denominational uniformity, at least till the early nineteenth century.

The evolution of the German state system was interpreted in different ways by contemporary thinkers. Johannes Althusius (1557-1638) envisioned a state built on federal structures and the subsidiarity principle, and Ludolf Hugo (1630-1704) a confederacy. Of the observers whose interpretations are known, Samuel Pufendorf (1632-94) was the most critical of the development he was witnessing. In his *De statu Imperii Germanici*, published in 1667 under the pseudonym Severinus de Monzambano, he called German federalism a 'monster' (*monstro simili*). However this word was not meant in a derogatory sense: he was suggesting that the German state system could not be positioned within any established category, but was an irregular entity (*systema irregulare*), a peculiar amalgam of more or less sovereign principalities. This was not conducive to the creation of the confederacy which Pufendorf advocated.

So one can conclude that between 1648 and 1806 the German Empire lacked structurally based cohesion, although feelings of solidarity with the empire were not totally absent. In 1745 Johann Jacob Moser, the German savant of constitutional law, argued that 'the Holy Roman Empire would undoubtedly be the most powerful in all Europe if its Estates, particularly the strongest

---

[51] Both France and Sweden preferred a divided Germany.

ones, were united and were more interested in the common good than in their own private interests.'[52]

In 1803 far-reaching changes swept the empire, brought on by the Napoleonic wars. Napoleon's 'territorial revolution' began after his victories and the Peace of Lunéville of 1801. This involved the making of new, medium-sized states at the expense of the ecclesiastical principalities and smallest states, whose support had been indispensable to the Holy Roman Empire. Power relations now shifted. The newly-created kingdoms, grand-duchies and electorates could assert their political independence only under French protection. The electorates of Baden and Württemberg were among the reformed states, and became respectively a grand-duchy and a kingdom.

In 1806, the Holy Roman Empire was formally abolished as the *Rheinbund* was created. This new organisation comprised sixteen south and west German princes who had entered Napoleon's protectorate, and before 1811 an additional twenty princes had joined.[53] The significance of the *Rheinbund* was intensively discussed within the context of contemporary international law and political science. Some commentators described it as a federation, while others argued that it was a confederation of autonomous states – the more widely-accepted view.[54]

Napoleon was thus the first to implement a policy of integration in Germany, and the newly formed grand-duchy of Berg and kingdom of Westphalia (with his brother Jerome as king) were intended to serve as model states. There, as well as in Bavaria and Baden, rational administrative structures, uniform legal principles and uniform monetary, weights and measures systems were introduced. In addition the levying of domestic customs was abolished, and the educational system standardised.[55] Thus Napoleon's so-called 'mental conquest' involved the construction of a new, solid

---

[52] See n.44.

[53] Not surprisingly, the powerful states of Austria, Prussia, Kurhessen and Braunschweig (Brunswick) did not enter this *Rheinbund*.

[54] See Michael Dreyer, *Föderalismus als ordnungspolitisches und normatives Prinzip* (Frankfurt am Main, 1987), pp.62-80.

[55] See Hellmut Berding, 'Staatliche Identität, nationale Integration und politischer Regionalismus', *Blätter für deutsche Landesgeschichte*, vol.121 (1985), pp. 371-93.

identity and engendered a sense of belonging in the new states. It was this loyalty to land and leader that made possible the reforms implemented in Prussia and *Rheinbund* states.[56] School, church and the military all served as identity-forming elements, as did the new constitution. Particularly in the southern states of Baden, Württemberg and Bavaria, the parliaments and the progressive form of government, with a strong Liberal opposition, were integrating factors. Political debate was closely followed by the public.[57]

In Prussia an entire mythology had been constructed around the still fresh memory of an age of splendour – of Frederick the Great and his enlightened despotism – and it was in conjunction with this that a new Prussian identity began to emerge. Other factors contributed to this development: an effective state bureaucracy, liberal economic policy, high educational standards and a functioning judicial system. Nearby Hannover, on the other hand, witnessed a different development: in the quest to foster a sense of internal cohesion, its distinctiveness *vis-à-vis* Prussia was emphasised. Instead of the militarism, sense of duty and respect for authority that were associated with Prussia, Hannover highlighted its dynastic connection to England, endorsing the notion of liberty and the right to decentralised self-rule.[58]

How important were the historic stem communities in building the new integrated state identities of the nineteenth century? First, a sort of 'stem renaissance' occurred during this time, with a new interest in linguistic research, dialects, stories, regional folk music and folk art. German historiography was increasingly focused on the history of the stems, and this led to the creation of historical associations, learned societies, academies and journals.[59]

However, the amalgamation of several entities into a larger state was not always followed by a successful 'mental conquest'; many individuals wished to be free of the new loyalties and rulers that had been imposed on them, and thus resorted to historically rooted microregional affiliations: the notion of the 'stem' was

---

[56] Ibid.

[57] Ibid.

[58] Ibid.

[59] See, for instance, Hellmut Kretschmar, 'Reichsgeschichte und Landesgeschichte in der Neuzeit', *Blätter für deutsche Landesgeschichte*, vol. 98 (1953), pp.1-16

projected forward as the basis for a new (micro)regional identity. The pertinent developments in each newly-formed state indicate that historical continuity is least tangible in those states that needed the largest dose of integrative measures. Thus it proved impossible to create a sense of historical cohesion between Rheinland and Westphalia on the one hand and Prussia on the other where two distinct microregional affinities evolved. For example, the Rheinlanders objected to the introduction of a new Prussian tax law that was utterly incompatible with their own, traditionally French system. And in Westphalia an emerging awareness of a historical landscape was rooted in the Saxon stem of the ninth century.[60]

Likewise Frankish, Swabian and Palatine histories were all brought into the regional consciousness in protest against the consolidation of those regions with the Bavarian state. In the Bavarian Palatinate the recurrent antagonisms led to violent efforts at secession.[61] One impediment to integration was the sheer physical distance between the political centres and areas to be integrated. Another was the persistence of denominational contradictions. Differences in the judicial systems and social structures were also major obstacles. As a result, regionally based opposition arose in the provincial assemblies of Bavaria, Württemberg and Hessen-Darmstadt.

Parallel to the Napoleonic 'territorial revolution', which involved both a concentration process and the 'stem renaissance'/regionalism, many hoped that abolition of the weak Empire would pave the way for a unified German state. The humiliation of the French occupation and the formal dissolution of the German Empire provided the proponents of unity with new arguments for their cause. However, hopes for a unified state were again thwarted, although the Congress of Vienna in 1815 steered developments in that direction: the German Confederation (*Deutscher Bund*) was formed, consisting of thirty-seven principalities and four free imperial cities (parts of Austria and Prussia lay outside the boundaries of the *Bund*).[62]

---

[60] Berding, 'Staatliche Identität', p.377.

[61] Ibid., p.376.

[62] A twenty point constitution was adopted for the Bund. However, the difficulty in coordinating interests was reflected in the fact that while Prussia remained absolutist Baden steered a course towards liberal democracy.

Continued disunion was defended by, among others, Wilhelm von Humboldt, the Prussian delegate to the Congress of Vienna: 'The existence of Germany is based on the preservation of a certain balance of power by an internal force; this force would possibly be destroyed if the number of European states was compounded by a larger Germany – in addition to those German states that already exist.[...] There would be nothing to prevent Germany too from becoming a conquering state – something which no true German wishes to see.'[63]

The *Bundestag* in Frankfurt am Main was the highest authority in the *Deutscher Bund*, and its resolutions had to be passed unanimously. But there existed no superordinated state authority, and no central organs such as a supreme court, a military administration or even a department for foreign affairs. Each state was to be sovereign and have a constitution of its own and accordingly the *Bund* was to function as the guarantor of the states' mutual autonomy and external security.

The term '*Bund*' itself invoked the principles of federalism, and in the next half century the German states would accumulate experiences relevant to federalism, in their interaction with each other and within the framework of the *Bund*.[64] The rivalry between Austria and Prussia was a major factor during this period. Until 1848 they governed the *Bund* jointly as a sort of dual hegemony, with Prussia as the more decisive actor.

The *Bund* initially served to preserve the *status quo*, safeguarding the continued existence and territorial sovereignty of the principalities, and a federal structure that contrasted with the liberal-democratic national currents of the period up to 1848-9. The populations of the states met the prevalent conditions: they were first and foremost Badeners, Prussians and Hannoverians rather than Germans. It would be a long time before the national movement became a popular movement. Indeed, it was only when the liberal-democratic forces aligned themselves with the (micro) regions in the coercively incorporated new states that the national movement truly gained momentum among the people. If they could not longer be Franks or Palatines and were forced to be

---

[63] Quoted in Gordon Craig, *Über die Deutschen* (Munich, 1985), p.26.

[64] See Thomas Nipperdey, *Nachdenken über die deutsche Geschichte* (Munich, 1990), p.82.

Bavarians, they might just as well be Germans. As has been noted by Thomas Nipperdey, 'particularism was a sociocultural reality.'[65]

The creation of the *Zollverein* (customs union) in 1834 provided a federalist alternative to the *Deutscher Bund*, since this economic union was more solidly structured. The driving force behind the *Zollverein* was Prussia, which thus reinforced its own hegemony, but it represented a milestone for the liberal-democratic opposition, since the majority of those who strove for a unified Germany supported evolution rather than revolution. Referring to both Switzerland and the United States as examples, they called for a federation instead of a confederation, i.e. for the preservation of a federal structure, though with a far wider sphere of authority for the central power, and in addition a common constitution, government, parliament and head of state.

Sovereignty was to be divided between the central government and the individual states, in accordance with the various models of a federal state laid forth by Carl Theodor Welcker, Paul A. Pfizer, Friedrich von Gagern, Johann Kaspar Bluntschli, Georg Waitz and Constantin Frantz, all of whom propounded comprehensive theories on the subject.[66]

The bourgeois revolution of 1848/9 was a great moment for the opposition: an assembly was held in the Paulskirche in Frankfurt am Main, a parliament established, and a constitution decided. From now on the term '*Reich*' was used in an attempt to avoid the rather weak-sounding '*Bund*'.[67] During the two years that the March revolution lasted events followed one another in rapid succession. The revolution ultimately failed in its chief objectives, and thus the struggle for unification was thwarted. A contributing factor was the polarisation between the democratic and social revolutionary forces and the conservative (particularist) interests. The constitution drafted in Frankfurt was a compromise solution.

The other major impediment was the Austrian–Prussian contest for power. Here was the main problem: a stronger central government could not be divided between two states. So which of the two would thus assume leadership? The Catholics and liberal-

---

[65] Ibid., p.86

[66] See, for instance, Constantin Frantz, *Der Föderalismus als das leitende Prinzip für die soziale, staatliche und internationale Organisation* (Mainz, 1879).

[67] Nipperdey, *Nachdenken*, p.98.

democrats in the southern German states did not want to see Austria excluded, and therefore recommended a 'Great German' solution. Conversely, the north endorsed the exclusion of Austria to the benefit of Prussia – the so-called 'Little German' solution.[68]

Those who advocated a 'Great German' solution applied the term federalism to the construction they themselves contemplated, while wrongly describing the Prussian solution as 'unitarist' and 'caesarist'. This made the Prussian solution appear more centralistic than it actually was. The tensions in the dual hegemony of Austria and Prussia spiralled into open warfare, in 1866, and Austria was defeated. Prussia now launched the *Norddeutscher Bund* (North German Confederation). Both the former *Rheinbund* and the *Norddeutscher Bund* exemplified macroregional solutions: several states and regions joined in order to safeguard both political and economic interests.[69] (As will be discussed later, the idea of fusing several *Bundesländer* in a North German association was revived in the 1990s.) The constitution of 1867 confirmed Prussia's hegemony.[70]

As we have seen, increasing efforts toward unification and a burgeoning German national awareness proceeded parallel to a rising interest in regionally and locally anchored history, a sort of 'stem-renaissance'. Since the latter movement mainly involved a cultural-historical perspective, it was not at this level that the tensions between the striving for unity and the striving for continued particularism were played out – quite the contrary. By invoking the uniqueness of what was Frankish, Frisian, Swabian, and so on there was an attempt to capture elements that were characteristic of Germanism, such as diversity. It became increasingly common for individuals to perceive themselves as, for instance, both German and Swabian. This could be described as a consciousness-raising process that in fact was first activated by Napoleon's policy of aggrandisement and 'territorial revolution'.

[68] The 'Great German' solution (including the whole German language area) was put forward by Austria. The 'Little German' solution was put forward by Prussia, mainly by Bismarck.

[69] On macroregions, see note 8, Lindeborg, pp.25-35.

[70] The south German states were not included in this constitution, although they were closely tied to the Norddeutscher Bund through the customs union. Their relations with France were sundered by the Franco-Prussian war, and Bismarck could thus complete the consolidation of the empire. A new constitution was adopted in 1871.

A question that has generated much discussion is that of which of the federalising forces during this period had the greatest centrifugal effect: those that involved the 'stem-renaissance' and the culture-historical dimension, or those that correlated to the tradition of the (small) state and dynastic politics. As has been seen, both of these forces dominated at various times and in different places.[71]

Following victory in the Franco-Prussian War (1870-1), the southern German states promptly aligned themselves with the *Norddeutscher Bund*, and Germany was unified in accordance with the Prussian solution. The king of Prussia, Wilhelm, became German Emperor, and Otto von Bismarck, who had been Prussia's Prime Minister since 1862, became Chancellor. The new German Empire was a federally structured *Bundesstaat* comprising twenty-two monarchies, three free imperial cities and the imperial land of Alsace-Lorraine (conquered from France in the 1870 war). The constitution of 1871 was similar in essence to the 1867 North German version. On unification, it was first necessary somehow to bring together the various political currents that existed, namely the unitarist-national, federalist and liberal forces. However, Bismarck refuted the idea of an imperial ministry, and instead gave the highest executive power in the new Germany to the *Bundesrat*, composed of the main ministers of the individual states and cities.

Power was later transferred to the Chancellor, and the *Bundesrat* lost its political centrality. The period up to the First World War saw a consistent strengthening of the nation-state at the expense of the *Länder*, but the German state nevertheless retained a federal structure. The *Länder* had separate constitutions and administrations, and a certain degree of legislative authority (e.g. in police, local government, ecclesiastical and educational matters), and even military independence. Moreover, they exercised significant financial autonomy with fiscal rights. The *Bundesrat* provided a forum in which the *Länder* could participate in the central decision-making process. Up till 1918, five systems of civil law existed in the country alongside uniform commercial law.

A growing number of functions and spheres of authority were successively transferred to central organs. The parliament and

---

[71] See Hellmut Kretschmar, 'Reichsgeschichte und Landesgeschichte in der Neuzeit', *Blätter für deutsche Landesgeschichte* (1953), pp.7-10

imperial bureaucracy thus showed centralising tendencies. This in turn led to a stronger national identity at the expense of the historical regional ones. By the outbreak of the First World War, it was evident that the majority of the population saw itself as German rather than, e.g., Frankish or Badener.[72]

Thus federalism in Germany proved relatively successful. Regional pluralism was recognised as a fact, but it fell short when the formation of a dynamic unification policy was in question. This was because certain states such as Bavaria, Württemberg, Baden and Saxony were more privileged than others. Moreover Prussia's hegemony within the empire was problematic. Prussia, which covered 65 per cent of the land surface and accounted for 62 per cent of its total population, was the seat of the unitaristic authorities, namely, the Emperor, the Chancellor and the conservative-military complex. On the other hand, Prussia was also the most powerful of the *Länder* and consequently the primary defender of the federal system.

One factor that proved important to regional development in the nineteenth century was industrialisation. This period witnessed the growth of the new functional industrial type of region exemplified by the Ruhr, Harz, Oberschlesien and western Saxony. In such areas what remained of 'stem'-awareness quickly faded.[73]

The war of 1914-18 accelerated the unification process: The Germans were now politically, socially and nationally united: the people shared the experience of war and would share the distress and destitution that followed it. The war effort itself required the centralisation of the economy, administration and labour. However, as the tide of the war turned in the last year of the conflict, an agitated population searched for scapegoats: the establishment, the leaders and the central administration in Berlin were condemned for failing the people. Pro-federalist sentiment spread at first throughout the country, most strongly in Bavaria, the heartland of federalism, but soon waned. Shortly before the end of the war, the democratisation process contributed to fostering a new vision of the future which included a stronger central power. The *Reichstag* would

---

[72] Nipperdey, *Nachdenken*, p.105.

[73] According to Kretschmar, this 'stem'-awareness continued to exist in the primarily agrarian area of southern Germany. See *op. cit.* p.14.

replace the *Bundesrat* as the centre of power, although the basic federal structure would remain.[74]

Under the constitution of the Weimar Republic a 'decentralised unified state' was to be established. Its main foundation would still be federalistic, but the Empire's monarchically-governed states would be superseded by free states and subsequently by *Bundesländer*. The scope of their authority was now much reduced, although they retained some control over legislative affairs, as in the educational system. The *Bundesrat* became the *Reichsrat*, a titular change that symbolised the new circumstances, but one Bismarck had carefully avoided. Finance was centralised, and in 1923 a financial equalisation law was applied to the *Länder*. In newly-created agencies such as the labour administration the borders between the *Länder* ceased to exist.[75]

Article 18 of the Weimar constitution stipulated that a new division of territories could be implemented against the background of economic, traffic policy and demographic considerations, notably in the middle regions of the republics. The proposal reflected the need for modern regional structures. It was likewise necessary progressively to eradicate the discrepancies between privileged and non-privileged free states and *Bundesländer*, although this idea was vehemently opposed in Prussia and Bavaria. In other parts, like Rheinland and Hannover, there was much separatist activity in the early 1920s. In sum, the Weimar Republic was generally characterised by tension between heightened centralist tendencies, and the efforts of the *Bundesländer* to preserve and enhance their rights.

Divergent trends were abruptly halted in 1933 with the coming to power of Hitler and the National Socialists. This destroyed the federal structure and created a totalitarian state under one party and one *Führer*.

From this historical overview tracing developments from the Middle Ages to 1933 we can see, first, that particularisation, *Kleinstaaterei* or regionalisation, was a key element in the German cultural space; only in 1871, with the Prussian solution, was a German

[74] Nipperdey, *Nachdenken*, p.106.
[75] Ibid., p.109.

nation-state with a federal structure formed, but no centrally-governed, unitary state existed till after the fall of the Weimar Republic. Secondly, it is clear that the foundations for, and circumstances around the development of, territorial and political particularisation varied from one period to another. However, geographical and topographical conditions were remarkably unimportant as particularisation factors, given the German area's relatively cohesive geography.

The background to particularisation was thus largely defined by cultural and political factors. The cultural dimension involved development from the 'stems' of the Middle Ages to the 'stem renaissance' of the nineteenth century, and the growth of a (micro)regional and local sense of belonging based on cultural and denominational distinctions and often formed in opposition to surrounding regions. The notion of kin was also present, involving the solidarity of the *Sib*, firm connection to local networks and an equally strong loyalty to the *Heimat*, all of which were actualised through inheritance, the division of joint property and dynastic politics. Political factors leading to particularisation in Germany included the creation of the 'stem' duchies, the decentralisation of powers in an often weak empire, the feudal system, war, the rise of powerful cities, and intervention by other states.

We can also see that regional deep structures have survived till today. Identity in a small principality and later in regions was generally determined by cultural, political, economic, denominational and, in rare cases, geographic aspects. Moreover, it appears that early political occurrences of decisive importance eventually become a part of the region's historical identity.

From 1933 to 1945

The Nazis' rise to power is sometimes attributed partly to the German *Sonderweg*, a widely controversial question among German historians. According to the prominent *Sonderweg* theorists such as Fritz Fischer, Hans-Ulrich Wehler, Heinrich August Winkler, Jürgen Kocka, Ralf Dahrendorf and Kurt Sontheimer,[76] a direct

---

[76] See, for instance, Fritz Fischer, *Griff nach der Weltmacht* (Düsseldorf, 1961), which triggered the first major post-war debate among historians, the so-called Fischer controversy. The work included an extensive list of sources, and Fischer

line runs from the Wilhelmine Empire to Hitler's Third Reich. The belated emergence of the nation-state and of democracy resulted in Germany pursuing a course distinct from that of its neighbours to east and west.

This *Sonderweg* served to reinforce ideas that the path being pursued was not only different from that of other states and peoples but superior to it. The Germans believed that they had a vocation to perform certain duties, and this perception ultimately found expression in calamitous national arrogance. This attitude was strengthened by the real or alleged threat posed by the European states surrounding the 'land in the middle'. The specific components of the *Sonderweg* 'theory' itself are not generally disputed: the continuing controversy is around whether these specific components justify a whole *Sonderweg* theory.[77]

Heinrich von Treitschke (1834-96) had at an early stage advocated a 'Borussianism', where the main seat of power should be in Prussia, and rest on three main structures: the military, the bureaucracy and the semi-absolutist imperial power (successor to the Prussian monarchy), as well as on the conviction that Prussia's future was dependent on expansionism.[78] These Prussian legacies were adopted in Germany as Prussia was progressively incorporated into the Empire, a process that culminated in Franz von Papen's *coup d'état* in 1932, which resulted in the removal of the Prussian government and the establishment of a *Reichskommissar*. Federalism was thus dealt a death-blow. Bavaria and the ousted Prussian government attempted in vain to salvage the rights of the *Länder* vis-à-vis the encroachment of the Reich.[79]

While the *Gleichschaltung* that was initiated when the Nazi came to power razed the federal structure, a *Heimat*-regionalism anchored in the '*Blut und Boden*' mythology subsisted. In addition, the Nazi

---

attributes the rise of the Nazis to the Empire's early plans for military expansion and the support of the leading circles for such plans. In 1992 Fritz Fischer published *Hitler war kein Betriebsunfall* (Munich), and here too he emphasises the continuity between the Empire and National Socialism.

[77] See, for instance Helga Grebing, *Der deutsche Sonderweg in Europa, 1806-1945. Eine Kritik* (Stuttgart, 1986).

[78] See Heinrich von Treitschke, *Historische und politische Aufsätze* (Leipzig, 1865), pp.444-52.

[79] Nipperdey, *Nachdenken*, p.111.

revolution from below resulted in the creation of regional National Socialist power centres, in each of which a *Gauleiter* (regional leader) resided. To counteract a possible regional expansion of power, Hitler established a governorship (*Reichsstatthalter*) that would carry out the orders of the central power. However, despite the proclamation of a unified state, regional bastions of power remained.[80] Hitler exploited this situation by refraining from firmly establishing centrally governed authorities, and instead retaining for himself a supreme position through which he would personally mediate between various agencies in political conflicts.

During the war of 1939-45 the antagonism between the centrally governed administration and the *Gauleiter* became ever more accentuated. The annexed areas – the Saar, Alsace, Lorraine, Austria and the so-called *Reichsgaue* in the east – were directly subordinated to Hitler and the party, and were thus outside the jurisdiction of the central state administration. The whole Nazi period, 1933-45, was characterised by 'state centralism and particularism'. For the history of federalism in Germany, this period was an interlude, which in a certain way 'contributed to the "federalist renaissance" in Germany after 1945.'[81]

Federalism and Regionalisation in Germany after 1945

'Nothing will alter our belief that the centralistic unitaristic state system is completely unsuitable to Germany and thus leads to catastrophe. [...], It is not true that the federal organism was forced upon us by the Allies. Federalism *per se* is not an import; it is a basic concern where German conditions and essentials, and the German conception of the state, are concerned.' (Hans Ehard, Prime Minister of Bavaria, in 1952)[82]

In contrast both to the empire of 1871 and to countries like Switzerland, Canada and later Belgium, where the principal aim was to integrate heterogeneous regions into a federation, postwar German federalism was geared to establishing an internal balance through a vertical distribution of power. It is described today as 'cooperative federalism': decision-making involves cooperation

---

[80] Ibid., p.113.

[81] Ibid., p.115.

[82] See Doris Fuhrmann-Mittlmeier, *Die deutschen Länder im Prozess der europäischen Einigung* (Berlin, 1991), p.91, n.227.

Regional Deep Structures in the German Cultural Space 83

between the *Bund* and the *Länder*, or among the *Länder* themselves via the *Bundesrat* and ministerial conferences.[83] Within the framework of German federalism, (micro)regionalism involves the rediscovery of distinctive regional roots in the (cultural) historical landscape e.g. in the history of the 'stems', such as the East Frisians, the Saxons, the Sorbs and the Alemanns.[84] Micro-regionalisation, on the other hand, also entails a political action, in which some political power is indirectly distributed among smaller spatial entities on the subsidiarity principle (e.g. the ZIM-regions in Nordrhein-Westfalen).[85]

The Allied victory in 1945 marked the definitive end of Bismarck's German empire born in 1871. The victors were now confronted with the task of determining how the post-war German republic was to be configured. The problem was essentially resolved already in 1945. The Allies, with the exception of the USSR, agreed that the German state was somehow to be broken up, perhaps through federalisation or decentralisation. This view, often advocated by Germans in exile, was supported primarily in the

---

[83] Since the early 1960s there has been much debate over the nature of German federalism. For instance, in her *Der verkappte Einheitsstaat* (Opladen, 1992), Heidrun Abromeit has argued that German federalism is spurious. Since reunification in 1990, it has often been proposed that the Federal Republic needs to be re-federalised. Likewise, in a speech on the sixth anniversary of German reunification in October 1996, President Roman Herzog (former president of the Federal Constitutional Court) spoke of the weak structure of German federalism. Among other measures, he proposed an expansion of the role of the *Bundesländer* in the financial sphere.

[84] In several institutes for research on federalism in Central European universities (for example in Innsbruck and Tübingen), the concept 'regionalism' designates (popular) movements from below, a manifest process rooted in a sense of regional affinity, which ultimately translates into demands for cultural and often political autonomy.

[85] ZIM: *Zukunftstinitiative Montanregion*. Regionalisation is a process aimed at creating or further developing a region. Thus, it is often an answer from above to demands and claims within the framework of regionalism from below. For instance, the decision to regionalise France was taken by the central government, but most of the regions created through this process have a distinct sense of regional affinity, which is the platform for regionalism. Another kind of regionalisation process is economically based. The division of Nordrhein-Westfalen into ZIM-regions is regionalisation that is mainly functionally determined to create greater economic efficiency via polycentrism.

southern parts of the country. In the north the preservation of a unitary state was endorsed despite the devastating Nazi experience.[86]

The main question was how decentralisation and federalisation could best be achieved, and what criteria should determine the direction of the process. The Allies had differing views on the matter. The Soviets increasingly supported the idea of a unitary – and implicitly socialist – Germany which could pay its war indemnity to the USSR and would also wish to do so. The French advocated a loose confederation of German states, while Britain at first showed sympathy for the North German wish to reestablish a unitary state. However, as the Cold War broadened, it became important for the British to distance themselves from the Soviet position. Thus they drew closer to Washington's position, which supported a federal structure and indeed, once the Soviets had withdrawn from the Allied Control Authority in the winter of 1947-8, the remaining victors could unite around the American proposal. The Western powers proceeded to outline the federal basis for the new West German constitution.[87]

The territorial criteria for federalisation did not pose a problem, since by 1948-9 *Länder* already existed. It had been decided at Potsdam that decentralisation and reconstruction would proceed from below.[88] The occupying powers had formed *Länder* in order to make the administration of the various areas more effective. Bavaria, Hamburg, Bremen and Schleswig-Holstein retained their historical borders, while the boundaries of all the other *Bundesländer* were arbitrarily redrawn by the Allies, partly on the basis of their

[86] Fuhrmann-Mittlmeier, *Die deutschen Länder*, pp.77-8, n.102.

[87] The new constitution was formally adopted on 23 May 1949 in Paris.

[88] In the immediate post-war years, developments in the *Bundesländer* were also determined by the different policies of the occupying powers in their four zones. In the Soviet zone, which was not included in the new constitution, eleven central administrative bodies were formed in addition to the *Länder*. These authorities effectively exercised power in the zone, and the authority of the *Länder* was curtailed, to be totally abolished in 1952. In the American zone, three *Länder* coordinated a *Länder* council as a first step towards a federal structure. In the British zone, the overarching administration was centralist, and numerous conflicts developed between the *Länder* and the zone administration, other central authorities and the political parties. See Nipperdey, *Nachdenken über die deutsche Geschichte*, pp.115-30; Fuhrmann-Mittlmeir, *Die deutschen Länder*, pp.80-99; Ernst Deuerlein, *Föderalismus* (Bonn, 1972), pp.221-90.

Regions in West Germany

zones of occupation. With the introduction of political parties, elections, parliaments and separate constitutions, the *Bundesländer* were granted significant political authority, and in the early post-war years political matters largely developed through them. The prime ministers and parliaments of these areas were of far greater relevance to the population than were the various agencies of the occupying powers.

In the American zone of occupation, as well as the old region (free state) of Bavaria, two new *Bundesländer* were created in September 1945: Baden-Württemberg and Gross-Hessen. The division of the American zone into three regions was based on the need to establish relatively large vital regions, and on the presence of a certain degree of historical cohesion. Although the representatives of the British zone essentially shared the American views, the circumstances were more complicated in their zone of occupation, partly because of the struggle among the victorious powers over the Ruhr, and partly because of the collapse of Prussia. The creation of the region of Nordrhein-Westfalen can thus be described as artificial. However, certain microregional identities and cultural spaces have flourished within this region, thus serving as the foundation for a common and overarching though not intensively experienced identity.

The French military government preserved the political-administrative boundaries in Süd-Baden and Süd-Württemberg and consolidated the remaining areas in its zone into Rheinland-Pfalz.[89] Article 1 and 2 of the so-called *Verordnung* no. 57, signed by the French on 30 August 1946, stipulated the formation of a new *Bundesland* comprising the Palatine and the *Regierungsbezirke* (administrative areas) of Mainz, Koblenz, Montabaur and Trier.[90] The following year, an interim government drafted a proposal for a constitution, which was adopted on a 53 per cent 'yes' vote in a referendum.

---

[89] Rheinland-Pfalz consisted of Rheinhessen, the Palatinate, Koblenz, Trier and four *Kreise* in Nassau.

[90] Cf. Rheinland-Pfalz Staatskanzlei (ed.), *Rheinland-Pfalz. Unser Land* (Mainz, 1990), p.8; also Lindeborg, 'Regionalt samarbete i Europa', pp.415-37.

Although Rheinland-Pfalz was an amalgam of disparate fragments where both the Catholic and Evangelical churches were strong, a certain Rheinland-Pfalz identity has nevertheless evolved. Up to the mid-1970s there were discussions not only about the borders of Rheinland-Pfalz but also about whether this *Bundesland* should exist at all. A referendum of 1975 showed massive popular support for the preservation of Rheinland-Pfalz within its existing borders,[91] and since then this issue seems to have been settled once and for all.

The Saar at first had special status under a provisional French government, lasting till 1954 when it was decided that the area should become an autonomous region under a supranational European authority. However, in a referendum 68 per cent of the respondents voted against this decision, and after further negotiations Saarland chose Germany, officially becoming a West German *Bundesland*[92] on 7 June 1959.

The new *Bundesländer* were intended as transitional solutions, but with the exception of Baden-Württemberg all of them have remained unaltered since their conception. In its interpretation of the constitution, the *Bundesverfassungsgericht* (Federal Constitutional Court) determined in 1961 that the division of the Federal Republic's territory was the responsibility of the *Bund*, the federal state's central authority. The following criteria are stipulated in the constitution: consideration of historical and cultural identity, economic capacity, social organisation and the extent of local and regional grassroots associations.

Throughout the 1950s, 1960s and 1970s there was recurrent discussion of whether the division into eleven *Bundesländer* was the ideal one, and several commissions were set up to investigate the question. In the early 1970s, for instance, it was proposed that the number of *Bundesländer* be reduced from eleven to five or six, but various efforts to redraw the boundaries of the

---

[91] Ibid., p.9

[92] The delay meant that the Saar, which had not reaped the benefits of French reconstruction, also did not participate in the intensive reconstruction of Germany under the Marshall Plan. Thus in a sense French and German neglect has helped to foster a strong regional identity in the Saar through it being left on its own.

Bundesländer have so far met with adamant opposition on the ground, not least in the city-states and Saarland.[93]

Europeanisation was another factor that contributed to the rapid crystallisation of German federalism. The emergence of a new West Germany was seen as running parallel to the evolution of a European union. With the subsidiarity principle as a fundamental element, West German politicians of various political persuasions spoke of the importance to post-war European cooperation of a federal West Germany. Leo Wohleb and Hans Ehard, chief ministers (*Minister-präsident*) respectively of Baden and Bavaria, were among the first to express a vision of German regional policy within a wider European framework. Ehard argued that 'the federative incorporation of a truly federal Germany into the European community is both a necessity and a goal for a universally oriented federal policy.'[94]

Another factor behind the strong focus on both a federal structure based on *Bundesländer* and a European union was bequeathed by Hitler and the Second World War: the Germans felt the need to distance themselves clearly from all that was nationalistic and pro-national unity. The only territorial strata where German identity-policy was 'permitted' to develop were the regional and the European.[95]

In contrast to the situation in West Germany, the *Länder* in the Soviet zone – subsequently the GDR – had very limited political, social and economic freedom, and such freedom as existed was terminated in 1952. The GDR existed in a constant tension between the state-ordained GDR-identity and the regional or provincial roots that continued to exist. However, the regional perspective was coloured exclusively by cultural-historical aspects, such as the promotion of a Sorbian culture through the erection of various institutions, namely Sorbian schools, people's theatres

[93] The small *Bundesländer* and city-states fear being engulfed by others in case of a fusion of several *Bundesländer*. Bremen, for instance, strongly endorses its own city-state status.

[94] See Fuhrmann-Mittlmeir, *Die deutschen Länder*, p.60, n. 102.

[95] The question of a 'permitted' German identity had been debated since the 1960s. According to the philosopher Jürgen Habermas, only a '*Verfassungspatriotismus*' ('constitutional patriotism') should be allowed to develop. A historically charged identity was to be avoided, and contemporary German identity was to be based on the history of the post-war Federal Republic.

and a national theatrical ensemble, cultural institutes, publishing houses, Sorbian radio and so on.[96] Even the concept of *Heimat* was socialised, although its Marxist definition, e.g. as propounded by Jürgen Hofmann, did not differ significantly from the interpretations that emerged in West Germany during the 1970s and '80s, except in the ideological and socialist aspects.[97]

It is clear that regional deep structures were entrenched in the German cultural space. How important did these structures become for West German – and subsequently also East German – (micro) regionalisation after the initial phase of the late 1940s and the '50s?

In accordance with the conceptual definitions of region sketched out in the introduction, the eleven *Bundesländer* can be described as political, administrative and functional regions rather than cultural regions, with the exception of Bavaria, Saarland and the old Hanseatic cities of Hamburg and Bremen, which embody strong cultural and historic qualities. Following from the definition of the *Bundesländer* as normative regions, we should consider the following aspects of the German constitution.

First, the *Bundesländer* have the right to decide on their own organisation and administration. Each has its own constitution – which, however, is not as significant as the overarching German one. Every fourth year the *Bundesländer* elect a parliament (*Landtag*), and a government headed by a *Ministerpräsident*, often called '*Landesvater*'.[98] Secondly, the *Bundesländer* exercise power in certain spheres, although these have been successively curtailed. In an analysis conducted in 1990, Fritz Ossenbühl noted that 'the transfer

---

[96] See Benedikt Dyrlich, 'Vom sanften Verschwinden in die Geschichtslosigkeit', *Frankfurter Rundschau*, 21 Dec. 1994, and Bernhard Honnigfort, 'Warum nicht auch Sherlock Holmes?', *Frankfurter Rundschau*, 13 March 1996.

[97] See Jürgen Hofmann, 'Heimat als Realitätsbezug. Überlegungen zum marxistischen Heimatsbegriff', *Widerspruch: Münchner Zeitschrift für Philosophie*, no.14 (1987), pp.24-30.

[98] The elections in the *Bundesländer* take place at different times. The label '*Landesvater*', which has been attached to several chief ministers including Johannes Rau in Nordrhein-Westfalen and Kurt Biedenkopf in Saxony, reflects the role's consolidating and symbolic importance to the people.

Regional Deep Structures in the German Cultural Space 89

of authority upwards has resulted in minimal range of authority.'[99] Nipperdey has likewise emphasised that the Federal Republic has become increasingly unitary since 1949.[100]

This transfer of power upward was caused by several specifically German questions that required resolution at the centre, e.g. the post-war settlement, international issues such as relations with the EC, the UN, NATO and Israel, as well as a series of other problems. It was caused also by the fact that the *Bundesländer* were functional entities rather than traditional, historical ones. Functionality has thus been the main consideration, and the *Bundesländer* have not protested where it was apparent that a particular case was best solved centrally. To compensate for this reduction in the authority of the *Bundesländer*, the institutional side of federalism has been notably solid: within the framework of an increasingly strong *Bundesrat*, these regions have the right to participate in the decision-making process in (federal) matters, not least where the EU is concerned. In this context no government decision can be implemented without the approval of the *Bundesrat*.[101]

The *Bundesländer* have also undergone interesting developments in their capacity as cultural spaces. Since the war these artificially constructed regions have forged distinct political profiles and distinct identities. One factor behind this phenomenon is the conscious promotion of polycentrism on the basis of existing, historical microregional identities within the *Bundesländer*. In several instances these microregions extend across the borders of several *Bundesländer* (e.g. Rhein-Neckar-Dreieck – the former Kurpfalz in the border area between Hessen, Baden-Württemberg and Rheinland-Pfalz). In the microregions, the historical landscapes and regional deep structures have influenced the course of developments.[102]

---

[99] See Fritz Ossenbühl, *Föderalismus und Regionalismus in Europa* (Baden-Baden, 1990), p.126.

[100] Nipperdey, *Nachdenken*, p.122.

[101] If the majority of the *Bundesländer* are of a different party affiliation to the central government, as was the case up to 1998, legislative procedure can be deadlocked. When the *Bundesrat* votes against a decision reached in the *Bundestag*, a mediation process is initiated. If no compromise is reached, the proposal is abandoned. Moreover, the *Bundesrat's* legislative power has increased since 1949. The approval of the *Bundesrat* was originally required for only 10 per cent of all proposed bills. Today it is required for 60 per cent of them.

[102] Another example is provided by Rhein-Main-Gebiet, comprising portions

This has been evident in Nordrhein-Westfalen, Europe's most densely populated region where the leadership has actively sought to forge a distinctive identity with the slogan '*Wir in Nordrhein-Westfalen*'. The absence of a Nordrhein-Westfalen identity was not previously seen as a disadvantage, but today a strong regional identity is a marketable asset – hence, the efforts to form one and to emphasise a certain unity despite Nordrhein-Westfalen's characteristic diversity, polycentrism and heterogeneity. Thus it may be valuable to foster a 'we' feeling in the more clearly demarcated of the nine microregions, such as the Ruhr, Rheinland, Lippe and Ost-Westfalen, all of which have strong historical identities.[103]

In the Ruhr, as the Federal Republic's principal industrial region, the almost exclusive concentration on coal and steel has produced a monolithic economic and social structure. Thus the current structural transformation from a traditional 'dirty' industrial community to a knowledge society has been particularly dramatic and problematic for the Ruhr, and the search for regional deep structures has been especially relevant. What was the Ruhr before it became an industrial region? How can the pre-industrial and industrial legacies contribute to the forging of a new forward-looking identity?

The answer to such questions lies partly in early history. In the tenth century the Ruhr was an important part of the German Empire – as a political core area and as a commercial centre with Duisburg to the west and Dortmund to the east. It also occupied a key position between Saxony, Lotharingia and Franconia.[104] Furthermore, the area was polycentric, being jointly governed by several local families. Some 1,000 years later, this polycentrism is being invoked in regional planning where the focus is on small planning entities (*kleinräumige Orientierung*). Since the Ruhr is being launched as an information, cultural and media region, it is also increasingly associating itself with an ecclesiastical legacy from the Middle Ages and cultural heritages dating from the early nineteenth century.

---

of Hessen and Rheinland-Pfalz.

[103] The remaining five microregions in Nordrhein-Westfalen are Niederrhein, Bergisches Land, Sauerland, Siegen-Wittgenstein and Münsterland, all of them historical regions, often composed of amalgamations of still smaller regions with historical identities.

[104] See Hans-Werner Goetz, 'Das Ruhr-gebiet im frühen Mittelalter', *Blätter für deutsche Landesgeschichte* (1990), pp. 123-39.

Regional Deep Structures in the German Cultural Space 91

In the Carolingian period Rheinland was an imperial centre, comprising the coronation town of Aachen and the former Roman strongholds of Cologne (later an archiepiscopal see) and Bonn. In the predominantly Protestant Nordrhein-Westfalen of today, Rheinland continues to bear the imprint of Catholicism, manifested in the carnival period preceding Lent. However, it was not until Prussian rule began in the 1820s that Rheinlanders began to develop a distinctive regional identity. Strongly influenced by all things French, they found Prussian culture totally alien. Industrialisation and proximity to the Ruhr caused Rheinland to evolve also as an economically viable region.

The Rheinlanders' strong identification with their region was manifested during the French occupation after the First World War. In protest, a Rheinland republic was proclaimed in Aachen on 21 October 1923 (it survived only till 2 November). Within Nordrhein-Westfalen, the Rheinlanders are considered more flexible and creative then the Westfaleners. This is highlighted today not least because Rheinland and Cologne are the driving forces behind the rapid growth of Nordrhein-Westfalen's media, cultural and knowledge character. Ost-Westfalen, on the other hand, is generally considered more northern, and the people are known for their pragmatism. A Westphalian identity was soon forged, and was clearly manifested when the Westphalian reaction to Prussian rule was stronger and more uncompromising than that of the Rheinlanders.[105]

In contrast to both these areas, which lack the experience of self-rule, Lippe, the smallest microregion in Nordrhein-Westfalen, enjoyed political sovereignty from the Middle Ages onwards. It contained one of the Hanseatic League's important cities, Lemgo, which however burned down during the Thirty Years War. Between 1802 and 1820, under the rule of Princess Pauline, it enjoyed a golden age. After the principalities were abolished under the Weimar Republic, an identity crisis developed in Lippe: the political vacuum was exploited by Hitler, and in 1932-3 it became a testing-ground for the Nazi propaganda machine. As the result, the Nazis achieved a remarkable electoral success there on 15 January 1933.

---

[105] Regarding Nordrhein-Westfalen, see Roland Günter, *Im Tal der Könige* (Essen, 1994).

When the war ended, Lippe was made part of Niedersachsen, but its leadership had other plans. The newly-created Nordrhein-Westfalen offered it the disposal of what remained of its princely possessions. Backed by the authorities in the British occupation zone, its politicians chose to join Nordrhein-Westfalen. Since the 1980s the people of Lippe have turned to their former princely rulers to animate their newly-awoken identity. The result has been increasing microregional self-confidence, paving the way for the current structural transformation of the region with investment in its spas and other forms of tourism.

Another method for promoting a forward-looking identity is to engender a 'we'-feeling around a specific common project. This is possible especially in areas where a tangible transformation process is taking place. In Nordrhein-Westfalen the search for identity has been accelerated by its traumatic transition from an industrial to a service- and knowledge-based society.

Fifty-five per cent of the labour force is today employed in the tertiary sector, and the trend appears to be escalating. The project of transforming Nordrhein-Westfalen into Europe's leading media region has contributed to exactly such 'we'-feeling as mentioned above. Moreover, the historical landscape is also evident in this type of identity-construction. The main centres of gravity for the development of media and culture are the microregions of Rheinland and the Ruhr, areas traditionally both urban and culturally rich.

Frisia also illustrates the relevance of regional deep structures to the process of microregionalisation. It is in the peripheral border-area between northern Niedersachsen and Dutch Groningen. In the eighth century the Frisians had a kingdom of their own, a progressive judicial system, and a distinct language and culture. Today it is both nationally and regionally fractured: East Frisia is in Niedersachsen, North Frisia in Schleswig-Holstein and West Frisia in Groningen. However, cross-border cooperation in the so-called Ems Dollart-region has regenerated a Frisian identity and culture.[106] It appears that this recovered identity will have increasing significance in regional developments, as people become ever more conscious of their historical roots. For instance, the East Frisians are represented

---

[106] On the Ems-Dollart region, see Lindeborg, note 8, pp.224-51.

in an institution of their own, the *Ostfriesische Landschaft*, structured as a parliament with forty-nine members.[107]

Regional cohesion across the North German–Dutch frontier is tangible not only in physical terms – in its low-lying and moorland landscape and red-brick churches – but in long-forgotten historical and cultural phenomena. For example, the East Frisian nobility became Dutch Calvinist rather than German Lutheran while the Dutch West Frisians and the German East Frisians share a symbolic common ancestor in the learned Ubbe Emmius (1547-1625).

In the 1990s the common Frisian cultural heritage – institutional and architectural – has been rediscovered by Frisians on both sides of the border.

Regions in East Germany

As has been discussed earlier, the East German government ordained a conformist unitary identity, but regional history and the sense of belonging proved sufficiently pervasive to survive this oppression from above. The deep structures were preserved via regional and local periodicals founded in the 1950s – *Natur und Heimat* (1952), *Heimatliche Blätter*, *Sächsische Heimatblätter* (1954), *Zeitzer Heimat* (1954) and several Sorbian journals. The regime consequently tried to adapt this interest in regional history to socialist ideology, to somehow correlate it to Marxism-Leninism. A decisive event took place in 1961 when at a state-sponsored conference of historians in Görlitz, a new association – the Arbeitsgemeinschaft für Heimats- und Landesgeschichte – was formed to study regional history in relation to the labour movement. With this programme regional research in East Germany was to be distinguished from its counterpart in the Federal Republic, which was described as an instrument in the struggle against the working classes. The creation of the *Jahrbuch für Regionalgeschichte* in 1965 was intended to provide a theoretical foundation for the campaign to reinforce the socialist individual's awareness of *Heimat*.

From 1980 onwards there was another change in the official East German attitude towards the regions and towards the writing of their histories. In an article written by a member of the Academy of Sciences, it was concluded that 'research on regional history

[107] Ibid.

has grown to a mass movement', and that this should affect the development of a socialist historical consciousness.[108] Thus the histories of various regions could be explored – but only within the framework of certain given aspects and without the promotion of regional characteristics. The history of Saxony was to be first, and publication happened to coincide with other significant events – in 1989.[109]

The reunification of 1990 ushered in a new era. The five new *Bundesländer* in the east were no longer forbidden to invoke regional deep structures. The history of the former 'stem' duchy of Thuringia could now be recovered. The Roman Flavius Vegetius Renatus employed the name 'Thoringi' as early as *c.* AD 380.[110] The Thuringians did not join the great migrations of the time, choosing instead to remain in their homelands. In AD 531 Thuringia was incorporated into the Frankish empire and, after the division of this domain and during most of the Middle Ages, was governed by margraves and provincial counts. From 1190 to 1217 Wartburg was a stronghold for the poetry of the High Middle Ages, and Luther's presence in Erfurt and Eisenach hastened the Reformation in Thuringia.

In the following centuries Thuringia was broken up into increasingly tiny states, and was largely ruled by Saxon princes. In the late eighteenth century Jena and Weimar became centres of German Classicism and early Romanticism. In 1848 efforts were made to consolidate the various small states into a unified Thuringia, but did not succeed till 1920.[111] However with the *Machtübernahme* in 1933 Thuringia ceased to exist: it was re-created in 1946, only to disappear again in 1952. In 1990 it was established for the third time in a century as a regional structure.

Thuringia is today seeking to forge a new, contemporary identity, by underlining its advantageous location at the centre of Germany and of Europe, '*das grüne Herz Deutschlands*' (the green heart of Germany), a bridge between east and west. This had formerly been a burden due to the risk of war, but in an increasingly

---

[108] Helga Schultz, 'Zu Inhalt und Begriff marxistischer Regionalgeschichtsforschung' in *Zeitschrift für Geschichtswissenschaften*, 10 (1985), p.875.

[109] Karl Czok (ed.), *Geschichte Sachsens*, Weimar, 1989.

[110] See Landeszentrale für politische Bildung, Thüringen, *Blätter zur Landeskunde* (Erfurt, 1995), p.1.

[111] Ibid., p.8.

integrated Europe it should be an asset. The term 'growth region', applied to present-day Thuringia, highlights effective infrastructure and the rising number of 'growth industries' such as Zeiss-Jenoptik and the Opel factory in Eisenach. A new sense of identity is being forged by underlining the attractiveness of Thuringia – not only its scenery, but also its remarkably rich cultural heritage. It is symptomatic of this trend that the majority of Thuringia's cities are involved in the tourism project, '*Klassikerstrasse Thüringia*' (the classical itinerary of Thuringia).[112]

Mecklenburg-Vorpommern provides yet another example of the developments we are considering. The area was consolidated as a *Land* in 1945 but, like Thuringia, was dissolved in 1952.[113] Reunification has resurrected Mecklenburg-Vorpommern, and here as in many other areas the search has begun for historical roots that will free the region from the weight of both the Nazi and GDR past. In 1995 Mecklenburg celebrated its millennium, and this event focused on the region's cultural heritage, its growing tourism and its transformation into a high-tech economic zone with emphasis on small and medium-sized enterprise. This concentration on smaller units corresponds with both the traditional demographic structure and earlier forms of industrial production in the region.

Mecklenburg is known for its weak democratic tradition. It was a Nazi bastion even before 1933, and the communist dictatorship likewise established an early and solid foothold there. Because of this background, the region felt an imperative need to turn to its earliest history, which includes both the Hanseatic League and Baltic collaboration. Mecklenburg-Vorpommern is today a highly active member of both the new Baltic cooperation and the Union of Baltic Cities.[114]

Without discussing Saxony's long and complex history in detail, we can say that it is an example, among European regions, of a

---

[112] See Thüringer Ministerium für Wirtschaft und Infrastruktur, Referatsgruppe Tourismus, *Klassikerstrasse Thüringen* (Erfurt, 1995).

[113] See Thomas Wupper, 'Es muss mehr geben als lange Strände und schöne Landschaften', *Frankfurter Rundschau*, 2 Sept. 1995, and Otto Jörg Weiss, 'Die Landesgrenze als Abrisskante des Bewusstseins', *Frankfurter Rundschau*, 6 Sept. 1995.

[114] On the Union of Baltic Cities, see Lindeborg, *Regional Collaboration in Europe*, pp.331-3.

symbiosis of a defined territory with traditionally strong autonomy and a cultural space. The historic occurrences specific to Saxony's past have served to reinforce Saxon consciousness, functioning as consolidating factors. This in part explains the remarkable preservation of a Saxon identity. One event of decisive importance was the inauguration of the first ruler of the Wettin dynasty as margrave in Meissen, as a part of Saxony, in 1089. This ruling house subsequently governed the state of Saxony for 829 years up till the end of the First World War, and was thus the longest-ruling of the German princely dynasties, outstripping the Habsburgs, Hohenzollerns and Wittelsbachs.

When the last Wettin ruler, King Friedrich August, died in 1932, his funeral cortège was accompanied by 700,000 grieving Saxons. Sixty-four years later, in the summer of 1996, the Wettins again attracted attention when Friedrich August's grandson Prince Emanuel announced that he was contemplating a return to Saxony. Emanuel's claims to the dilapidated palace of his ancestors met with both favourable and unfavourable reactions. At the time of writing, this chapter in Saxony's resuscitated regional history remained unresolved.

In the former GDR the government capitalised on the presence of a Sorbian population to demonstrate its own tolerance of minorities. An estimated 60,000 Sorbs reside in the microregions of Ober- und Niederlausitz (some in Brandenburg, others in Saxony), and the group is today redefining its role as it emerges from East German oppression. The Sorb youth seek to distance themselves from the folkloric dimension of their society in an effort to adapt to the new knowledge society. However, they wish simultaneously to preserve their culture. The Sorb daily newspaper is thus being modernised, and the publication of current non-fiction and fiction in Sorb is also planned.[115]

The *Bundesländer* in eastern Germany are in the process of rediscovering forgotten (micro)regional cultural space and forging a new sense of regional belonging. This reflects the profound desire of their populations to escape the label 'East German' ('*Ossi*'). Individuals refer to their identity as, for instance, Brandenburger,

---

[115] See n.96.

Saxon or Mecklenburger – anchored to a specific region. Thus the people of the former GDR use the regional path on their way to both West Germany and the Europe of the EU.

German Regions on the Eve of the 21st Century: the Significance of Deep Structures for Regional Development

'A regional identity is a stabilising component, often rooted in past structures. Since regional identity is not primarily determined by economics, economic criteria should not determine new possible structures of the *Länder*.' (Klaus Töpfer, former Minister for Planning and Housing, from a speech in Hanover, 9 May 1996)

The presence of regional deep structures, or the (micro)regional cultural-historical heritages, is of increasingly importance in the (micro)regionalisation processes in the Federal Republic. The identities that are being formed are mostly attached to the cultural-historical realm as well as to the heritage of a particular past in the sphere of economy. In this way, completely artificial constructs have been avoided. While references to tradition can sometimes appear far-fetched, they are nevertheless often based on a reality of some sort.

In the late 1990s discussions on continued (micro)regionalisation in the Federal Republic intensified. Even comparatively strong regions such as the German *Bundesländer* must be further reinforced because of the new and demanding dual role of both entrepreneur and partner within the framework of Europe of the Regions. A solid regional identity represents an invaluable resource for both of these roles. In the introduction to this essay we mentioned the many forms of identity that exist parallel to one another in different regional contexts. Each region is thus confronted with the task of consistently finding new channels for expanding and strengthening its regional identity, not least by turning to the historical record.

In the Federal Republic a key issue is that of the internal boundaries between the regions. The question of how many *Bundesländer* should exist in Germany has been revived over the contemplated fusion of Berlin and Brandenburg. As we have seen, Article 29 (1) of the German Constitution stipulates that the Federal Republic's territory may be re-divided if the purpose is to enlarge the *Länder* so that they are strong enough to carry out their functions. Many of the smaller *Bundesländer* do, after all, live off of the large ones.[116]

Numerous proposals have been made to merge several *Bundesländer* so that there would be only six or seven rather than sixteen. In 1996 the 'old' idea of forming a northern *Land* consisting of Schleswig-Holstein, Niedersachsen, Mecklenburg-Vorpommern and the city-states of Hamburg and Bremen was rekindled. While it had wholehearted support from the governing mayor of Hamburg, it was vehemently opposed by his colleague in Bremen. Since both are Social Democrats, the divergence could not be attributed to party-political considerations. Likewise, a spatial reorganisation of the five *Bundesländer* in eastern Germany has also been discussed. The historian Karlheinz Blaschke drafted a plan that would reduce their number to three. One element in the proposal is the merging of Saxony and Thuringia, and Blaschke supported this suggestion by pointing to the fact that the two regions coexisted under the Wettin dynasty for some two centuries before their separation in 1485. However, politicians and scholars alike object to such plans, so underlining the importance of identity.[117]

Hence there are numerous examples of the significance of regional deep structures to regional evolution in regions, microregions and cross-border cooperative regions. Here the case of Baden-Württemberg is a particularly significant example since it currently displays a fruitful interaction between the regional, microregional and cross-border perspectives that go beyond its self-evident status as a *Bundesland*. A balance has been achieved between awareness of the cultural and historical heritage, effective administrative structures, and functional obligations like establishing institutions and locating industries, and this balance is being used as a resource for fresh synergies.

---

[116] The so-called *Finanzausgleich* (financial equalisation) means in the current situation that the 'wealthy' *Bundesländer* such as Hessen, Baden-Württemberg and Bavaria now pay for the 'poor' ones such as Saarland and Bremen.

[117] For instance, in the spring of 1996, in a new debate on the possible fusion of these regions, the Social Democrat chief minister of Sachsen-Anhalt, Reinhard Höppner, argued that 'regional identity is more important than money' (*Das Sonntagsblatt*, 8 March 1996, p.4). On 4 October 1996 he was joined by his Christian Democrat counterpart in Thuringia, Bernhard Vogel. In a speech before the Thuringian assembly in Altenburg, Vogel said that regional identity is the central factor to regional development (Deutschlandfunk, 4 October 1996).

Regional Diversity: Baden-Württemberg

'The new *Bundesland* which has just been created from the Länder of Baden, Württemberg-Baden und Württemberg-Hohenzollern will be called Baden-Württemberg. The final name will be laid down in the Constitution.' (from the legislative documents for the prospective *Bundesland* Baden-Württemberg, para. 1, 1952)[118]

The *Land* of Baden-Württemberg officially came into existence on 25 April 1952 at 12.30 p.m. At the same moment the Baden-Württemberg assembly elected its first chief minister, who in his inaugural speech proclaimed that the decision of 4 May 1951 to unify the three hitherto independent regions of Baden, Württemberg-Baden and Württemberg-Hohenzollern into one *Bundesland* had now been realised.[119] With these words he sealed a highly complicated political process: the fusion of the two historical regions of Baden and Württemberg, each of which exhibited enduring and tangible regional distinctiveness.

The lengthy and emotional debate that had preceded the creation of this new *Bundesland* was coloured by the recollection of deep structures. Prominent politicians and economists had already emphasised in the 1920s the economic and infrastructural benefits that such a fusion would bring. However, the populations were concerned over a possible loss of identity. How could two such dissimilar regions be bonded together? How would their disparate historical experiences be consolidated into a common foundation on which to build? How would differences and mutual antipathy (often overstated) be reconciled? The south Baden president Leo Wohleb told his counterparts in Württemberg-Hohenzollern that the Danube itself was so adamantly opposed to the fusion with Württemberg that 'the moment it reaches the Württemberg area, it trickles off, disappearing into Badian Hegau'.[120] The Badeners for their part were afraid that Baden would be totally engulfed by Württemberg, fears that were reinforced by the Württembergers'

---

[118] Reinhard Mussgnug, 'Die Anfänge Baden-Württembergs in verfassungsrechtlicher und verfassungsgeschichtlicher Sicht', *Zeitschrift für württembergische Landesgeschichte* (1985), p. 373.

[119] The division of south-western Germany was carried out by the Allies in 1945: Württemberg-Baden was in the American zone, Baden and Württemberg-Hohenzollern in the French zone.

[120] See Klaus Koziol, *Badener und Württemberger* (Stuttgart, 1987), p.10.

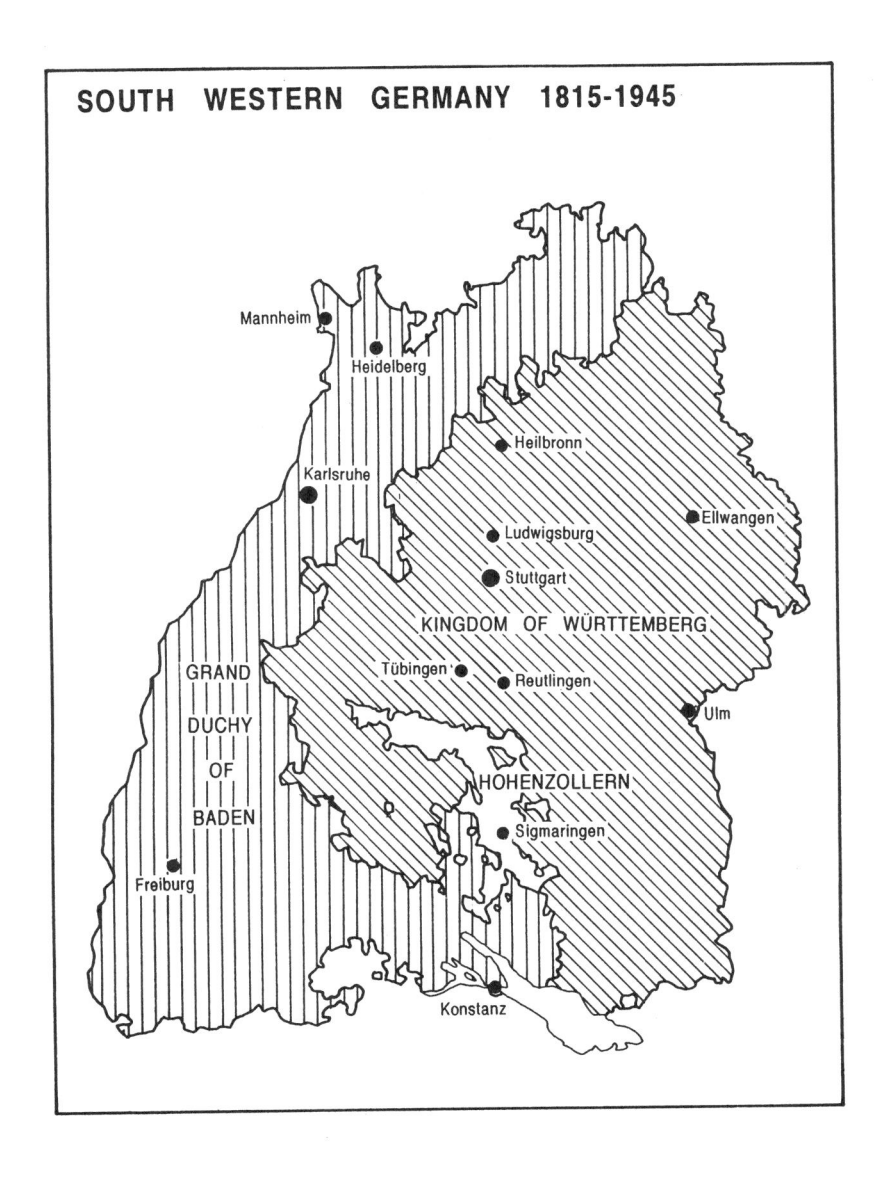

SOUTH WESTERN GERMANY 1815-1945

attitude to a region they sarcastically described as the '*Spätzle* democracy'.[121]

The referendum of 9 December 1951, which preceded the political decision, confirmed that Badeners were far more apprehensive about proposed fusion than Württembergers. Although a majority of 77 per cent voted in favour of the merger, most of the 'yes' responses, some 92 per cent, came from the Württembergers. In southern Baden 62 per cent voted against. The referendum in northern Baden – where 57 per cent voted in favour – was thus decisive.

Nearly a half a century after the consolidation of the two regions, the historic antagonism continues, though largely below the surface. Hence it is perhaps puzzling that Baden-Württemberg has capitalised so effectively on the synergy that resulted from the fusion. Among all European regions, this *Bundesland* is often held up as a sort of model, as expressed in the term '*Musterländle*'.[122] Indeed, a new sense of shared regional belonging has evolved in Baden-Württemberg, although older identities are still evident. The population has proved able to accommodate several strong identities.

How has this rapid assimilation, following strong opposition and involving no loss of the regions separate identities, been possible? Which historical experiences in Württemberg and Baden have survived as constituent components of both separate and shared identities? And finally, what constitutes a new common identity? Before we can suggest answers to these questions, we must first define briefly what is Württemberg and what is Baden in terms of the significant events that have molded these two core regions.

WÜRTTEMBERG

'During the past three centuries Württemberg has been marked by a high degree of political and social continuity.'[123]

---

[121] *Spätzle* is a famous pasta-style dish popular in Baden.

[122] The concept '*Musterländle*' means 'small model *Land*'. The suffix '- *le*' is a diminutive peculiar to the Baden dialect. See the section on Baden below (pp.105-10).

[123] Hartmut Lehmann, 'Pietismus und weltliche Ordnung in Württemberg von 17. bis zu 20. Jahrhundert' (Stuttgart, 1969), cited in Koziol, *Badener und Württemberger*, p.60.

'As compared to Baden, Württemberg was always inland; with its horizon blocked it was directed inwards and in that self-confident and disarmingly direct way was even self-important. [124]

What was once the duchy of Württemberg is an enclosed space, surrounded by three 'walls' – Odenwald and Stromberg in the north, Schwarzwald in the south-west, and Schwäbische Alb in the south-east. Although these forested mountain areas are no more than so-called *Mittelgebirge* with no high peaks, the absence of roads and other communications long caused them to be considered impenetrable. For centuries Württemberg was thus rather isolated and far from major routes. Hence the history of the region is marked by continuity and stability and therefore comparatively easy to grasp.

Württemberg can be called Swabian land, since it is the place of origin of the Swabian 'stem'. Before Württemberg itself existed, present-day Baden-Württemberg, Alsace and western Bavaria were divided among the Frankish 'stems' in the north, the Swabians in the south, and the bishoprics of Speyer, Strasbourg, Würzburg, Augsburg and Konstanz. During the tenth and eleven centuries, a duchy of Swabia was established in the area. Since the dukes were closely related to the imperial Staufer dynasty, the duchy had a position of power. When the last of the German Staufers, Konrad, was executed in 1266, the duchy of Swabia came to an end. Various attempts were made to reestablish it or to enfeoff the area to another prince, but all were thwarted, partly due to resistance from the Swabian nobility. A sort of power-vacuum characterised this part of south-western Germany until the mid-fifteenth century, after which portions of Swabia came to be incorporated into Württemberg.

The name 'Wirtenberg' belonged to an aristocratic family and attached to its castle already by the end of the eleventh century. Württemberg evolved into a countship and by the late fourteenth century was the largest in Germany. It had the standing of a duchy and acted as a stabilising influence in the southern part of the empire. In 1441 the brothers Ludwig and Ulrich, counts of Württemberg, who had governed jointly for eight years, decided to divide the countship between them. The resulting partition proved short-lived, and in 1482 an accord was signed at Münsing

---

[124] Amadeus Siebenpunkt, *Deutschland deine Badener* (Hamburg, 1978), p.13.

the result of which was reunification of the countship, which was made a duchy in 1495. The decision had important repercussions: here was a territory that was reunified not for dynastic reasons but because it had acquired a value in its own right. The Treaty of Münsing also had a psychological relevance by demonstrating that a decisive historical event could occur through peaceful means. The historian Hans-Martin Maurer underlines the treaty's importance to Württemberger regional identity:

This historical structural transformation...affected the population: it fostered a sense of solidarity, certain collectively anchored values, a sense of cohesion, and a new foundation for identification with the land. During the war-ravaged period of the sixteenth century, the Württembergers were carried through by their sense of self, of pride and of solidarity *vis-à-vis* dynasty and country. However the phrase '*Hie gut Württemberg*' (here the good Württemberg) has developed; it expresses the strong and solid regional awareness of the time.[125]

On the basis of the Münsing treaty, the duchy of Württemberg was organised into local communities (*Gemeinde*) and the somewhat larger *Ämter* (similar to *Kreise*) in the late fifteenth and sixteenth centuries. The residents had the right to choose their own sheriff, and in certain communities this was done through elections conducted on the majority system. The competences of the *Ämter* included certain overarching administrative affairs so that the *Ämter* were in fact self-ruling units responsible for their constituent counties. Some 100 of these 'microregions' were scattered throughout Württemberg until the nineteenth century. Remarkably the residents defined themselves according to the *Ämter* rather than to the community itself. An *Amt* assembly convened regularly, and here certain prominent residents were involved in the decision-making process. This further cultivated a sense of cohesion within the area, the matters to be decided often concerned not only local affairs, but proposals that applied to the entire duchy.

In addition, the division into *Ämter* served to neutralise the differences between urban and rural areas. The absence of large cities was counterbalanced by the great number of small towns. Württemberg lacked economic centres and large-scale industry

---

[125] See Hans-Martin Maurer, 'Von der Landesteilung zur Wiedervereinigung: Der Münsinger Vertrag als ein Markstein württembergischer Geschichte', *Zeitschrift für württembergische Landesgeschichte* 43 (1984), p.115.

and was largely a region of peasants and craftsmen. The small-scale experiences that characterised Württemberg ultimately produced the most democratic municipal laws in Germany. A law of 1849 decreed that all men over twenty-five who were liable to taxation were to be enfranchised. In 1868, Württemberg instituted a 'universal' (albeit limited to males) direct and secret ballot for elections to the second Chamber of the *Landtag*.

Another component of the democratisation process was already introduced in 1514, when the Tübinger *Landtag* decided to take over the debts of Duke Ulrich, which at this point threatened to bankrupt the entire duchy. As compensation the *Landtag* requested the right to political participation in both legislative and certain fiscal matters. In addition, it was decided that each new duke would be obliged to approve the *Tübinger Vertrag* (treaty) in order to be recognised by the Estates. For nearly three centuries this contract between prince and people served as a type of constitution.[126]

The impact of the Reformation was crucial to the future of Württemberg. Given its relative physical isolation nearly all of Württemberg remained Protestant – characterised by Pietism and the Lutheran work ethic – for several centuries. The resulting diligence, orderliness and rigorous social controls sometimes turned into intolerance.

The next profound change was triggered by Napoleon's regional interventions. Württemberg expanded three times over, and its population increased from 600,000 to 1.4 million. The integration of the new areas was eased by denominational affinity. The writing of regional history had an upswing in the 1820s, and this proved significant for the successful integration of the new Württembergers. Christoph Friedrich Stälin's *Wirttembergische Geschichte* (1846) was a milestone in this context.

For the rest of the nineteenth century, Württemberg was spared the violent revolutions and wars that erupted throughout Europe. The kingdom's incorporation into Germany likewise proceeded smoothly. While other principalities were torn a part by internal strife and war Württemberg made social progress. In 1906 democratisation reached its culmination when the privileged members of the *Landtag* were excluded from the Second Chamber, which was transformed into a Chamber of Commons. One of

---

[126] See Klaus Koziol, *Badener und Württemberger*, Stuttgart, 1987, p.16.

the factors behind the stable conditions in the *'königliche Republic Württemberg'* was that in general the monarchy was highly regarded, even by the Social Democrats.

During the Weimar Republic, Württemberg suffered lower unemployment and fewer bankruptcies than other regions. This comparative good fortune may partly explain Württemberg's position on National Socialism: in the *Reichstag* elections of 1932, the votes in favour of the Nazis were 7 per cent below the national average. Another reason for this result was a traditional conservatism that shied away from new ideas. The centralising ideology of Nazism also contributed to Württemberg's negative stance towards the party, since it went against the region's five centuries of decentralisation and microregionalisation. In contrast to Saxony, which was recurrently drawn into major international events, and to Baden, small-scale politics continued to be the norm in Württemberg, particularly through the *Ämter*.

As has been pointed out, Württemberg lacked a tradition of large-scale trade and industry. Up to the mid-1800s Württemberg was a predominantly agrarian area. It nevertheless comprised a large group of craftsmen who were known for their inventiveness and this segment of the population constituted a base for the small and medium-sized enterprises that flourished in the late nineteenth century and which carried Württemberg through various economic crises. By 1875 Württemberg had a greater number of small industries than any other German region. Precision mechanics, electronics, and engine-, car-, aircraft- and ship-building (associated with such names as Daimler, Benz, Dornier, Bosch and Zeppelin) were the major growth industries in the early twentieth century. In the 1920s about a century after poor harvests had triggered an emigration from Württemberg, industrial growth generated a stream of migration to the region. In sum, Württemberg as an economic region has seen both continuity and consistent progress.

BADEN

'The people of Baden were never a self-contained internal unit. Its northern and southern parts are very different, which is one reason why it is difficult to summarise its traditions.' (Eugen Fehrle)[127]

[127] Eugen Fehrle, *Badische Volkskunde*, 1924 (reprint – Frankfurt am Main, 1979),

'From the political, religious, cultural and social points of view, the grand-duchy of Baden was a diversified conglomeration.' (Paul Rothmund, *Die Anfänge des Liberalismus in Baden*)[128]

In direct contrast to Württemberg, Baden has been geographically open and marked by political discontinuity. Its position along the east bank of the Rhine has made it the object of a number of unfortunate descriptions, e.g. 'a blood sausage, stuffed at each end and empty in the middle.' The Rhine is portrayed either as the 'backbone' of Baden or as its 'corset rod'. Independent of these characterisations the fact remains that the Rhine has not been an inhibiting frontier but rather an essential communication route westward to France and Switzerland. There has thus been a steady influx of new ideas and people – merchants, craftsmen, artists and scholars. 'For over a hundred years, Paris was closer to Baden than Berlin.'[129] Thus, unlike Württemberg, rural and enclosed, Baden was urbanised and open to the world.

It could almost be seen as symbolic that the margravate of Baden originated in a division within one of the foremost ruling houses of the Middle Ages, the Zähringer.[130] In *c.* 1070 Hermann I of this dynasty, who was also margrave of Verona, became the first margrave of Baden. Further divisions came between the twelfth and fourteenth centuries. The oldest part of Baden, comprising the cities of Besigheim and Backnang, remained a core-area, but it was lost (partly to Württemberg) in the early fourteenth century, and the margravate's core shifted to the areas surrounding the cities of Durlach, Ettlingen and Pforzheim as well as the fortress of Baden-Baden, from which the wider area took its name. Like the ruling dynasty in Württemberg, that in Baden was related to

---

p.ix. Cited in Koziol, p.116.

[128] Cited in Koziol, p.98.

[129] Siebenpunkt, *Deutschland deine Badener*, p.11.

[130] The geographical origins of this aristocratic dynasty lay in the Black Forest but the House of Zähringer also eventually produced dukes of Carinthia and Swabia. In the eleventh century it brought under its rule most of the Black Forest, founding fortresses and cities. Theodor Mayer has argued that the Zähringer state, where the fief system was not widespread, was 'a peculiar state-formation based on individual performance in a given area, and a certain degree of political liberty'. See Theodor Mayer, 'Die Ausbildung der Grundlagen des modernen deutschen Staates im hohen Mittelalter' in Hellmut Kämpf (ed.), *Herrschaft und Staat im Mittelalter* (Darmstadt, 1964), pp.306-7.

the Staufers and so had a position of power. After the Staufer era the margrave of Baden remained powerful in spite of later divisions. The core land was actively supported by the smaller princely dynasties of Baden through various leagues and alliances.

In 1535 the margravate was divided between two family branches in Baden-Durlach and Baden-Baden, against the will of both the people and the Estates. This division, which turned into open hostility, held for 250 years, and as the result the two Badens went their separate ways – also denominationally. The Reformation penetrated Baden-Durlach, which aligned with Sweden during the Thirty Years' War, but Baden-Baden remained Catholic and was allied with the Habsburg Emperor. In 1771, with no male heirs in Baden-Baden, this half of the margravate was reunited with Baden-Durlach.

Again like Württemberg, Baden benefited from Napoleon's 'territorial revolution.' Its ground area was increased fourfold, and the population from 165,000 to 900,000. Baden became a grand-duchy in 1806, the same year as the German Empire was dissolved. In contrast to Württemberg, the new principality was not formed around the older 'stem' lands but was artificial, being an amalgam of disparate territories and traditions. The historian Lothar Gall has described its establishment as 'a continuation of the discontinuities within all areas'.[131] One result of this development was the eruption of conflict between city and countryside, triggered by denominational friction: the traditionally privileged urban centres of commerce and industry were predominantly Protestant, whereas most of the rural population, and indeed of the whole grand-duchy, were Catholic.

The new entity was organised on the French model, with a centralist bureaucratic structure. The division of the grand-duchy into nine *Kreise* in 1810 was based on pragmatic considerations such as surface area, population size and economic conditions, and the regional deep structures were ignored. The leadership in each *Kreis* executed the orders from above, and this also recalled the French system of prefectures. Unlike in Württemberg, decentralisation and self-rule played no role.

To accelerate the difficult and slow-moving integration process,

---

[131] See Lothar Gall, *Der Liberalismus als regierende Partei. Das Grossherzogtum Baden zwischen Restauration und Reichsgründung* (Wiesbaden, 1968), p.13.

and bind together diverse components, the grand-duke of Baden resolved to draft a 'modern constitution'. A representative state system, introduced in 1818, was thought of as 'the most liberal in Germany'. However, opposition was already substantial by the next year, and resulted in repression of the liberals. Liberalism did not have its true breakthrough in Baden till the 1860s; before this time, Baden had fluctuated between two extremes, namely revolution (in 1830 and again in 1848-9) and reaction.

The surrounding world watched as the revolutions broke out in Baden, which had been regarded as a political model. However, much of the vaunted liberalism of Baden was myth, or at least an exaggeration: a considerable distance separated the strong, centralised state and its administration from the private individual. Furthermore, in contrast to Württemberg, the population had not obtained the right to political participation. Baden remained an *Obrigkeitsstaat*, a state ruled from above, even after the reforms of 1860.[132] Moreover while Württemberg introduced a limited franchise and the direct ballot in 1868, only the following year did Baden pass a similar law, albeit a far more restrictive one (for example, involving indirect election).

The new constitution of 1818 did not allow for municipal self-rule: in the cities that had previously belonged to the former Empire's Austrian section, and been incorporated into the new grand-duchy in 1806, whatever self-rule had existed was now abolished. However, the French July Revolution in 1830 had reverberations in Baden, and municipal self-rule was at last institutionalised, although it was only in 1863 that the local communities were genuinely able to exercise the privilege. Despite the presence of revolutionary tendencies, the people of Baden were unable to seize a greater share of power: their civic rights were always conferred upon them, as gifts from the authorities.

However, in another aspect Baden enjoyed a literally 'boundless' freedom: its boundaries were open for the import of revolutionary notions and other ideas from the outside world. We thus find a consistent discrepancy between political claims and political reality. The realm of industry was the first effectively to put foreign ideas into effect during the first phase of industrialisation, in the late nineteenth century – a significant part of industry was in the hands

---

[132] Ibid., p.38. The concept of the *Obrigkeitsstaat* is more generally applied to Prussia.

of Swiss and French immigrants and was tied to Swiss capital. Since the grand-duchy was renowned for its natural beauty, the charm of its cities and its health resorts, people from Britain, Holland, Poland and Russia had settled there.

This tolerance had no parallel in religious matters. Between 1827 and 1918, the Protestant state power (representing nearly one-third of the population) and the politically powerless Catholic Church (representing just over two-thirds) were in a state of perpetual conflict, which was exacerbated after 1860 when the Protestant liberals took power and initiated the so-called *Kulturkampf*, whereby they strove to subordinate the Catholic Church to the state. These attempts resulted in the political institutionalisation of the Catholic Church into the Catholic Liberal Party, founded in 1869 and reorganised in 1888 under the designation 'Badische Zentrumpartei'. Although in the 1880s the *Kulturkampf* was toned down with the adoption of various legal compromises, the divergence between the Protestant and Catholic positions remains to this day: while the Christian Democratic Union (CDU) of other areas serves as a rallying-point for all Christians, in Baden it is still dominated by the Catholics.

The process of industrialisation engendered the shared identity of *Musterländle*. Technologically – e.g. in railway building – Baden stood well ahead of Württemberg and was one of Germany's most industrialised states in the two decades before the First World War. By 1907 only one-third of the population still lived by agriculture. The aftermath of the war brought a period of comparative decline; during the Weimar Republic Baden was a partly demilitarised border-region, and this status contributed to the depression, with potential investors reluctant to commit their assets to the area. In addition, Baden's industries were not adaptable. Thus, the global economic crisis had different repercussions on Baden and Württemberg. The result was a striking adherence to National Socialism, in contrast to Württemberg: in elections support for the Nazis was 1.5 per cent above the national average. After the end of the Second World War, northern Baden found itself in the American occupation zone while the south was administered by the French.

Opposition to the subsequent proposal for fusion of Baden and Württemberg grew out of the political uncertainties in the former grand-duchy. Given its heterogeneity, division and lack of sense of cohesion, the population feared that its region would be virtually engulfed by a far more stable Württemberg. However, those concerns ultimately proved unfounded. In 1975 the head of government in Freiburg, Hermann Person, who had once objected to the amalgamation, noted that the identification of southern Badeners with Baden was stronger than ever before, and that the cultural Alemann tradition was more apparent and prevalent than at any time since the end of the war: 'The Badian question is solved; today we live as proud Badeners without hang-ups in the *Land* of Baden-Württemberg.'[133]

BADEN-WÜRTTEMBERG

'Today Europe of the Regions is part of European reality and everyday European politics. [...] In this context Baden-Württemberg was always in the vanguard.' (from a speech by Erich Schneider, former President of the Landtag in Baden-Württemberg, 3 July 1991, Stuttgart)

Since it was consolidated in 1952 Baden-Württemberg has experienced a highly positive development. Assimilation too has been a trouble-free process. In the 1950s opponents of fusion were assured that a referendum on the region's continued existence would eventually be held. When this came to pass on 7 July 1970 any remaining doubts about the success of the merger were removed: no less than 81.9 per cent of the respondents in Baden (79.1 per cent of these in the former opposition stronghold in the south) voted for the preservation of Baden-Württemberg.

Several of Württemberg's experiences continue to influence the evolution of Baden-Württemberg. First, the federal structures and decentralised administration within the *Bundesland* are linked to its history. Although the grand-duchy of Baden had a centralist structure, Württemberg's decentralised system has prevailed. Thus, the regional diversity in Baden could be preserved after the fusion. Baden-Württemberg is today divided into four *Regierungsbezirke* (administrative districts), which have controlling powers over the *Kreise* and local communities in such issues as budgetary planning. There are nine municipal *Kreise*, thirty five *Länderkreise* and 1,110 communities. Reforms implemented in 1971, 1973 and 1975 gave

[133] In Paul Sauer, 'Die Anfänge des Landes Baden-Württemberg', *Zeitschrift für württembergische Landesgeschichte* 44 (1985), p.371, from a speech delivered at the opening of the *Landtag's* exhibition '25 Jahre Baden-Württemberg' in 1977.

the *Kreise* and communities increased self-rule and a wider sphere of authority. A genuine polycentrism has arisen from this process of political and administrative decentralisation, and this has encouraged a kind of regional renaissance including the building of prestigious new educational facilities and cultural institutes.

Inner balance and stability, pragmatism and political and social continuity are other major legacies Württemberg brought to Baden-Württemberg. The political spectrum is dominated by the centre, although right and left are represented in the *Landtag*. For most of its existence, Baden-Württemberg has been governed by the CDU, at times in coalition with the Social Democrats and the Liberals; this has been made easier by the fact that the CDU in Württemberg has a strong dash of social liberalism. The focus on education is also derived from the Württemberg tradition. An emphasis on diligence and orderliness have permeated the educational system, which is of an exceptionally high standard both at compulsory school level and in the universities. Baden-Württemberg is home to several colleges and universities of high international standing, including Heidelberg, Tübingen, Freiburg and Ulm.

Baden has also contributed important elements to the new identity. First, an openness to the outside world has influenced the successful development of the new *Bundesland*, and defines Baden-Württemberg in both the European and international contexts: more than any other region of the Federal Republic, it is known for its extensive regional cooperation. The region has thus played a leading role in the Assembly of European Regions. Moreover, its openness to the outside world has promoted the influx of new ideas and impulses, as was the case when Baden stood on its own. Its former chief minister Lothar Späth sought to transform Baden-Württemberg into a centre of culture and high technology.[134]

Secondly, Baden's tolerance towards outsiders is one of its main contributions to the *Bundesland*. Instead of homogeneity being the norm, pluralism and regional diversity are seen as valuable resources. The label '*Musterländle*' invokes Baden's third contribution. The former grand-duchy was long plagued by a split personality:

---

[134] That Lothar Späth was indeed a pioneer in the realm of regional cooperation is shown, for instance in his initiation of a collaboration between Baden-Württemberg, Catalonia, Lombardy and Rhône-Alpes.

an inferiority complex rooted in a sense of a territorial and political insignificance and at the same time the desire to be a *Musterländle*. The ambiguity has been resolved in the new *Bundesland*. The whole of Baden-Württemberg is today viewed as a model for other European regions.

All in all, the experiences of Baden and Württemberg complement each other, and the new *Bundesland* has shown itself capable of capitalising on this compatibility in the forging of a new, common identity. The forces of disintegration have yielded to the principle of cohesion. However, the new identity involves not only complementary elements, but some genuine similarities. The first shared experience was that of the fusion itself. Both regions strove to show the outside world that they were fully capable of succeeding in the new situation. A second resemblance was in the economic structures: both northern Baden, with the city of Mannheim, and northern Württemberg, with Stuttgart, were heavily industrialised, while the southern portions of both regions were predominantly agricultural. Industrialisation had been delayed in both Baden and Württemberg due to a shortage of raw materials. Industrialisation arrived late in these regions, but then motor-car, engine, electronic and high-tech industries became integral in the *Bundesland's* future.

We have seen not only how regional deep structures have survived in present-day Germany, but also the significance of identities in forging a new and modernised regional awareness. Four or five centuries ago, a particular region may have been known for its intense Protestantism, its prominent mining industry or its easy accessibility via roads and rivers. Today's regions market themselves by highlighting their attractive cultural life, their high-tech image or their effective infrastructures. We have examined several identity-related factors that shaped them from the Middle Ages to the present.

The world stands on the threshold of a new economic revolution. This phenomenon entails the transition from a traditional industrial society to a knowledge society with an increasingly significant third sector, namely the social economy and social capital. In this context the importance of regions and microregions is increasing. In an emerging economy that fosters globalisation, Europeanisation and regionalisation and as the nation-state consequently declines in importance, the regions and microregions are leading actors.

The regional arena allows for new regional-political developments. In Baden-Württemberg microregionalisation of the entire *Bundesland* is contemplated, as part of a quest to enhance the area's autonomy and boost public involvement. It has become clear that some kind of historical connection is necessary for such a process to succeed. Thus the importance ascribed to regional deep structures is not surprising. As they face the future, the regions and microregions are experiencing 'the return of history'.

THE AUSTRO-HUNGARIAN EMPIRE 1867-1918
Russia
Bohemia
Germany
Silesia
Galicia
Moravia
Bukovina
U. Austria
L. Austria
Hungary
V.
S.
Tyrol
Styria
Carinthia
Transylvania
Carniola
Croatia - Slavonia
Istria
Italy
Romania
Bosnia
Dalmatia
Herzegovina
1908
Serbia
Bulgaria

PART THREE

REGION, CULTURAL IDENTITY AND POLITICS IN THE LATE HABSBURG MONARCHY

Fredrik Lindström

In today's perspective the organisation of Central Europe into nations appears self-evident, even natural. However, the origins of these nations lie in the political construction of national communities in the nineteenth century, when the complex patterns of languages and cultural identities were interpreted discursively and presented as discrete, internally coherent entities. Compared with other parts of Europe, those areas of Central and Eastern Europe that were organised politically under the Habsburg dynasty exhibited a remarkably complicated pattern, and the political construction of national community therefore had particularly dramatic consequences. In the political arena, this led to severe antagonism between nationalist parties, which finally became all-pervasive in the Habsburg Monarchy's domestic affairs. The result for society as a whole was that older forms of cultural identity were challenged, re-evaluated and reinterpreted in national terms. In some areas there was a strong trend towards assimilation.

However, the political construction of national communities took place within the Monarchy's stable parameters of political/administrative institutionalised regions. These regions formed the institutional framework for nascent modernisation, since the process was channelled through their socio-economic and eventually also their political framework. They were generally corporative, territorial entities with no cohesive cultural identity. This proved to be a problem when the construction of national communities also required definition in terms of national space. Thus, during modernisation tension escalated between the institutionalised spaces and political efforts to launch various national interpretations of the existing patterns of cultural identities. This tension was an important element in what is often called the nationality problem under the Habsburg Monarchy. Before 1914 it was not clear how such tensions could be alleviated. The Monarchy played host to an intense political contest in which the future political organisation of society into cultural communities and spaces was a central question.

In this chapter we deal with several projects that operated in this arena, particularly the roles played by institutionalised *regions* in the political construction of cultural communities under the Monarchy of the later nineteenth and early twentieth century. The concept of *place* is used as an instrument to highlight the strain between older expressions of cultural identity and political constructions of cultural communities.[1] Historically, the relationship between different institutionalised space in Central Europe,

---

[1] The point of departure for this approach to nationalism in general, and the so called nationality problem in the late Habsburg Monarchy in particular, is that the old and persistent dichotomy in theories on nationalism between *Staatsnation* and *Kulturnation* (Friedrich Meinecke, *Weltbürgertum und Nationalstaat*, Munich and Berlin, 1907), the Western and the Eastern type of nationalism (Hans Kohn, *The Idea of Nationalism: A Study in its Origins and Background*, New York, 1944), or the Civic and Ethnic type of nation (Liah Greenfeld, *Nationalism: Five Roads to Modernity*, Cambridge, MA, 1992), to mention a few influential examples, is seen as problematic. The basic idea here is instead to treat the relationship in nationalism between (politically institutionalised) territory and cultural community as general, and to focus the role of older spatial structures, already established at the time of the breakthrough of nationalism. Institutionalised regions functioned at different levels as the spatial containers of modernisation, and were the units that carried the gradual development of modern political and administrative institutions. This process was initiated without regard to the cultural definition of space, and with the growing strength of nationalism, with its idea of organising the political system on the basis of cultural community, tension developed between cultural identity and institutionalised space. These ideas are discussed in the present author's 'Region och kulturell identitet. Ett kalejdoskopiskt perspektiv på det habsburgska Centraleuropas historia före 1900' (unpubl. ms., Dept. of History, University of Lund, 1995) and 'Institutionalized Space and the Political Construction of Cultural Community during Modernization: A Theoretical Perspective' (unpublished ms., Dept. of History, University of Lund, 1996). Important inspiration comes from Anssi Paasi, 'The institutionalization of regions: a theoretical framework for understanding the emergence of regions and the constitution of regional identity' (*Fennia* 164:1, 1986), concerning the concept of region, and John Agnew, 'Representing space: Space, scale and culture in social science' in J. Duncan and D. Ley (eds), *Place/Culture/Representation* London and New York, 1993, concerning the concept of place.

principalities of different sizes and dignity, was unclear and multi-faceted. It was not formalized in any systematic way (they were neither parts of a uniform intra-state administrative system, or sovereign parts of an inter-state system). For example, the relationship between Bohemia and Moravia within the Habsburg Monarchy was unclear. They were both provinces of the Monarchy and they had a history of common statehood, but their mutual relationship in this period was a matter of dispute. This state of affairs was also used politically in different ways.

Furthermore, in Central European history institutionalised spaces could be included in different subdivided spatial hierarchies. In the nineteenth century Bohemia and Moravia were part of both the German League and the Habsburg Monarchy. A further complication was that changes in the organisation of space had left spatial remnant structures that were still relevant and could be activated politically.

However, the most important of these spatial structures were those that functioned as sustaining structures in the political organisation of space. Under the Habsburg Monarchy in the nineteenth century, these were organised into *Kronländer*,[2] or provinces, and the Habsburg state (Austria and later Austria-Hungary) as a whole. After outlining the development that gave rise to a certain organisation of space and cultural identities in the early phases of modernisation, we look at several political projects and their construction of cultural community in relation to the institutionalised spaces.

Region and Cultural Identity in a Long-Term Perspective

In the areas of Central Europe within the Habsburg Monarchy the organisation of space went through numerous changes from the Middle Ages to the nineteenth century. At the same time the kingdoms, principalities and duchies established in the Middle Ages continued to provide a basic pattern in the political organisation of space. A certain continuity can be discerned, mainly in the symbolism associated with these political institutions and

---

[2] *Kronland* was the designation for the base entity around which the late Habsburg Monarchy's administration was built.

lands, but also to a lesser degree between actual institutions and territories. In addition the area had a turbulent history of wars and migrations, which provided an often intricate web of cultural identities within these institutionalised spaces.

For the sake of simplicity we can distinguish three major phases. The first involves the establishment in the period *c*. 800-1100, the medieval kingdoms and principalities that organised the space before the Habsburg era. The second spans the period from the establishment of Habsburg rule over the majority of these kingdoms and principalities in 1526-7 to the expulsion of the Ottomans from Hungary in the late seventeenth century. During this time particularist power interests and the dynasty balanced each other, and there was no significant integration into the larger dynastic entity. In the final phase, covering the eighteenth century, there was growing pressure for integration. The regimes of Maria Theresa (1740-80) and Joseph II (1780-90) introduces a broad project of reforms with the object of forging a unified Austrian state. In this period the greater part of the independent status of the lands was eliminated, so, from this point on we have provinces within a larger state rather than constitutionally-defined entities bound together by a dynasty.

In some cases, the demarcation of regions, the emergence of a regional institutional sphere and the development of a regional system of symbols can be traced back to the Middle Ages. The duchy of Carinthia is an example, involving not only a regional system of symbols, with 600 to 1000 years of history but also extensive transformation in terms of institutions and territory.[3]

Bohemia and Moravia. Numerous regions in the late Habsburg monarchy had a history of regional institutionalisation and symbolism comparable to that of Carinthia. However, there were also regions that vanished and those that became institutionalised relatively late.[4] Bohemia can be described as one of the most

---

[3] See Tom Gullberg's chapter (pp.154-65, below) for a thorough discussion of Carinthia.

[4] By way of comparison with Carinthia, Gullberg deals with another example that falls outside the chronological limits of this chapter, namely the institutionalisation of Burgenland beginning in 1918. Burgenland was formed on the basis of an earlier role in the spatial organisation of western Hungary.

solid spatial structures in the organisation of Central Europe. It was caught in the tensions between the Holy Roman Empire, of which it was a part, and the Bohemian kings' constant efforts to expand their power to the east and south. Internal development was naturally affected by periodic dependence on the Emperor and by expansionary projects that resulted in war with neighbouring areas.[5] However, much of the driving force behind the regional institutionalisation came from the internal situation.

The political-institutional structure of the Bohemian lands was crystallised in the High Middle Ages (c. 1100-1300). Power was divided between the royal authority, a Council and the Estates. The Council represented the high nobility and the Estates, the church, the numerically strong gentry and a number of towns. Power shifted among all three in various ways, but the main tensions were in the relationship between the royal power and the Provincial Assembly in which the gentry had early become the dominating force. In the fifteenth century a weak and vacillating royal power left the Assembly in almost total control of Bohemia. Recurring royal attempts to consolidate its power over the land led to an expansion of the institutional sphere, which towards the end of the Middle Ages had granted Bohemia an institutional framework which was well developed and consolidated.[6]

The term 'Lands of the Bohemian Crown' (*Corona Bohemiae*) was introduced in the fourteenth century to apply to those lands answering to the Bohemian king and ruled from Prague, although they contained their own political and administrative bodies. During the reign of Charles IV in the mid-fourteenth century Moravia, Silesia, Lausitz, Brandenburg and a number of areas in the Rhineland were included in this constellation.[7] Later, the term

---

[5] See Ferdinard Seibt, *Deutschland und die Tschechen. Geschichte einer Nachbarschaft in der Mitte Europas* (Munich, 1993), pp.89-97. Bohemia's position in the Middle Ages has been much debated in Czech and German nationalist history. In his *Böhmen/Mähren und das Reich* (Cologne, 1959), Wilhelm Wegener provides perhaps the final effort to show that Bohemia was truly 'German' in medieval times. Seibt discusses this complex of national-historical problems.

[6] On the development of the institutional structure, see Ernst Hellbling, *Österreichische Verfassungs- und Verwaltungsgeschichte* (Vienna, 1974) pp. 152-83. Seibt provides a historical overview (*Deutschland und die Tschechen*, pp. 89-162).

[7] Seibt, *Deutschland und die Tschechen*, pp. 121-34.

came to signify a smaller entity: Bohemia, Moravia and the section of Silesia (Austrian Silesia) that remained after the War of the Austrian Succession in the 1740s. In 1527 a new phase in Bohemian history began, as the Estates voted to install Ferdinand I of Habsburg as king. Between then and 1618 the nobility maintained a strong position in Bohemia, but the Habsburgs progressively and methodically curtailed it. The upheaval of 1618 was partly due to an attempt by the Bohemian nobility to shed the increasing weight of Habsburg influence. However, the effort failed, and instead prompted the rapid expansion of the royal institutions. The power of the nobility was diminished.[8]

Germans migrated over several centuries to Bohemia and Moravia from different areas of the Holy Roman Empire. This began in the early Middle Ages and had grown to substantial proportions in the twelfth century, when the Bohemian kings sought to develop various sectors of society with the help of colonists. A few centuries later Charles IV eagerly enlisted colonists to expand trading and industrial centres and help to create agricultural communities. The latter were also often established under the aegis of the Church and great land-owners.[9]

Hungary and Transylvania. Another region as important politically as Bohemia, if not more so, was the kingdom of Hungary, where a political structure involving extensive power of the nobility in the local arena was created in the Middle Ages. The division of administrative counties remained in place till 1918 and was dominated by the Hungarian nobility for most of its existence. The main difference from Bohemia was that between 1526 and 1689 Hungary was divided into three parts. The effect of the Turkish invasion was devastating in many respects, and one result was that about half of the land came under Turkish control. It was during this period that Transylvania in the east became institutionalised as a region, while a strip of land in the west and north became part of the growing Habsburg dominion, as the remaining Hungarian nobility chose Ferdinand I as king of Hungary after the Turkish victory in 1526. The weakening of the Hungarian

---

[8] Hellbling, *Österreichische Verfassungs- und Verwaltungsgeschichte*, pp.210-82; Seibt, *Deutschland und die Tschechen*, pp.163-190.

[9] Seibt, *Deutschland und die Tschechen*, pp.59-88.

nobility, and the leading role of the Habsburg dynasty in the reconquest at the end of the seventeenth century meant that Hungary was increasingly tied to the developing central power in Vienna. However, the Hungarian nobility held on to much of its control at the county level and the historical symbolism of the Crown of St Stephen became a unifying element in the notion of preserving Hungary.[10]

The medieval migrations also affected Hungary. German colonists – known as Saxons – came to Transylvania in the twelfth and thirteenth centuries, and were soon granted privileges directly from the Hungarian king.[11] Their representative body communicated directly with the royal power through the 'Count of the Saxons' (*Sachsengraf*), an official appointed by the King. These colonists founded agricultural communities and market towns, which in parts of south-western Transylvania were united in a continuous territory[12] but in others were dispersed in enclaves. The terms 'enclave' and 'continuous territory' are not wholly valid since Magyars, Szekles, Romanians and others often lived among the Germans in these settlements.[13] However, the Saxons were corporatively demarcated in Transylvania and could in part be defined by territory.

As we saw above, Transylvania was institutionalised as its own region under the Turkish occupation, and the political institutions were built around the privileges distributed in the area. Up till 1863 three recognised nations can be distinguished in Transylvania:[14] the free Saxon community, the free Szekelian community

---

[10] On the institutional structure, see Hellbling, *Österreichische Verfassungs- und Verwaltungsgeschichte*, pp.184-282. A historical overview is provided by, for example, Péter Hanák (ed.), *The Corvina History of Hungary* (Budapest, 1991), pp.11-82.

[11] The original charter is dated 1224. See Hellbling (1974), p.209; also Ulf Irheden, '"Bän ä sakse äm Sakseland". Tysk etnisk-regional identitet i Transylvanien', unpubl. master's thesis, Dept. of History, Lund University, 1996.

[12] This area was originally called Siebenbürgen, but over time this term came to be used as a German synonym for Transylvania. See Irheden, op. cit.

[13] See, e.g., Friedrich Göllner, *Die Siebenbürgische Militärgrenze. Ein Beitrag zur Sozial- und Wirtschaftgeschichte, 1762-1851* (Munich, 1974), pp.9-17, for the strain between the judicial-territorial organisation into nations and the ethnic-linguistic affiliation.

[14] The three nations are understood to have been created under an agreement

and the Hungarian nobility in the area. The three groups were collectively represented in the Transylvanian Estates. The Hungarian nobility reflected no particular cultural identity, but the Saxon and Szekel communities comprised cultural identities with corporative rights. However, more than half the population were peasants who spoke various Romanian dialects and who like the Magyar peasants did not have political representation.[15]

In the central and southern parts of Hungary proper, the recurrent struggle against the Turks resulted in virtual depopulation. Only after the Habsburg reconquest were these areas significantly repopulated, partly through a massive colonisation project again dominated by Germans.

Austrian integration and de-integration. In the sixteenth and seventeenth centuries the Habsburg dynasty made efforts to consolidate its possessions. However, these remained scattered, and did not have the clear, geographically demarcated borders of nineteenth-century Austria. However, the core areas – the Austrian hereditary domains and the domains of the Bohemian Crown – became increasingly closely tied during this time. The notion of a closely interconnected complex of Habsburg territories did not truly gain momentum till after the successful wars against the Ottomans in the late seventeenth century. One of the first important steps in that direction was taken by Charles VI, who through the Pragmatic

---

of 1437, see Göllner, *Die Siebenbürgische Militärgrenze*, p.15, and Mathias Bernath, *Habsburg und die Anfänge der rumänischen Nationsbildung* (Leiden, 1972), pp.9ff. 'Nation' here represents a variation of the medieval concept of nation not to be confused with its modern usage. However, such a corporation could well protect, or indeed create, a cultural identity. In 1863 the Romanian people were given political rights, and thus can be said to have constituted a fourth nation from that point on. But the arrangement was short-lived, since the political constitution was abolished in 1867 due to the Hungarian effort to make Hungary a unified Magyar state (see Keith Hitchins, 'Die Rumänen' in vol.II of A. Wandruszka and P. Urbanitsch (eds), *Die Habsburger Monarchie, 1848-1918*, Vienna, 1980). With the abolition of the corporate-judicial system, the Szekel nation practically disappeared as a cultural community distinct from the Magyars.

[15] Göllner, *Die Siebenbürgische Militärgrenze* pp.9-17. The gentry represented in the Estates were not only of Magyar origin, but included those of other origins, including Romanian. In practice, a stratification developed in the Saxon and Szekel corporations, so that these groups too developed a kind of gentry. On the Romanian social structure at this time, see Bernath, *op. cit*, pp.139-46.

Sanction secured recognition of the Habsburg right of inheritance in all the territories, and firmly established the bonds tying those areas together.[16]

However, it was only in the reign of Maria Theresa and Joseph II that the expansion of the central power truly gained momentum. The imperial objective was to abolish particularist institutions and integrate the Habsburg dominions into a unified, centrally governed state. The spheres of finance and administration were joined and transformed into a single system that applied to the entire Monarchy. The transformation of former princely competences into royal, ducal and other such chancelleries, and then into uniform Court Chancelleries, had already gone on for some time. These were all now transferred to Vienna, and a kind of subdivided Ministry of Domestic Affairs was founded. The administrative structure was turned into Governorships (*Statthalterei*) taking their orders from the ministry in Vienna. Thereafter the composition of the Ministry of Domestic Affairs was simplified, being reduced first to three Court Chancelleries and then to two (*böhmisch-österreichische Hofkanzlei* and *Hofkanzlei für Ungarn*). Finance was made into a uniform system, but only in 1816 was an Austrian national bank founded. In 1780-90, the final ten years of this reform period, Joseph II, Maria Theresa's son, attempted to realise a radical reform programme. He wanted to complete the formation of a modern, well-integrated unified state, but the highly accelerated pace of his reforms was resisted from various directions. After his death in 1790, significant elements of his achievements were dismantled. Austria entered the age which had been ushered in by the French Revolution as a half-finished state project.[17]

However, the Theresian–Josephian reforms did result in the creation of a superordinated political structure. The Austrian state was to experience numerous crises and transformations during the

---

[16] On the early institutional integration, see Hellbling, *Österreichische Verfassungs- und Verwaltungsgesichte*, pp.210-82, and on its impact on Bohemia, E. Hassenpflug-Elzholz, *Böhmen und die böhmische Stände in der Zeit der beginnenden Zentralismus* (Munich and Vienna, 1982).

[17] For the projects launched by Joseph and Maria Theresa, see Hellbling, *Die Österreichische Verfassungs-und Verwaltungsgeschichte*, pp.283-322.

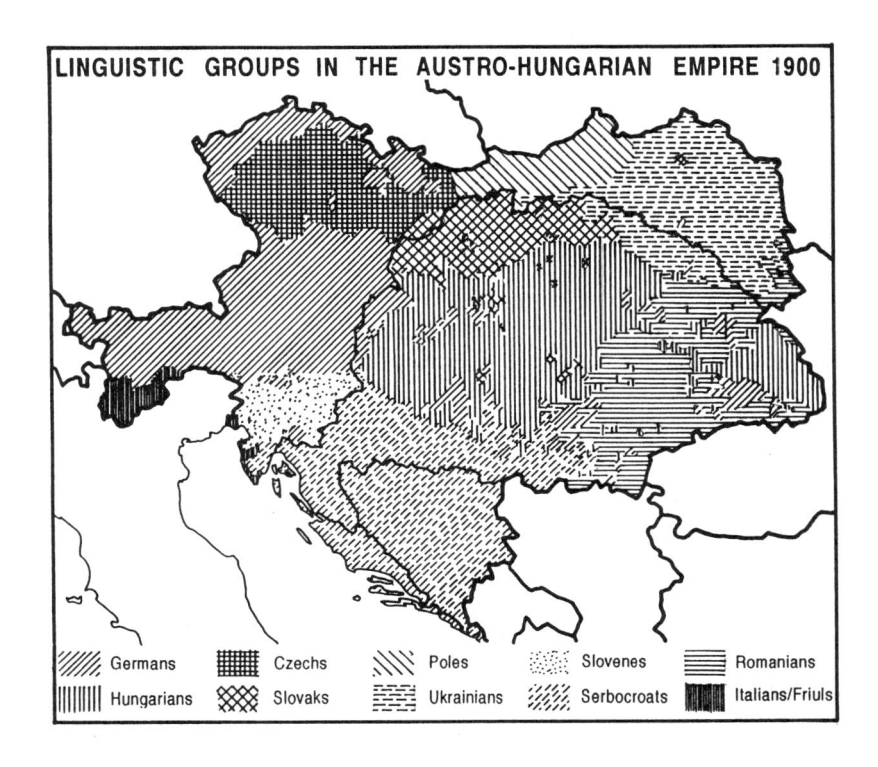

LINGUISTIC GROUPS IN THE AUSTRO-HUNGARIAN EMPIRE 1900

Germans, Czechs, Poles, Slovenes, Romanians, Hungarians, Slovaks, Ukrainians, Serbocroats, Italians/Friuls

nineteenth century, especially the latter half. The most critical of these were the revolution and civil war of 1848-9, the war against Prussia in 1866 and the consequent division of the Austrian empire into an Austrian and a Hungarian part. These upheavals and their repercussions on the domestic arena brought the spatial structures and cultural identities that history had fostered in the area into immediate focus.

Place and Cultural Identity in the Nineteenth Century

Bohemia and Moravia. The migrations to the Bohemian lands over a long period contributed to the shifting of boundaries between Germans and Czechs. Hence various places and localities developed 'layered' histories involving extensive spheres of contact between what was German and what was Czech, and a degree of integration was thereby promoted.[18] For some parts of these lands there is evidence of bilingualism already in the sixteenth and seventeenth centuries, although it is difficult to grasp the extent of it during this early period.[19] The distribution of corporative privileges in the late Middle Ages in connection with the cultivation of new land and the founding of towns promoted both integration and fragmentation – a Bohemian mix between German and Czech, as well as distinct German and Czech cultural identities – in different parts of these lands. A distinction between cultural identities within the two main groups, especially the Germans, also evolved, probably because the Germans arrived over a long period, were from different parts of German-speaking Europe, settled in different parts of the new countries and adopted different occupations.[20]

By the mid-nineteenth century the element of integration in Bohemian society appears to have grown strong. Gary B. Cohen's study of the Prague Germans focuses on the emergence of a German ethnic identity in Prague at that time and concludes that cultural identity was defined by aspects other than 'German' or 'Czech' in the 1840s and '50s. Bilingualism was frequent and doubtless necessary in a society with a German *bürgerlich* culture mixed with definite Czech elements.[21] It emphasises that those

---

[18] Seibt (*Deutschland und die Tschechen*) highlights this mixed history of the 'place'. He belongs to a smaller group of German historians who have sought to move between the images and counter-images of the national narratives in Bohemian history. A number of Czech historians have made similar attempts in recent years. See, for example, Jan Kren, *Die Konfliktgemeinschaft. Tschechen und Deutsche, 1780-1918* (Munich, 1996).

[19] On southern Bohemia and southern Moravia during this time, see, for instance, Vaclav Buzek, 'Zum tschechisch–deutschen Bilinguismus in den böhmischen und österreichischen Ländern in der frühen Neuzeit', *Österreichische Osthefte* vol.335, no.4 (1993).

[20] See Seibt, *Deutschland und die Tschechen*, pp.62-88.

[21] There was another phenomenon known as *Kuchelböhmisch*, a mixed language spoken, for example, in the Bohemian state administration in its contacts with the people. See, for instance, William Johnston, *The Austrian Mind* (Berkeley, CA, 1972), pp.265-7, and Barbara Plewa Törnquist, 'Language and nationalism in Europe: Eastern Central Europe', unpubl. paper, Department of Slavic Studies, Lund University, 1995, p.24. It can also be assumed that some of the observed

who climbed the social ladder were socialised into this culture, independently of whether their background was German or Czech, or best described simply as Bohemian, and thus pinpoints the importance of class (*Stand*) to cultural identity in Prague during this time. Cohen also suggests that, in society at large, Bohemian integration between the cultural identities only slowly gave way to the political polarisation between Czech and German.[22]

According to Cohen, 1860 was the watershed year in German and Czech becoming primary components of cultural identity in Prague. That year saw the introduction of the constitutional era, with a shift in state policy towards recognition of the politicised national identities. However, the distribution of national rights was no simple matter in the absence of reliable statistics on national affiliation. From 1880 a population census was to be conducted every tenth year as a basis for nationality policy. Respondents were asked to state the 'everyday language used' (*Umgangssprache*), so precluding the possibility of declaring bilingualism. Neither did the question involve national identity.[23] Thus the censuses reveal nothing about bilingualism or the possibility of Bohemian integration as part of cultural identity. However, official investigations in response to grievances concerning inaccuracies in the census presumably shed light on these questions.

In the first censuses, numerous respondents ignored the instructions and claimed two or more everyday languages. However, the pattern was later broken since the authorities would accept only one listed language. If in doubt, people were asked to say which language they used most often. The census material shows interesting changes over time, with the same individuals claiming different languages in different censuses. There appeared to be great uncertainty among those arriving from rural areas; some merely opted for the dominant language in their current environment.

---

bilingualism was the result of lack of fluency in either language. However, there is evidence of genuine bilingualism, as is discussed below.

[22] Gary B. Cohen, *The Politics of Ethnic Survival: Germans in Prague, 1861-1914* (Princeton, NJ, 1981), especially pp.19-51 and 274-82 and 'Ethnicity and urban population growth: the decline of the Prague Germans, 1880-1920', in K. Hitchens (ed.), *Studies in East European Social History* (Leiden, 1981).

[23] For an analysis of the population censuses and their role in policy-making, see Emil Brix, *Die Umgangssprachen in Altösterreich zwischen Agitation und Assimilation* (Vienna and Graz, 1982).

The turbulence of urbanisation and industrialisation makes a clear assessment of the reasons for the obvious ambivalence difficult, but bi- or multilingualism was clearly widespread.[24]

Gerald Stourzh has examined legal cases that followed the implementation of national rights in society, e.g. concerning the division of institutions along national lines. Schools were now to be defined by nationality. The appointment of members to the board of education and requests by parents to transfer their children from one school to another with a different language of instruction resulted in court proceedings which in turn often gave a national definition of the individual in question. The court records show that many individuals were bilingual and unwilling to choose either 'Germanness' or 'Czechness'.[25] Thus it seems clear that some degree of social and cultural integration between diverse cultural identities, within the Bohemian framework, had taken place.

Although, the effects on cultural identity are more difficult to estimate, one can at least conclude that the German and Czech elements were intertwined in many areas of Bohemian society. Certainly some parts of Bohemia had an overwhelmingly Czech character, while others were primarily German. Thus, variations in the cultural element of sense of place, and the degree of significance the institutionalised regional levels were ascribed from different places, are important to an understanding of how the regional elements in the different national constructions were received on the ground.

[24] In Bohemia and Moravia bilingualism was widespread, while Silesia and the Littoral in the south (German *Küstenland*, consisting of Istria, Trieste, Gorizia and Gradisca but not Dalmatia) were more multilingual. See Brix, *Die Umgangssprachen in Altösterreich*, pp.118-42 and 251-352. More detailed investigations were sometimes conducted, e.g. when the shifts in claims were thought to be strong enough to cause concern. For instance, the population censuses of 1880, 1890 and 1900 showed that the Moravian community of Schwanenberg had a marked German, then Czech and then again German majority. Emigration and immigration were evidently too slow to be considered as explanatory factors. An investigation by the governor's office in Brno/Brünn showed that all the residents of Schwanenberg spoke both languages and that factors other than ethnic identity determined which language they chose to list. On Schwanenberg, see Brix, *Die Umgangssprachen in Altösterreich*, pp.332ff.

[25] Gerald Stourzh, *Die Gleichberechtigung der Nationalitäten in der Verfassung und Verwaltung Österreichs, 1848-1918* (Vienna, 1985).

Hungary and Transylvania. In the parts of southern and central Hungary that were newly populated after their conquest from the Turks an intricate web of cultural identities emerged. One of the largest immigrant groups in southern Hungary consisted of the so-called Swabians,[26] Germans who arrived in several phases during the eighteenth century.[27] The influx was more rapid than that of the Germans in Bohemia and Moravia but, as in those lands, the immigration originated from diverse parts of German-speaking Europe, occurred over a long period and resulted in the newcomers being dispersed throughout southern Hungary. A constellation of German-language cultural identities evolved with very different versions of German being spoken and diverse traditions forming under the social influence of the place of origin and the new environment.[28] German organisations and institutions within the economic, cultural and political spheres of society also gradually evolved.[29]

---

[26] The designation *Schwaben*, or Swabian, became a collective label for the German groups who arrived in Hungary from the eighteenth century onward, while Saxon was the name given to the colonists who had come during the Middle Ages, for example the Saxons in Transylvania mentioned earlier. Consequently, there were, for example, *Zipsersachsen* in Hungary proper, as there were Transylvanian Swabians. However, these labels do not indicate any homogeneous connection to a particular geographical origin: both Saxons and Swabians came from diverse parts of Germany. See Gottas, 'Die Deutschen in Ungarn', pp.340ff.

[27] The immigration process continued throughout the nineteenth century, to be superseded by a widespread emigration in the late nineteenth century and the early twentieth century. See Gottas,'Die Deutschen in Ungarn', pp.350ff.

[28] Jørgen Kühl, 'De tyske minoriteter i Østeuropa og Asien, 1918-1993' (unpublished doctoral thesis, Flensburg, 1993) notes that High German was considered a foreign language by portions of the German-Hungarian groups in the final decades of the Habsburg Monarchy. The local German dialect and Hungarian were the main languages. See p.188.

[29] Most of these institutions were of economic character and were successfully developed during the late nineteenth century, and to some extent served the objectives of nationally oriented policy. See Gottas, 'Die Deutschen in Ungarn', pp.373ff. The organisation of churches in Hungary did not promote Swabian identity, since the Catholic Church was organised at a higher level. It was also used to some degree in an effort to encourage the Magyarisation of Germans in Hungary (ibid., pp.356ff.). On the Germans in southern Hungary, see Gottas and Ingomar Senz, *Die nationale Bewegung der ungarnländischen Deutschen vor dem ersten Weltkrieg: Eine Entwicklung in Spannungsfeld zwischen Altdeutschtum und un-*

The Saxons in Transylvania preserved a more clearly demarcated identity than the Swabians. With their status as a corporatively defined group, their cultural identity was directly linked in the political institutions of the region. In the Reformation they underwent a collective conversion, and the Saxon Lutheran Church became yet another important institution clearly connected to cultural identity. These Saxons remained a distinct group till the end of the Monarchy.[30] The Romanians did not fall under the Transylvanian privileges and were long excluded from the institutional sphere, which they sought to enter at an early stage. A Romanian cultural identity had some institutional support from the Greek Orthodox and Uniate churches, as well as from the Transylvanian Military Border communities introduced under Maria Theresa partly to counterbalance the local power of the Hungarian nobility.[31]

The Region and National Space

If we shift to the regional perspective, we observe that the institutionalisation of the Bohemian lands gave the region — Bohemia and Moravia — a relatively uniform character. Its corporative structures directly tied diverse places and cultural identities to the regional institutional spheres. Bohemia and Moravia were first and foremost politically institutionalised territories that did not reflect the cultural identities. This presented no problems as long as the corporative structure remained, but when this structure began to dissolve, the relationship had to be redefined.

Hungary likewise had a history of relatively uniform in-

---

garischen Innenpolitik (Munich, 1977). On the Hungarian political-institutional structure and its relation to the cultural identities, see George Barany, 'Ungarns Verwaltung, 1848-1918' in vol.II of A. Wandruzska and P. Urbanitsch, *Die Habsburgermonarchie, 1848-1918* (Vienna, 1975).

[30] On the Saxons (before 1848) see Göllner, *Die Siebenbürgische Militärgrenze*, especially pp.9-18; (after 1848) see Gottas, 'Die Deutschen in Ungarn', pp.340-62 and 376-9; and Irheden, op. cit.

[31] See Mathias Bernath, *Habsburg und die Anfänge der rumänischen Nationsbildung* (Leiden, 1972) and Göllner, *Die Siebenbürgische Militärgrenze*.

stitutionalisation, where the political-institutional structure exhibited stability and continuity. Here the institutional sphere did not either reflect identity. Not even the Magyars can readily be bound to this structure. However, the situation differed from that in Bohemia and Moravia because the regional symbolism was directly connected to the Hungarian Nation of the Nobility, *Natio Hungarica*, which derived its own historical legitimacy from the Magyar warrior tribes that allegedly founded the kingdom. Furthermore, the Magyars were the largest single group within the culturally mixed historical kingdom. A principal issue in Hungarian politics in the nineteenth century concerned the exact relation between the political structure and Magyar cultural identity.[32] Other cultural identities, such as the Swabian, were not reflected in the institutional sphere. Thus, the problems that emerged were similar to those of Bohemia and Moravia, but the bond between the political structure and the Magyar element produced a rather different effect.

The institutional sphere in Transylvania was distinct from that in Hungary, Bohemia and Moravia, since to an extent it reflected the complex structure of places and cultural identities. The region was defined on the basis of the three nations. Although the Romanian-speaking majority was not included, its political leaders worked actively for recognition within this framework rather than by trying to destroy it. In 1867 Transylvania was incorporated into Hungary, but the region nevertheless continued to affect the political construction of cultural-national community and space.

Bohemia and Moravia. Before 1848, politics in Bohemia were based on the concept of the bilingual Bohemian nation. This older concept of nation was preserved by the Bohemian Estates, then wholly dominated by the nobility, which had an interest in the ancient notion of the 'lands of the Bohemian Crown' which

---

[32] See, for instance, Tofik Islamov, 'From Natio Hungarica to Hungarian nation', in D. Good and R. Rudolph (eds), *Nationalism and Empire* (New York, 1992); Emil Niederhauser, 'The national question in Hungary' in M. Teich and R. Porter (eds), *Nationalism and National Identity* (Cambridge, 1993); and Péter Lászlo, 'Language, the constitution and the past in Hungarian nationalism', in R. Robertson and E. Timms (eds), 'The Habsburg legacy', *Austrian Studies* 5 (Edinburgh, 1994).

they wanted to use in their aim of consolidating the three Crownlands into one entity. But they showed little interest in the cultural dimension. Those who did put this matter on the agenda were liberal politicians such as František Palacký, who became a principal advocate for enhancing the Czech element in a Bohemian society dominated by German culture and language. However, Palacký made little effort to distance himself from the Bohemian movement and its trailblazer, the conservative thinker Bernard Bolzano, who argued for the expansion of the older nation of the Estates into a more widely defined, bilingual Bohemian nation.[33]

With the revolution of 1848 came the first signs of a fracture between the Czech and German elements in Bohemian society. However, the way the revolution developed in Prague, and later in other parts of Bohemia, suggests that this schism did not partition society along any clear-cut lines. The first manifestation in Prague was the founding of a revolutionary committee (the Vaclav or Wenzels Committee), which after a month was re-named the National Committee. This organ served to express Liberal and Radical efforts, and the absolutist state was its main adversary. The nation represented by the committee was more Bohemian than anything else, but this factor was secondary in the early weeks of the upheavals. The Frankfurt parliament's request to the Bohemians to send representatives to the German *Reichstag*

---

[33] Czech historiography has recently worked through a number of national impediments in the reading of Bohemian history. It is no longer seen as controversial to observe that there was no Czech national identity to speak of before the nineteenth century. In cooperation with German historians, there has been an attempt to re-evaluate the idea that the Czech–German tension was an omnipresent interpretive framework in the writing of history. See especially the material from the German–Czech historians' conference held in Prague in 1994 ('Unsere Geschichte. Die tschechisch-deutsche Vergangenheit als Interpretationsproblem'). The strain between Bohemian and Czech nationalism in Palacký's thinking remained up to the time of his death, but is clearly weighted towards Bohemianism before 1848. His actions in the revolution of 1848-9 are described in this perspective by Jan Kren in his 'Palacky's Mitteleuropavorstellungen, 1848-1849' in V. Precan (ed.), *Acta Creationis* (Prague, 1980). On Bolzano, Palacký and Bohemianism, see W. Johnston, *The Austrian Mind* (Berkeley, CA, 1972), pp.269-281, and Jiri Koralka, *Tschechen im Habsburgerreich und in Europa, 1815-1914: Sozialgeschichtliche Zusammenhänge der neuzeitlichen Nationsbildung und der Nationalitätsfrage der böhmischen Ländern* (Vienna, 1991), pp.51-63 and 175-200.

prompted Palacký's famous response that Bohemia was an autonomous land within the Austrian Monarchy and did not wish to be part of the new Germany. His reply included an emphasis on the Czech element, which alienated certain German Liberals within the National Committee. Most important, however, was the hostile reception of the National Committee's position in other parts of Bohemia. In the summer of 1848 German parties were organised for the first time in Bohemia and these partly defined themselves as being against the Czech element, although it was more probably against the Bohemian-Austrian policies being implemented by the National Committee in Prague.[34]

However, the observable reactions were scarcely uniform, and we have to look at specifically local responses to understand more clearly how this antagonism arose. In Prague, the Liberal and Radical endeavors were the most important, as reflected in the mainly moderate position adopted over the German and Czech questions.[35] In Prague there existed a Bohemian integration and a social structure which helped to bring issues of political rights and economic and social reform to the fore. This could be achieved within the existing institutional framework and by opposing the ruling absolutist regime. A reformed Bohemian society within a reformed Austrian state appeared the most direct road to the desired end, although a number of German-minded Liberals would have preferred developments to be guided by the Frankfurt parliament. This pattern was presumably replicated in several other Bohemian towns with conditions similar to those in Prague.

However, in other parts of Bohemia, especially the west and north, the position of the National Committee was forcefully rejected. This reaction went with an appeal to nationality, and German-Bohemian parties were formed as an organised form of resistance to developments in Prague.[36] These localities had diverse German cultural identities moulded throughout a lengthy history, in which contact with the Czech element had been limited. When

---

[34] Peter Bugge, 'Czech Nation-Building: National Self-perception and Politics, 1780-1914', unpubl. Ph.D. thesis, Aarhus University, 1994, pp.26-34; Cohen, *The Politics of Ethnic Survival* pp.26-34, Koralka, *Tschechen in Habsburgerreich*, pp.90-3; Kren,' Palacky's Mitteleuropa-Vorstellungen', *passim*.

[35] Cohen, pp.30ff.

[36] Ibid.

these local responses were projected upwards to a larger space, one of the most important spatial structures was the region of Bohemia. The Bohemian policies being pursued in Prague were received there as an imposed Czech element in a space seen as German. This was aggravated by the fact that these policies called for the severance of the important link between these localities and another spatial structure or remnant structure – the German League, heir to the Holy Roman Empire.[37]

The national mobilisation in the political arena depended largely on this triangular relationship between Prague, Vienna and Frankfurt, and should not be seen only in terms of the Czech–German national conflict within Bohemia. However, Bohemian–Moravian antagonism escalated. The Moravian Estates convened in March 1848 and were quickly expanded to include representatives from the towns and rural areas. In Moravia it was noted that Bohemia-centered tendencies were evident in Prague, and the suggestion to establish Bohemia–Moravia–Silesia as one country with Prague as its capital met with strong reservations. In mid-May an election was held, further expanding the representation of the Estates, and when they met on 31 May they contained a substantial number of peasants. In addition, there was roughly equal representation of Germans and Czechs. This assembly drafted a liberal constitution for Moravia, which was presented in January 1849. Among its major stipulations were that the Czech and German languages had equal status and that Moravia would be an independent province, 'bound solely and organically to the constitutional Empire of Austria'.[38]

The intricate political situation of the Bohemian lands also had a pan-Slavic angle. In June 1848 a pan-Slav congress convened

---

[37] The varied reception of the political developments was reflected in the varied success of German parties in different parts of Bohemia. In Prague, which at this time was wholly dominated by German culture and language, success was scant, as was evident at the joint German–Bohemian meeting in Teplitz/Teplice in the late summer of 1848. After the collapse of the Frankfurt parliament, the German identification waned. See Cohen, *The Politics of Ethnic Survival*, pp.25 and 33. In this context a spatial remnant structure like Egerland, which had tangible ties across the borders with Lausitz and Saxony and was strongly marked by Germanness in its cultural identities, offers an interesting comparison.

[38] Bugge, 'Czech nation-building', p.39.

in Prague, which the Czech leaders succeeded in orienting towards an Austro-Slavic policy. Besides this tension, there was also a fluid affiliation between the Slavic and the national, where Slavism was sometimes divided by regional affiliation and sometimes founded upon a cultural definition of nation. Moravian members seem to have played on both these aspects, and their nation was described as a distinct one standing at the junction between cultural identity and region.[39]

The revolution of 1848 caused spatial and cultural structures to be highlighted during a quite short crisis period. In the spring of 1849, Austria entered a decade-long phase of absolutism during which these structures again came under a cloud. When the political arena was reopened in 1860, ushering in the constitutional period, the mobilisation of language-defined nations grew dramatically. Yet notable differences between Bohemia and Moravia continued till the dissolution of the Monarchy. The Moravian evolution, which was characterised by willingness to compromise and led to the Moravian Settlement (*Mährische Ausgleich*) of 1905,[40] was reflected in a German–Czech polarisation in Bohemia. The German-national parties long adhered to the notion that the Austrian hereditary domains and the lands of the Bohemian Crown should become one entity, and that areas such as Galicia, Bukovina and Dalmatia should be severed and granted a status similar to Hungary's, within a loose dynastic state-formation. The Czech nationalists were equally adamant in promoting 'Bohemian State-Rights', emphasising the integrity of the Bohemian Crown lands. In 1899 the German national parties in Austria adopted the so-called

---

[39] Ibid., pp.71-9. Numerous problems over categorisation arose during this congress. In one interesting instance, all the present Silesian representatives chose to leave the broadly defined Bohemian-Moravian-Silesian-Slovakian section and moved to the Polish-Ruthenian section.

[40] This was an agreement between the German and Czech political parties in Moravia, sponsored by the government in Vienna, which *inter alia* ensured the two languages equal standing, established the main structure of the political system, and gave the German minority a veto right concerning revision of the settlement. But it also contributed to the institutionalisation of a national dichotomy in Moravia, and 'Moravianness' was subsequently counteracted by the institutional sphere. However, the measure also stabilised the relationship between cultural identity and political structure in a way that had the potential to forestall the political construction of overlapping and mutually exclusive cultural spaces. On the *Mährische Ausgleich*, cf. Koralka, *Tschechen in Habsburgerreich*, pp.159-64.

Pentecost Programme (*Pfingstprogramm*), advocating the partitioning of the Bohemian lands according to national demarcations. The Czech response was to endorse the integrity of the Bohemian lands still more firmly.[41]

The influence of the spatial structures on the political construction of cultural/national spaces in the Bohemian lands seems to have been quite tangible. Regarding the manner in which space was constructed from a German-Bohemian sense of place, the Holy Roman Empire as a remnant structure played a significant role by the middle of the nineteenth century. The senses of place were presumably projected on to Bohemia. However, thereafter the spatial hierarchy was divided and leant towards Vienna on the one hand and Frankfurt on the other. This situation is not likely to have been experienced as a conflict at the time. The reaction was therefore rather strong when the policies pursued in Prague suggested a severance of one of these bonds, while Bohemia was also being provided with a cultural content that was unacceptable at the local level.

After 1866 the German element in Bohemia eventually adapted to the fact that this tie had in fact been severed. Vienna subsequently assumed an increasingly prominent role in the construction of the cultural space. Bohemia remained an important structure, but the Austrian core lands, and by extension the western half of the Dual Monarchy, played a greater role. The shaping of the German-Austrian cultural/national space was first geared towards incorporating Bohemia and Moravia into this space, while demarcating the areas from the Slavic-dominated regions in the east and south. After 1899 the idea of Bohemia as a spatial structure in this construction was downplayed, and the cultural/national

---

[41] For an overview of the 'Bohemian State Rights' and political development from a Czech perspective, see, for instance, Bugge, 'Czech nation-building', pp.103-306. On German activity during this time, see Berthold Sutter, 'Die politische und rechtliche Stellung der Deutschen in Österreich, 1848 bis 1918', in vol.III of A. Wandruszka and P. Urbanitsch (eds), *Die Habsburger Monarchie, 1848-1918* (Vienna, 1980), pp.182-304. The two main programmes from the German national side were the Linz Programme (1882) and the Pentecost Programme (1899). These are reproduced in Klaus Berchtold (ed.), *Österreichische Parteiprogramme, 1868-1966* (Munich 1967), pp. 198-203 (the Linz Programme), and pp.210-25 (the Pentecost Programme).

space became as much German-Austrian as German-Bohemian. The Czech element in these spaces was consistently subordinated to the German one, a notion which could not be tolerated in places where cultural identities were characterised by Czechness.

The Czech national space was initially defined by the bilingual Bohemian nation. The Bohemian integration and the uniform structure of the region served to neutralise the spatial opposition to a German-Bohemian space. In short, one might conclude that there existed a Bohemian national space that was also a Czech cultural space. During the revolution of 1848 the problems inherent to this construction were revealed, and opposition to a German-Bohemian space developed. However, this opposition did not play a concrete role until after 1860. It was then that the discrepancy between the political constructions' interpretation of society in terms of exclusive, linguistic-cultural categories and the existing patterns of cultural identity became highly relevant to the evolution of conflict. Bohemian integration made it difficult to draw cultural boundaries in such a definitive manner. Forging a cultural/national space was therefore quite problematic. How was one to draw the spatial boundary when it had proved difficult to draw the cultural one?

The institutionalised spatial structures thus became crucial spatial points of reference particularly for the Czech national construction, and this resulted in an overlap with the corresponding German constructions of space. The Czech national space filled the institutionalized spaces in the area, perhaps in part due to the fact that it was difficult to construct such spaces in any other way.[42] Czech national space was also to be oriented upwards in the politically institutionalised spatial hierarchy, and great importance was attached to the Austrian level. However, the Austrian space appeared in this context more as a Slavic cultural space. The overlap between the two constructions was therefore reproduced higher up in the spatial hierarchy, which presumably did little to

---

[42] The division of Bohemia that was briefly advocated by Palacký during the period of the Austrian *Reichstag* (1848-9) involved a more far-reaching reorganisation of the 'Habsburg' space, in which the Slovakian parts of northern Hungary were to be fused with the Czech areas of Bohemia and Moravia, in a new institutionalised 'Czech-Slavic' national space. This approach can be understood as a reflection of the construction of the German-Austrian space, but its role was not noteworthy before 1914. See, for instance, Koralka, *Tschechen in Habsburgerreich*, pp.190-94.

mitigate the frictions between the national-political parties in the Monarchy's western half.

Two structures that remained concealed were the Bohemian/Moravian integration in certain places and the politically institutionalised space of Moravia. In some places these interacted with one another, e.g. those bound to the Moravian institutional sphere and affected by Moravian integration. Here a quite strong counterforce against the Czech–German dichotomisation of society, which often proceeded from the Bohemian situation, may have developed. This would explain the distinct development of Moravia compared to the path taken in Bohemia (in the political realm this combination was not a practicable construction). The other structure, cultural Bohemianism, was greatly affected by the polarisation and ultimately subordinated to the partitioning of society into German and Czech spheres.[43]

Hungary and Transylvania. The evolution towards a national dichotomisation of Bohemian society was fostered by Austrian nationality policy, and the interaction between the national movements and the state was politically significant in the transformation of space and cultural community in the western half of the Monarchy. For Hungary the key period for analysing the issues which concern us here is the period of the Dual Monarchy. The Hungarian political leadership played a similar role after 1867 *vis-à-vis* the minorities in the eastern part of the empire. The main difference with regard to Austria was that nationality policy in Hungary was geared to assimilating the minorities into the Magyar cultural community and transforming the politically institutionalised space into a Magyar national space. Reactions to this policy varied according to the way the institutionalised spaces and the cultural communities had been formed by history.

The *Ausgleich* of 1867 also caused the region of Transylvania

---

[43] See Brix, *Die Umgangssprachen in Altösterreich*, and Stourzh (see note 25). These studies reveal how the German–Czech dichotomisation suffused society. The population censuses of 1900 and 1910 were succeeded by veritable 'national' election campaigns, including door-to-door canvassing, fliers and pressure to 'vote for the right nation'. Court proceedings consulted by Stourzh suggest that the Austrian state ascribed an ethnic/national identity to every individual with whom it came into contact.

to disappear as a political structure and become integrated into the Hungarian political structure, and this directly influenced the position adopted within the Saxon political establishment. The Saxon cultural identity had hitherto involved a stable spatial dimension since it was directly anchored in the regional institutional sphere. In addition, certain parts of Transylvania were also *territorially* institutionalised under the Saxon corporation. With the obliteration of the direct institutional anchor in 1867, the Saxons preserved their political autonomy within smaller territories, and in the ensuing years the safeguarding of these last remnants of their politically unique position became a high priority, although some anticipated that only an alliance with the political leadership in Budapest would secure the perpetuation of the cultural community. In 1876 this foresight was proved correct as the abolition of Transylvanian special rights was completed and the Saxons had no choice but to fall back on their religious and cultural institutions.[44]

After 1867 the German element in southern Hungary started an accelerating assimilation and acculturation with the Magyars. This resulted in political activities specifically designed to halt this process, e.g. the development of Swabian economic institutions in southern Hungary as a future base for a political organisation, and political action in Budapest and Vienna. The initial measures were partly successful, with the Swabian economic institutions becoming crucial components in the southern Hungarian economic infrastructure. However, in the political sphere the measures fared less well, and only a few local bodies were successfully organised. The Swabian politicians had to turn to Budapest to secure influence. The southern Hungarian German element furthermore became the principal source of support in the quest to consolidate the whole German-Hungarian population politically. The German-Hungarian politician Edmund Steinacker was particularly known for his efforts to create a joint political platform for all Germans in Hungary, and in the closing decades of the nineteenth century he laboured both politically (in the Budapest parliament) and journalistically (by founding a German-Hungarian newspaper) for the cause, which he continued to promote from Vienna after his retirement in 1891.[45]

---

[44] Gottas, 'Die Deutschen in Ungarn', pp.387ff.

[45] Ibid., pp.353ff and 373ff. On the German-Hungarian movement see also

The creation of the Ungarnländische Deutsche Volkpartei (UDVP) in 1906 again propelled Steinacker into Hungarian politics as he quickly became a leading force in the party. At the same time he became active in the shadow cabinet of the Emperor's next heir, Archduke Franz Ferdinand, and took part in planning the transformation that would take place in Austria-Hungary upon the Archduke's succession. Steinacker secured a place for the German-Hungarian movement in this plan. The party was able to organise a substantial portion of the Hungarian Germans, and contact was also made with an opposition group within the Saxon political establishment in Transylvania. It grew for several years, winning widespread support in southern Hungary and Transylvania, but efforts to organise the German element in western Hungary, in and around Budapest, in Croatia-Slavonia and in northern Hungary generally failed.[46] The party was quite successful organisationally and at the local level, but floundered in the elections to the Budapest parliament. The only members who entered the parliament were elected in Transylvania, where two members of the small opposition body within the Saxon establishment were elected on the UDVP programme.[47] These endeavours were thus at least partly successful in the years leading up to 1914, but they failed to satisfy the primary objective, namely to have an effective influence on Hungarian politics at the centre to assure the Hungarian-German element a future as a politically organised cultural community.

After the last means of anchoring their cultural identity in political institutions had been lost, the Saxons officially adopted the course of entering a coalition with the governing party in Budapest. The Saxon cultural community hoped to secure its

---

Senz, *Die nationale Bewegung der ungarnländischen Deutschen.*

[46] There was also an attempt to consolidate the entire German element within the Habsburg Monarchy outside of the German-dominated core areas and Bohemia-Moravia-Silesia. The Karpatendeutsche Bewegung strove to link the Hungarian movement to German interests in Galicia and Bukovina (ibid., pp.408ff).

[47] Ibid., pp.397-410. This was partly because Magyarisation policy involved organised 'electoral rigging'. Dividing constituencies and active intervention of the state apparatus were both intended to steer the election in the desired direction, i.e. the creation of a primarily Magyar parliament.

survival by acting at the centre of power.[48] There was a Saxon group opposed to this policy, preferring an independent position outside the Hungarian governing party, but in 1893 it retreated from this position and drafted a national programme. In the early twentieth century this group obtained support among the young intelligentsia, who proved receptive to the German national message and began collaborating with the German-Hungarian movement. Following the Hungarian elections of 1910 it sent two members to Budapest, where they spoke in favour of the UDVP while adhering to the official Saxon position. Only in the spring of 1914 did these two individuals openly position themselves in favour of UDVP and withdrew from the Hungarian governing party.[49]

Up to 1914 the Saxon political establishment consistently sought to protect their cultural community through cooperation with the governing party in Budapest and maintained a strict dividing line between themselves and the rest of the Hungarian German element. In 1908 a prominent Saxon politician said of the rapprochement between Saxons and Swabians: '[W]ir wollen nicht Deutsche schlechthin, sondern Siebenbürger Deutsche sein' (We don't want to be German. We want to be Siebenbürger German). He declared that the Saxons were a distinct group and would not sacrifice themselves for the Swabians.[50] The boundary separating them from the remaining German element in Hungary was drawn with reference to cultural particularity, and on the basis of the regional dimension of Saxon identity. The institutionalised Hungarian space, with its increasingly Magyar cultural content, was not a part of Saxon cultural space.

In the local perspective, Saxon cultural identity was remarkably stable in the spatial dimension. The particular relationship between the institutionalised space and cultural identities in Transylvania likewise influenced the construction of cultural/national community in this region. In contrast to Bohemia and Hungary, the

---

[48] With the exception of 1897-1903, when protest against legislation on Magyar place-names prompted actual withdrawal from the coalition, the Saxons kept this collaboration alive from the 1890s to 1914. This was true independently of which party governed in Hungary (ibid., pp.288ff. and 407).

[49] Ibid., pp.387ff. and 407.

[50] Statement from *Siebenbürgisch-Deutsche Tageblatt* 5 May 1908, cited in Gottas, 'Die Deutschen in Ungarn', p.390.

region proved able to accommodate and serve as a cultural space for several cultural communities.[51]

The Swabians in southern Hungary lacked the clear spatial dimension of Saxon cultural identity, and this had divided them into several groups. Thus they were receptive to assimilation and acculturation with the Magyar element. There was no Swabian cultural space to stabilise a Swabian cultural community and thus counteract the project of transforming the whole of Hungary into a Magyar national space. The Swabians became Magyars, i.e. German-Magyars, or maintained some form of German-Hungarian identity through the limited institutional sphere shaped during the nineteenth century. The last strategy was furthered by the political work during the final decades of the century of Swabian politicians in southern Hungary, whose relative failure must have been partly due to the absence of an institutional spatial structure around which the Swabian community could be consolidated. The politically institutionalised structure of Hungary prevented any such spatial points of reference from being formed. Consequently, political activity was ever more geared toward the centre in the structure, and its orientation shifted from the Swabian issue to the consolidation of the whole Hungarian-German element into a single politically organised cultural community. After attempts to establish a small Swabian cultural space failed, the rhetoric and political activity were transferred upwards to the Hungarian level.

The aim to organise the Hungarian-German element met with some success, mainly in the two areas with the largest German population, namely southern and western Hungary.[52] In the towns outside these territories, transformation of the space to a Magyar national one had already gone so far that the German component in the cultural identity of individuals had largely faded. The situation was similar in the countryside of central and northern Hungary, and some headway was made among the Saxons in Transylvania,

---

[51] Saxon activities at the Versailles Conference are interesting as an afternote to the period considered here. The Saxons sounded out the prevailing climate of opinion and thereafter handed in their vote for incorporating Transylvania into Romania. See Macartney, p.223.

[52] See Gullberg's chapter (pp.148-78, below) on the organisation of the western Hungarian space and its relation to cultural identities during the transition to a nation-state system in 1918 and within the Austrian republic.

which suggests that the integration of this area in the wider Hungarian space had repercussions on the German element here too.[53]

However, Transylvania as a remnant structure also served as a barrier against the expansion of the German-Hungarian cultural space. The building of a German-Hungarian cultural community was thus obstructed both by spatial remnant structures and by the establishment of an antithetical Magyar national construction. This last factor may have been decisive, although to function effectively, the German-Hungarian movement had been propelled to a high level in the socio-spatial hierarchy. The cultural space became too large, and the multitude of cultural identities characterised by Germanness was too diversified to allow for a successful construction. In addition, the political-institutional sphere in Hungary was a uniform structure which, in contrast to that of Transylvania, did not promote the accommodation of several cultural/national spaces within the Hungarian space itself. Meanwhile, when the construction was raised to this level, it generated a decline in the force of political integration of the Swabian cultural community.

The Romanians in Transylvania were one of the groups in the Habsburg Monarchy least effectively organised as a cultural community. This was largely because connections to the premodern political structure in the area were absent. However, during the eighteenth century the Uniate Church had served as an institutional foundation for some form of cultural identity. The Uniate or Greek-Catholic Church had its roots in an imperial project of the 1690s, which aimed to integrate the Greek Orthodox subjects in the newly-conquered Transylvania with the Western, Catholic sphere. Many Romanians nevertheless remained Orthodox. The imperial power extended its recognition in the later eighteenth century by placing the Orthodox congregation under the Serbian Orthodox Church in southern Hungary. In 1716 a Transylvanian Military Border had also been formed, partly around the Romanian element in the region, with the intention of counter-

---

[53] Mobilisation was particularly successful among the lower strata of Saxon society. The restructuring of society and the widespread activation of these strata occurred at a time when the Transylvanian region had been eradicated for several decades. This may have contributed to channelling a growing number of societal activities within the existing Hungarian space. The youthful intelligentsia were especially receptive to the German-Hungarian movement.

balancing the power of the Hungarian nobility. The two churches and the Military Border came to play a key role in the forging of Romanian cultural community in the area, although this community long remained vaguely defined and equally weakly integrated.[54]

During the revolution of 1848 the Romanian regiments in the Military Border placed themselves on the imperial side, and for the first years of the constitutional era a Romanian national movement struggled for recognition as a fourth nation in Transylvania. In 1863 these Romanians obtained political rights and had thus effectively reached their goal. However, this success was only temporary because the constitution was suspended in 1865 and the political struggle within the Monarchy resulted two years later in the *Ausgleich*. As Transylvania ceased to exist as a politically institutionalised region, the Romanian movement lost almost all it had achieved. This experience may have contributed to making the reestablishment of the Transylvanian constitution and the regional institutions high priorities on the agenda of the Romanian-Transylvanian movement during the rest of the Dual Monarchy.[55]

This emphasis impeded cooperation with other Romanian movements in the Dual Monarchy. Romanians in the rest of Hungary organised their own parties, which collaborated with the Romanian-Transylvanian movement only periodically. In 1895 an effort was made to merge several of the Hungarian minorities into a single political grouping, in order to provide a stronger basis for the political demands being made in Budapest. This endeavour failed, and the political scene was once again fragmented. From 1905 the Transylvanian dimension was played down in the political programme, and policy continued up till 1914 to vacillate between cooperation with the Romanian parties outside the region, cooperation with the Slav minorities, and operating independently. One belief that remained consistent among the the political leadership between 1906 and 1914 was that the nationality problem

---

[54] On the earlier history see Bernath, *Habsburg und die Anfänge der rumänischen Nationsbildung*, and Göllner, *Die Siebenbürgische Mititärgrenze*, who particularly focus on the relevance of the Churches and the Military Border. The Military Border was created around two Romanian areas in the north-eastern and southern parts of the region, and a Szekelian area between these two in the east. The transfer of people gave these areas a certain 'ethnic' character.

[55] Hitchins, 'Die Rumänen', pp.585-95.

should be resolved within the framework of the Habsburg Monarchy. As with the German-Hungarian movement, there was close cooperation to that end with the office of Archduke Franz Ferdinand, the heir to the throne. This was partly why a wider Romanian cultural community, including cooperation across the border with the Romanian kingdom, was never actively promoted by the Romanian-Transylvanian movement.[56]

In comparison with the Saxon cultural identity, the Transylvanian Romanians were divided and integration long remained quite weak. This is likely to have been of some relevance to the vacillations in the political constructions of cultural community and space, and to have caused the spatial structures, especially the spatial remnant structure of Transylvania, to play such a clear role in the Romanian case. After its disappearance, this region continued to be highly significant in the political construction of the cultural space, in which Romanians on the other side of the older border with Hungary also tended to retain a distinct identity although they now lived within the same political structure. The cross-border ties can not be underestimated, but they played only a minor role politically before 1914.

Conclusions

In the political projects we have sought to highlight, the institutionalised regions have held a key position in the political construction of cultural community and cultural space, although their manifestations and effects have varied. The institutionalised organisation of space at different levels steered and channelled the effects of modernisation in the Habsburg Monarchy in the nineteenth century. Political ambitions to organise cultural communities and use these as foundations for political life, or what we call 'nationalism', had their breakthrough late in the nineteenth century. By this time, spatial institutionalisation was already widespread and highly significant to politics and society, and in fact decisively affected the way in which communities were forged.

In many instances, it determined the scale on which the political construction was to operate, and consolidated or demarcated cultural communities from each other. For instance, the Transylvanian-

---

[56] Ibid., pp.595-607 and 613ff.

Romanian movement insisted that the nationalities problem should be resolved within the institutionalised space of the Habsburg Monarchy, and emphasised a demarcation *vis-à- vis* other Romanian movements within this structure, based on reference to a (Transylvanian) regional dimension that no longer existed.

Another example is the German-Hungarian movement's political construction of a cultural community involving a multitude of highly diverse cultural identities, where the only common denominator was some form of Germanness as well as the fact that they could be spatially defined in relation to the institutionalised region of Hungary. In this latter case, such a construction presumably had fewer chances of success than one founded on southern Hungary Germanness, which showed a degree of integration both in the spatial and the cultural dimensions. However, such an evolution was most likely impeded by the lack of institutionalised spaces at the lower level that could support the construction of a cultural community of this type. Instead, the integrative force of various German-Hungarian cultural identities declined, and these identities were ultimately assimilated or acculturated into the Magyar national community and its homogeneously defined national space.

The Transylvanian German element under the name of 'Saxon' was a clearly demarcated cultural identity, defined according to both cultural and regional terms, and this group too, resided within the boundaries of Hungary after 1867. However, the Saxon construction of cultural community and cultural space continued to build on the spatial remnant structure of Transylvania, which functioned as it had for the Romanians, as a barrier against a wider German-Hungarian cultural community. It furthermore allowed the Saxons to distinguish themselves from the homogeneous Magyar national space and avoid the course on which the remaining Hungarian German element embarked. The region of Transylvania is of interest, too, insofar as its history of institutionalisation fostered the development of a base structure that made it possible to simultaneously sustain several cultural spaces during modernisation. However, the momentum of the time left them unable to withstand the pressure towards national homogeneous spaces, which after 1918 was anchored in the overarching Western political ideology.

Finally, the political construction of Czech and German-Bohemian, and German-Austrian cultural spaces, are the clearest instances of severe strain between the institutionalised space and the political construction of cultural community. In this case the perspective of place revealed the accentuated discrepancy between the political construction of cultural space and cultural identities in Bohemian society.

The evolution in Bohemia in particular showed the strongly destabilising effects of this process. The overlapping and mutually exclusive cultural spaces intensified polarisation and lack of cooperation at the political level, while rising intolerance towards the historically grown cultural Bohemianism forced people to forsake the Bohemian element in their cultural identity. The choice between a Czech and a German identity was complicated by the risk of exclusion or subordination in a homogeneous cultural space of the other kind. However, institutionalised spaces also impeded such a process, as in the region of Moravia between 1848 and 1914. Moravia was long an obstacle to the expansion of the overlapping Czech and German-Austrian spaces, and particularly at the beginning of this period the region directly influenced the construction of cultural communities/spaces. The Moravian element in the cultural identities also endured within the protective mantle of the institutionalised space, despite increasing outside pressure.

The First World War and the political transformation of space in 1919-20 profoundly altered the basis for the development of Central Europe, adding a score of new institutionalised spaces. These new constructions were independent states with absolute prevalence both upward and downward in the spatial hierarchy. It follows that all obscurities in lateral relations were eliminated. Moreover, these changes brought revisions of the factors for the construction of cultural space. In a general sense, it can be claimed that the overarching ideology adopted at the Versailles Conference in 1919 fostered the construction of mutually exclusive and often spatially overlapping cultural/national identities locked within a determined and uniform framework of politically institutionalised spaces. The older Central European structures, marked by more diffuse relations between such institutionalised spaces and by several important levels in the spatial hierarchy, had proved unable to accommodate the effects of modernisation in the ways we have discussed. However, the state of affairs since 1918 suggests that no better way was found at Versailles.

THE PRIMACY OF THE NATION AND REGIONAL IDENTITY
CARINTHIA, BURGENLAND AND STATE-FORMATION AFTER THE DISSOLUTION OF THE DYNASTIC SYSTEM

Tom Gullberg

Introduction

The period 1918–21 was one of dramatic transformation in Europe. The most profound change was the emancipation of nations from the old dynastic system: emerging from it, those nations could now form their own states in accordance with the principle of nationality. This development was particularly devastating for the Habsburg Monarchy, whose territory was broken up into seven separate nation-states, some of them new configurations cut out of the dismantled empire.

This way of viewing the period has been nourished mainly by the so-called 'nation-state historiography'.[1] Such a portrayal of twentieth-century post-dynastic history is by no means inaccurate where the visible results of the restructuring of the European state system after the First World War are concerned. However, it has tended to assume the character of a deterministic and unproblematised story of progress. For historians of the nation-state it has been self-evident that the nation should be presented as the primary basis for state-building. They have found investigating whether reality corresponds to their assumption neither necessary nor natural.

Tackling the subject in a critical-theoretical perspective prompts certain questions. Were national identities truly the primary consolidating factors in the nation-states created in the wake of the

---

[1] See, for instance, Max Engman, 'Historikerna och nationalstaten' in Christian Kvium (ed.), *Studier i historisk metod 21. Historien och historikerne i Norden efter 1965* (Aarhus, 1991).

First World War? Was there a vertically mobilised, ethnic-cultural mass movement actively endorsing the nation-state – or was it the notion of such a state, as formulated by a limited circle of intellectuals, that determined events towards the end of the First World War?[2] Did the inhabitants of the Habsburg realm really think it 'obvious' that they should abandon the structures that had been their inherent and stable frame of reference for centuries?

As has been detailed in earlier chapters, the Habsburg Empire experienced the evolution of national-political movements during the nineteenth century. However, this was not equivalent to a rise of nationalism in which the primary aim was the formation of a distinct state.[3] Demands for the Empire's ethnic and cultural diversity to receive greater consideration were mainly expressed through various proposals for federalisation on the basis of national aspects, but within the framework of the dynastic domain.[4] Among the internal population, the dynastic framework was seen as self-evident – so much so that the idea of abolishing it was never seriously considered. The structure was also widely recognised as a reality by the international community. Indeed, the Empire had

---

[2] The theoretical notions that are relied on here are presented by, for example, Anthony D. Smith, Miroslav Hroch and Ernest Gellner. For an overview, see Rune Johansson, 'Nationer och nationalism: teoretiska och empiriska aspekter' in Sven Tägil (ed.), *Den problematiska etniciteten. Nationalism, migration och samhällsomvälvning* (Lund, 1993).

[3] One should distinguish between efforts to create states in accordance with the principle of nationality and efforts based on politico-historical arguments. The latter is exemplified by the Magyar struggle of 1848-9, where the leaders sought to separate the dynastic Hungarian kingdom from the Empire, but did not seek to establish a Magyar nation-state.

[4] The Czech historian František Palacký's proposal for federalisation was presented to the Austrian *Reichstag* in 1848. He suggested that the Empire be divided into eight ethnic, federal entities. Although his proposal is generally considered the first of its kind, the Slovenes had earlier that year drafted a Pan-Slovene programme requesting an administrative entity of their own within the Empire. The Slovenes were later major advocates of a three-way German-Magyar-South Slavic solution. The Social Democratic Austro-Marxists also at first expressed federative notions, but eventually relinquished these in favour of the principle of personal autonomy. See J.F. Zacek, *Palacký: The Historian and the Nationalist* (The Hague, 1970); Janko Prunk, *Slovenski narodni program: Narodni programi v Slovenski Politicni misli od 1848 do 1945* (Ljubljana, 1987), pp.6-29; Øyvin Østerud, *Nasjonenes selvbestemmelserett: Søkelys på en politisk doktrin* (Drammen, 1984), p.84.

The Primacy of the Nation and Regional Identity 149

traditionally functioned as a buffer zone that checked Russian, Turkish and German expansionism.[5]

Concrete national-political goals were outlined mainly by small non-German groups in exile. However, the political circumstances were the key factor in the emergence of the new nation-states. A complicated diplomatic process began as the First World War neared its end. The Allies vacillated between signing a separate peace with Vienna in order to fracture the Central Powers and allowing the Empire to decompose. But the Empire's disintegration was already a *fait accompli* in October 1918: as part of their war strategy, the Allies recognised the Czechoslovak exile movement's demand that the 'Czecho-Slovakians' be permitted to found their own state. The primacy of the national assertion had now been affirmed.[6]

Diplomatic contrivances notwithstanding, the development received a positive response in numerous parts of Europe. After minor adjustment difficulties, Czechs in Prague, Poles in Cracow, Magyars in Budapest, Croats in Zagreb (Agram) and Slovenes in Ljubljana (Laibach) all accepted the territorial parameters of the new states. But these peoples would not necessarily have been

---

[5] For an illuminating discussion on the position and role of the Habsburg Empire, see Wilfried Fest, *Peace and Partition: The Habsburg Monarchy and British Policy, 1914–1918* (London, 1978). See also Max Engman, 'Restitutio imperii – om en europeisk nödvändighet', *Finsk Tidskrift*, no. 7–8 (1988), pp. 354-72.

[6] What brought recognition of the primacy of national arguments was Woodrow Wilson's Fourteen Points peace programme. This stipulated the national right to self-determination and was formally accepted by all parties in October 1918 as a foundation for the approaching peace negotiations. However, Wilson had never expressed support for state formation on the basis of ethnically and culturally defined nations. His programme did not include any element that suggested that he accepted the dissolution of the Habsburg Empire. The increasing emphasis on the principle of nationality had been fostered primarily by the British. The journal *New Europe* and the 'liberal nationalists' (especially R.W. Seton-Watson and Henry Wickham Steed) launched the idea of the dissolution of the dynastic system and the creation of states on the basis of the nationality principle. This group's escalating influence on British foreign policy and its contact with the non-German exile leaders from the Habsburg Empire resulted in the misconception that Wilson favoured the formation of states on the basis of nationality. See Fest, *Peace of Partition*, p.43; Kenneth J. Calder, *Britain and the Origins of the New Europe, 1914-1918* (Cambridge, 1976), pp.25-8; Harry Hanak, *Great Britain and Austria-Hungary during the First World War: A Study in the Formation of Public Opinion* (London, 1962). See also Hugh Seton-Watson, *The Making of a New Europe: R.W. Seton-Watson and the Last Years of Austria-Hungary* (London, 1981).

dissatisfied if they had continued to live within the framework of a reformed Habsburg Monarchy. The situation was not quite so straightforward even in the principal national-political centres. For example, neither Prague nor large portions of Bohemia and Moravia could be counted as uniformly Czech areas. However, faced by the prevailing circumstances, the affected populations were progressively transformed into what can best be described as political driftwood, and possible apprehensions regarding the new nation-state did not find expression. In addition, in many cases there was no other plausible alternative. The 'national core areas', as they were labelled, were not offered alternative courses to choose from, as were residents of the borderlands, between two projected nation-states. Independently of the affected population's position, it proved a tactical error for two competing nation-state projects not to demand a disputed territory with reference to the principle of nationality.

Only in two instances was the affected population in the defunct Habsburg Empire given the formal possibility to decide between alternative nation-states. The result was a shock to the nation-state ideologues. In southern Carinthia a referendum conducted in October 1920 revealed a 59 per cent majority in favour of the new Austrian republic, in spite of Slovenes making up 70 per cent of the population according to Habsburg statistics for 1910. It had thus been expected that southern Carinthia would vote for incorporation into the SHS state, i.e. Yugoslavia, on the basis of the principle of nationality.[7]

Approximately one year later, in December 1921, after a lengthy and complicated process, and a preparatory period that in no way satisfied the criteria for free and democratic elections, a referendum was arranged in a smaller area of western Hungary – the future Austrian *Bundesland* Burgenland – around Sopron (Ödenburg).[8]

---

[7] The statistics were based on *Umgangssprache* (language of daily use), which did not necessarily correspond to the respondents' mother-tongue. Thus the actual proportion of the national identities can not readily be concluded from these figures. For a discussion on language statistics as a phenomenon in the Habsburg Empire, see Emil Brix, *Die Umgangssprachen in Altösterreich zwischen Agitation und Assimilation. Die Sprachenstatistik in der zisleithanischen Volkszählungen, 1880 bis 1910* (Vienna, 1983).

[8] In the Treaty of Saint-Germain, Austria had been granted three of western Hungary's four *comitate* (countships). The fourth was Pozsony (Bratislava,

According to statistics, more than half of the population were German, but 65 per cent of the respondents nevertheless opted for Hungary (in Sopron itself, 73 per cent did so).

The outcomes of both these referendums thus departed from what had been expected in a Europe that was to be cast on the basis of the nationalities. Given the prevalent political currents it had seemed certain to the decision-makers at the peace conference that the affected population would vote according to their national identity. However, the result of the referendum implied that many were not prepared to accept the organisational principle of the new territorial states. In addition, the referendums revealed the tensions between what was new, namely the nation, and older, traditional structures – a phenomenon that can be described as a tension between national and regional identities.

The Historical Region as an Analytical Instrument

The expressed objective in the regional history approach is to avoid making anachronistic deductions from contemporary political-territorial organisation.[9] The fundamental principle underlying this view is that older political and mental structures exist which exercise greater influence on the spatial-social identity of individuals than is understood by the contemporary world, bound to and often blinded by its own worldview – e.g. the focus on the nation-state. Regional history instead concentrates on structures that have grown over the course of history but which are no longer relevant in the contemporary perspective but linger on as an older stratum of identity beneath the explicit reality of the present. In the nineteenth century the German geographer Friedrich Ratzel coined the term 'historical landscape' (*Geschichtslandschaft*) to describe what was historically conditioned in the spatial-social

---

Pressburg), which went to Czechoslovakia.

[9] Ernst Henrich has described the region as a geographic-social space that does not comprise a coexistent state-administrative entity. Otto Dann has likewise stipulated that the concept of region should be employed to designate spatial formations that are not characterised by sovereignty and related administrative units. Ernst Heinrich, 'Regionalgeschichte' in Carl-Hans Hauptmeyer (ed.), *Landesgeschichte heute* (Göttingen, 1987), p.18; Otto Dann, 'Die Regionen als Gegenstand der Geschichtswissenschaft', *Archiv für Sozialgeschichte*, XXIII (1983), pp.652-61.

REPUBLIC OF AUSTRIA [map showing Austrian states including Bregenz, Tyrol, Innsbruck, Salzburg, E. Tyrol, Carinthia, Klagenfurt, U. Austria, Linz, L. Austria, Vienna, Eisenstadt, Styria, Graz, Burgenland; neighbouring countries Germany, Czech Rep., Slov., Hungary, Slovenia, Italy, Switz.]

identity. In the 1990s Ratzel's 'landscape' has yielded to the new conception 'historical region'.[10]

The question of older, spatially related identities was not a topical one during the time of transformation in 1918–20, when the nation was considered the most 'natural' entity.[11] The referendums referred to earlier suggest that identification with the new nationally-defined territorial formations was not as strong as leaders of both the national-political movement and the great powers had presumed. The majority of the population in both areas rejected the supposed leading ideology, and instead chose inclusion into the state that corresponded most closely to the Habsburg structure they were used to. In considering how the populations in southern Carinthia and the Sopron area perceived the state-territorial transformations of the period, the region-historical perspective usefully complements the theoretical conceptions of the nation.

Anssi Paasi's model on the constitution of regions – by implication, historical ones – is a framework for the regional history

[10] The 'historical region' thus has nothing in common with the 'functional region', which economic historians and economic geographers have constructed as an analytical instrument for their own analyses. See Steen Bo Frandsen, 'Regionen i historien', and Carl-Hans Hauptmeyer, 'Regionalhistorie i Tyskland. Probleme, metoder og anvendelseområder', Den jyske Historiker, 68 (1994), pp.7-31 and pp.67-79; and Sven Tägil, Hans-Åke Persson and Solveig Ståhl, Närhet och nätverk. Regionernas återkomst? (Lund, 1994).

[11] For an introduction to theories on 'spatially-related identities', see Peter Weichhart, Raumbezogne Identität. Bausteine zu einer Theorie räumlich-sozialer Kognition und Identifikation (Stuttgart, 1990).

perspective in viewing the relation between national and regional identity.[12] Paasi particularly underlines that regions, like nations, must be seen as the result of a historical process. The emergence of regional identities is shown as the consequence of several interwoven factors: an awareness regarding a specific territory; the appearance of a system connected to the territory (its name, shared historical memory); and the development of an institutional sphere (administrative and legislative organs, associations, press etc.). A fully evolved region is described as a territorial unit that 'has specific structures of expectations which are constantly being reproduced by social institutions'.

While the conceptualisation of region is intended to illuminate older, spatial-social identities, the region, like the nation, can also be exploited for political purposes by the leadership. It is frequently 'added' to the national narrative in an effort to appear a particularistic regional identity. Through ideological construction the regional identity can be incorporated into the current national narrative, thus legitimising the region's state-territorial position. An example of a modern construction of a 'historical region' is the German *Bundesland* Nordrhein-Westphalia, whose territorial boundaries were not determined until the British occupation zone was established after the Second World War. It was incorporated into the new West German state as a federal unit.

This type of political-administrative construction of regions recalls a writing of history not unlike that of nation-state historiography where the regional formation is given a longer political-historical continuity than is accurate.[13] The message conveyed is that the region is a genuine and intrinsic part of the existing nation-state construct. Leaders can thus capitalise on the regional angle when they wish to highlight important spatial-social identities behind the overarching notion of national ideology. However, regional identities can equally serve the national ideology itself, and in the long run also the national identity.

---

[12] Anssi Paasi, 'The institutionalization of regions: a theoretical framework for understanding the emergence of regions and the constitution of regional identity', *Fennia*, no.1 (1986), pp.106-46.

[13] See Peter Steinbach, 'Zur Diskussion über den Begriff der "Region" – eine Grundsatzfrage der modernen Landesgeschichte', *Hessische Jahrbuch für Landesgeschichte*, no.31 (1981), p.187, and Frandsen, 'Regionen i historien', pp.22-4.

Carinthia: From Duchy to Bundesland

Carinthia was brought into the Habsburg domain as a duchy in 1335. Partly because of its geographical position, it had long been host to extensive population transfers and intricate political processes. The Slavic population moved into the former Roman province of Noricum in the late sixth century, and around 590 founded the independent duchy of Carinthia. As well as the area of present-day Carinthia, the entity comprised eastern Tyrol and portions of northern and central Styria. The duchy is thought to have been given formal protection by the neighbouring Avars up till the 620s, after which it became part of the mythical Slavic Samo kingdom.[14]

Carinthia and Bavaria signed a treaty in 730, stipulating mutual assistance in case of attack. This agreement is the first evidence of contact between the Carinthians and the Germanic sphere. Bavaria honoured its commitment and thwarted an Avar expansionist advance, so consolidating its own influence in the Slavic duchy. The Carinthian territory was thus brought into the western Christian structure.[15] Since Charlemagne likewise incorporated Bavaria into the Frankish empire in 788, Carinthia thus became a part of the Carolingian mark-system, and when the empire dissolved it was absorbed into Otto I's Holy Roman Empire. As a result of the Saxon House's efforts to weaken Bavaria, Carinthia was elevated to an autonomous duchy, with the German name 'Kärnten', in 976. One of the most important symbolic dimensions of regional awareness had thus been introduced, that is the name.[16]

---

[14] Claudia Fräsch-Ehrfeld, *Geschichte Kärntens. Band 1, Das Mittelalter* (Klagenfurt, 1984), pp.49–54. The nature of the relationship between the Slavic population and the Avars has been a controversial issue in Carinthian historiography. The German interpretation depicts the Slavs as the Avar's subjects, while the Slovenes interpret the relationship as an alliance. See Thomas Barker (with the collaboration of Andreas Moritsch), *The Slovene Minority of Carinthia* (New York, 1984), pp.21–3.

[15] Hermann Bruckmüller, *Sozialgeschichte Österreichs* (Vienna, 1985), pp.55–9; Fräsch-Ehrfeld, *Geschichte Kärntens*, pp.54–61 and 68–71.

[16] Ernst C. Hellbling, *Österreichische Verfassungs- und Verwaltungsgeschicte* (Vienna, 1974), pp.28–9. The name Carinthia/Kärnten is believed to have been in use already during the Roman Noricum period. It is presumably derived from the Celtic 'Karanta'. See, for instance, Barker, *The Slovene Minority of Carinthia*, p.25.

The Carinthian duchy would long continue to be territorially fragmented. In the High Middle Ages, because of the Saxon policy of enfeoffement, its political-territorial structure was something like a mosaic, and the Duke of Carinthia controlled only a fraction of its titular territory.[17] This changed in the thirteenth century, when the notion that territorial sovereignty should apply to a cohesive geographical space became established in the eastern parts of the German-Roman empire. In Carinthia, Duke Bernhard of Spanheim manifested this ambition by giving himself the title 'Land Prince' (*iudex et princeps terre*), which reflected an objective rather than a reality. In 1286 an all-encompassing legislation for the entire duchy, a *Landesrecht* ('Constitution of the country') was first mentioned, but only in 1338, three years after the Habsburg takeover, was the Carinthian legal system formally documented. This legal code stipulated that the duke ranked above all the remaining territorial lords in the duchy, and that any territorial lord whose principal seat was outside it was still subject to Carinthian law as far as their Carinthian domains were concerned.

Almost two centuries later, in 1530, territories outside the control of Carinthia or with administrative traditions outside its influence (Gorizia, Bamberg and Salzburg) were still subordinated to its legislation. The sluggishness of the legislative consolidation process was linked to the pace of Carinthia's territorialisation which proceeded far more slowly than that of its neighbours Austria and Styria. Once territorially integrated, Carinthia was till 1535 mainly composed of the central areas around St Veit (Virinium, the chief town in Noricum), Klagenfurt (Celovec) and Völkermarkt (Velikovec). Most of Salzburg's possessions could now be integrated, although a small area around Maria Saal (Gospa Sveta), the headquarters of the Archbishop of Salzburg, remained under his control till 1805. And Bamberg's substantial domains, including the important city of Villach (Biljak), were not definitively integrated until 1759.[18]

[17] During the first years of the German duchy, the ducal throne was occupied by the two dynasties of Eppensteiner (up to 1122), and Spanheim (1122–69). Thereafter, up to the Habsburg takeover, the Carinthian crown remained mainly within the house of Görtz. See Fräsch-Ehrfeld, *Geschichte Kärntens*, pp.133–6, 180-96 and 406–16.

[18] Otto Brunner, *Land und Herrschaft: Grundfragen der territorialen Verfassungsgeschichte Österreichs im Mittelalter* (Darmstadt, 1973), pp.21-212; Hermann Braumüller,

The territorial disintegration long acted as a brake on any further deepening of the institutional structure. Though an independent duchy since 976, and thus the oldest political unit among the Austrian hereditary domains, Carinthia was still remarkably fragmented at the time the Habsburg empire incorporated it; an important reason for this enduring disintegration was that the dukes had not been stationary in Carinthia since the Spanheim dynasty died out in 1286. Controls had to be consolidated over the areas that were only nominally part of the duchy, but incorporation into the expanding Habsburg system was considered more urgent. From 1446, Carinthia, Styria, Krain and Istria together made up the new administrative entity of Inner Austria, with Graz, Styria's chief town, as its centre. The administrative structure was further developed under the rule of Maximilian I (1493–1519), and together with the other Austrian corelands, Carinthia became a part of Lower Austria.[19]

In the south of the Habsburg realm increasing influence was concentrated in Graz. At a time when Carinthia was undeniably losing its independent status, there was one force that preserved the notion of its independence, namely the Estates Assembly (*Landtag*). The Carinthian Estates convened at their first Provincial Diet in 1457, twelve years after the Estates within Inner Austria, that included Carinthia, had met for the first 'general assembly' (*Generallandtag*). The enlarged activity of the Carinthian Estates was in reaction to the ever-intensifying centralisation being conducted by the Habsburgs. Before they had begun intervening in Carinthian affairs, these Estates had enjoyed substantial leeway and freedom of action, given the absence of the duke. Their independence received concrete expression in 1484 when they bought peace from the Hungarian King Mattias Corvinus, who thus began preparing for his successful onslaught against the Habsburg Emperor Friedrich III.

In 1521 the Estates were further able to defend Carinthia's

Geschichte Kärntens (Klagenfurt, 1979), pp.150-1 and 195-7; Wilhelm Neumann, 'Wirklichkeit und Idee des "windischen" Erzherzogtums Kärnten' in *Bausteine zur Geschichte Kärntens. Festgabe für Wilhelm Neumann zum 70. Geburtstag* (Klagenfurt, 1985), pp.81-2; Fräsch-Ehrfeld, *Geschichte Kärntens*, pp.406-16.

[19] See Hugo Hantsch, *Die Geschichte Österreichs*, vol. I (Graz, 1951), pp.181 and 224-8.

territorial integrity, refusing to accept Ferdinand I as duke unless he dissolved his agreement with his brother Charles V, Holy Roman Emperor with dominion over the dynasty's Spanish realm, stipulating that Charles would come into possession of Carinthia's western sections (Ortenburg, Pustertal).[20] A strong identification with both ruler and territory, *Landesbewusstsein*, thus existed within the Estates, and if it had not existed during this, the most critical period before 1918, no force would have struggled to preserve the notion of Carinthia's political-historical individuality.

Up to the Napoleonic wars, Carinthia was a subordinate element in Inner Austria, within the parameters of the Habsburg empire. In addition, the area was partitioned during the shortlived French-Illyrian period, the Villach district being governed from Laibach (Ljubljana) in Krain, and the Klagenfurt district continuing to come under Graz. In 1825, however, Klagenfurt was transferred to Krain and the four-centuries-long administrative connection to Graz ended. This arrangement proved brief, because in 1849 Carinthia was elevated to a crownland, with its principal centre in Klagenfurt. Carinthia's status was raised in this way because of its loyalty to the dynasty during the revolts of the previous year.[21]

The Tradition of Independence

Carinthia's tradition as an independent unit within the Habsburg Monarchy thus did not have a long history, but there was a widely-held view of Carinthia as a 'natural' entity. This was based primarily on a substantial historical-territorial continuity, which had been affirmed at the superficial level, i.e. through its name. The complex territorial sovereignty issues would not remain as interesting to posterity as the fact that a political entity called Kärnten had 'always' existed. The most concrete symbol of this historical narrative is the so-called 'ducal seat' at Zollfeld (Gosposvetsko Polje) near St Veit. The seat figured in the ceremonies in which every new Carinthian duke assumed office. The ceremony

---

[20] Bruckmüller, *Sozialgeschichte Österreichs*, pp.107-8 and 173-6; Fräsch-Ehrfeld, *Geschichte Kärntens*, pp.567-70; Wilhelm Neumann, 'Kärnten – Grundlinien der Landesbildung' in Neumann (ed.), *Bausteine zur Geschichte Kärntens*, pp.33-5.

[21] Hellbling, *Österreichische Verfassungs- und Verwaltungsgeschichte*, p.330. See also Martin Wutte, *Kärntens Freiheitskampf* (Weimar, 1943), pp.23-4.

has had a remarkably 'democratic' character ascribed to it, and this has been significant where the image of Carinthia's historical sovereignty has been concerned.

According to tradition the new duke would arrive in Zollfeld dressed as a peasant in order to mark that he was 'first among peasants'. The ceremony itself was led by the 'Kosezi' class (*Edlinger*), free peasants of high status. As early as the 1570s Jean Bodin described the Carinthian princely inaugurations as the foremost example of power being conferred on the sovereign by this subjects. Carinthia's contribution to classic works of state-theory has likewise reinforced notions of the uniqueness of its history. The ceremony originated in the ninth century and lasted for some six centuries, being abolished by the Habsburgs in 1414. Emperor Francis I visited the seat as late as 1830, and the ruling dynasty capitalised on its symbolic value a number of times. Demonstrating that 'nothing had changed' served a legitimising function.[22]

The National Histories

By the mid nineteenth century the image of Carinthian unity and continuity was confronted by two contending national narratives. The Slovenes claimed a Slavic character for the inauguration ceremony, which was conducted in a Slav language, and by thus highlighting Carinthia's Slovene tradition, they could present the medieval duchy as the first Slovene state-formation. The German so-called Carinthian *Landesgeschichte* ('regional history') tradition played down the Slovene element of Carinthian history, by developing the '*Windisch*' theory: in earliest Carinthian history this term meaning 'wind' signified the Slav population, but in the German national interpretation the Winds were described as German-influenced *'heimattreue'* Slavs – Slavs loyal to their own province. One of the principal arguments used to support this view was that the Slavic dialect, *Windisch*, was not Slovene – a claim convincingly refuted by modern scholarship. The argument was easily espoused at the time, since the Slovenes in Carinthia seldom

---

[22] Joseph Felician, *The Genesis of Contractual Theory and the Installation of the Dukes of Carinthia* (Klagenfurt, 1967), pp.20-36 and 91-4; Wilhelm Neumann, 'Der Kärntner Herzogstuhl im Wandel der Geschichte' in Neumann (ed.), *Bausteine zur Geschichte Kärntens*, pp.21-3.

identified themselves with the Slovene written language that had developed in Ljubljana.[23]

These opposite interpretations of Carinthian history fed the boundary conflict and the controversy that surfaced towards the end of the First World War. Although the national projections on Carinthia's early history are anachronistic and politically motivated, the importance of the ever more complicated ethnic-linguistic relations should not be minimised. From the ninth century Carinthia had become increasingly bilingual. The traditional 'Carinthian' structure was of a Slavic character, but the newer 'Carinthian' structure was German. In the Slovene national perspective, the princely inauguration was a clear indication of Slovene dominance, but the phenomenon can as easily be dismissed as a historical relic, perhaps an attempt by the German nobility to foster Carinthian cohesion. From the German viewpoint, Carinthia's Slavic legacy was made less dramatic by the *Windisch* theory, which also satisfactorily explained the Slavic element in Carinthia's history and reality. Besides its function as an instrument of German national propaganda, the theory could, if seen in a 'neutral' perspective, tend to denationalise Carinthia's history.[24]

Still, German social dominance in Carinthia was advancing. The trend is confirmed in linguistic statistics, compiled from 1846 which ultimately served German national ideology. In the first population census, 30 per cent of respondents claimed to speak Slovene. The following year, that figure had dropped to 26.6 per cent and by the the last Habsburg census, of 1910, was only 18.3 per cent. However, in the part of Carinthia that eventually became a referendum site, 67 per cent still apparently spoke Slovene,

---

[23] For the Slovene interpretation see Bogo Grafenauer, *The National Development of the Carinthian Slovenes* (Ljubljana, 1946), and for the German one Martin Wutte, *Kärntens Freiheitskampf* (Weimar 1943); On the Carinthian-Slovene language debate, see Theodor Robert Domej, 'Die Slowene in Kärnten und ihre Sprache. Mit besonderer Berücksichtigung des Zeitalters von 1470 bis 1848' (unpublished doctoral dissertation, Vienna, 1986).

[24] Barker, *The Slovene Minority of Carinthia*, pp.42-5; Domej, *Die Slowene in Kärnten*, pp.45-51; Neumann, 'Wirklichkeit und Idee des "windische" Erzherzogtums Kärntens', pp.85-91. For a theoretical discussion of the difficulties of dealing with Carinthian national historiography, see Robert Gary Minich, *Homesteaders and Citizens: An Ecology of Person and Self-Realization among Slovene-Speaking Villagers on the Austro-Italian Frontier* (Bergen, 1992), pp.12-14.

down from 79 per cent in 1880. The results are not conclusive on either linguistic or national identity. In 1846 respondents were asked which language they considered the most important for them, and the rest of the information was based on *Umgangssprache*, the language of daily use; the statistics did not indicate the mother-tongue (or language spoken in the home). The only clear conclusion from these statistics is that a growing number of Slovenes regarded the German language as important to them.[25]

German nationalist intellectuals like Martin Wutte could not see that national forces played no part in the Slovene adaptation of the German element, and that the process was primarily one of adjustment to a new social milieu. This adaptation had already begun in the thirteenth century, as the Carinthian cities were increasingly dominated by German merchants and craftsmen. By the end of the Middle Ages, two-thirds of Carinthia are estimated to have been German while the southern areas had a mixed German-Slovene population.[26] Conditions for agriculture were less favourable in the south than in the north and the Slovene farms were less prosperous than the German ones. This gave rise to a lasting tradition of northward labour migration.[27] In the 1820s Urban Jarnik, a Slovene national activist, lamented in an article that these migrations were 'a good school for learning the German language'.[28] This appeared in the journal *Carinthia*, which accepted both German and Slovene writings.

The modernisation process increased the interaction of the Slovene and German elements, and contacts between the two populations were revolutionised by the arrival of a rail connection

---

[25] Andreas Moritsch, 'Deutsche und Slovenen in Kärnten. Das nationale Bewusstsein in Kärnten in der zweiten Hälfte des 19. Jahrhunderts', *Österreichische Ostheft*, no.4 (1970), pp.234-5. In 1846 the population of Carinthia was 320,000. Thirty years later it was just over 362,000. See Barker, *The Slovene Minority in Carinthia*, p.88.

[26] Moritsch, 'Deutsche und Slovenen', p.234; Barker, *The Slovene Minority in Carinthia*, pp.6–8.

[27] Bruckmüller, *Sozialgeschichte Österreichs*, pp.186-214.

[28] See Urban Jarnik, *Andeutungen über Kärntens Germanisierung. Mit einer Studie und Anmerkungen von Bogo Grafenauer* (Slovenski Znanstveni Institut, Klagenfurt, 1984). Jarnik's article 'Andeutungen über Kärntens Germanisierung' was originally published in the journal *Carinthia* (issue 16, 1828). See also Moritsch, 'Deutsche und Slovenen', pp.237-8.

from the north. More Germans now began moving into the south of Carinthia, particularly the areas around Wörthersee (Vrbsko jezero), which German-run hotels turned into a popular vacation spot for wealthy Viennese. Development within the agrarian sector also strengthened relations between German and Slovene Carinthia.

Certain ingrained views on the Carinthian socio-economic structure, particularly that of the poor and isolated Slovene peasant, have recently been challenged. By the late nineteenth century, only part of Slovene agriculture was in the hands of self-sufficient small farmers, and few of these lived in isolation since their need for seasonal work obliged them to move about. Large-scale Slovene farming, mainly west of Klagenfurt and demarcated in the south by the river Drau (Drava), depended more on the market in that city. As for the relation between language statistics and Carinthia's economic geography: it appears that the Slovene areas most dependent on the market were also those with the strongest tendency to switch from Slovene to German. Thus national considerations seem not to have been central factors in this linguistic shift, but rather a consequence of the economic integration of the crownland of Carinthia.[29]

German influence also permeated education in Carinthia. The Church controlled elementary education following an ordinance of 1855; thus the medium of instruction was Slovene in all areas where Slovenes were the majority in the congregation. The German element expressed vehement opposition to the educational monopoly of the Church, which was the sole social sector in Carinthia dominated by Slovenes, partly because the seminary in Klagenfurt was long the only alternative for higher education available in their language. However, Vienna took the German protests to heart, as was reflected in the new school legislation of 1869, which stipulated that the individual counties were responsible for the maintenance of their educational sector and should also determine the language of instruction. According to the new bilingual 'utraquistic principle', areas with majority Slovene population were to introduce Slovene-language instruction in the lower

---

[29] See Andreas Moritsch (in collaboration with Marjan Sturmund und Sigilde Haas-Ortner), 'Die wirtschaftlichen und sozialen Verhältnisse in Südkärnten und die Volksabstimmung 1920', in *Kärnten-Volksabstimmung 1920. Voraussetzungen, Verlauf, Folgen* (Vienna, 1981), pp.103-7.

grades, but switching to German as soon as possible. Slovene was thereafter used in schools mainly as a vehicle for teaching German.[30]

The Political Dilemma of the Slovene National Identity

As explained above, the increasing use of German among Slovenes was an outcome of Carinthia's progressive integration. A contributing factor was the low degree of Carinthian-Slovene identification with the Slovene national movement in Carniola (Krain).[31] Slovene national awareness was growing in Carinthia during the nineteenth century, but in the cultural rather than the political sphere. For instance, the first Slovene publishing house, Druzba sv. Mohorja, opened in Klagenfurt in 1852, and began publishing mainly apolitical, religious and Habsburg-patriotic works. These writings were appreciated by the broad strata of Slovene society in Carinthia, being perceived as a counterforce to the expansion of German liberal principles. In an effort to strengthen identification with the Slovene written language, reading-rooms (*citalnice*) were opened in both Klagenfurt and Eisenkappeln.[32]

There was thus a tangible striving for a national or, more accurately, a linguistic institutionalisation, but it was not prominently manifested in political terms. Only in that year of turbulence, 1848, did the Slovenes in Vienna, Ljubljana and Graz formulate distinctly political demands – in the pan-Slavic programme *Zedinjene Slovenije* – for a unified Slovene administrative entity within the Empire. Along with this development, the newly created Slovene association in Klagenfurt spoke for the '*Beibehaltung der Landeseinheit*' (preservation of the historical integrity of the country). Unlike their fellow-nationals in Krain, the Slovenes in Carinthia took part in the elections to the Frankfurt parliament. After the Austrians lost the Slovenes in Venetia in 1866 and Prekmurje in

---

[30] Bernhard Perchinig, 'Wir sind Kärntner und damit hat sich's...' in *Deutschnationalismus und politische Kultur in Kärnten* (Klagenfurt, 1989), pp.40-1 and 53-5; Barker, *The Slovene Minority in Carinthia*, pp.67-74.

[31] For an overview of the development of the Slovene national political movement, see Carol Rogel, *The Slovenes and Yugoslavism, 1890-1914* (New York, 1977).

[32] Barker, *The Slovene Minority in Carinthia*, pp.78-80; Rogel, *The Slovenes and Yugoslavism*, pp.18-19; Moritsch, 'Deutsche und Slovenen', pp.240-41.

connection with the *Ausgleich* in 1867 a sense of crisis spread among the nationally-conscious Slovenes. As a result, they gathered at large, outdoor, meetings (*tabori*) several times between 1868 and 1870, and called for a unified Slovenia. However, in Carinthia, the Slovene peasantry's economic and social demands overshadowed the national dimension.

The political schism between the Slovenes in Carinthia and those in Carniola was accentuated through developments in Slovene party-politics during the late nineteenth century. In spite of the clerical-conservative bias of the Carinthia Slovenes, the Slovene Catholic Popular Party (*Katolska ljudska stranka*) could not consolidate them behind the party before 1909. In the election of 1911 many of the Carinthia Slovene peasantry thus voted for the German national agrarian party, whose political slogan was 'Peasants elect Peasants'. The Carinthia Slovenes had previously drafted their own list within the framework of the Catholic Political and Economic Association for Slovenes in Carniola (*Katolisko politicno in gospodarsko drustvo za Slovence na Koroskem*). Neither the Liberal National-Progressive Party (*Narodna napredna stranka*) nor the Yugoslav Social Democrats founded by Slovenes in Carinthia was able to establish a foothold in Carinthia. Slovene Social Democrats in Carinthia instead took part in the activities of the Austrian 'mother party'.[33]

This Slovene national reality makes the result of the referendum of 1920 more intelligible. The Slovenes preferred to vote '*für die Aufrechterhaltung der historischen Landeseinheit*' (the preservation of the historical integrity of the country).[34] It was the regional identity rather than Slovene Yugoslav rhetoric that formed the natural frame of reference for the Carinthia Slovenes, and was thus decisive in the referendum. However, in the German national perspective the referendum result confirmed the idea that the Carinthia Slovenes were Winds, who identified more with the German than with the Slovene and South Slav culture. It was therefore concluded

[33] Janko Prunk, 'Slovenski narodni programi' in *Narodni Programi v Slovenski Politicni misli uch 1858 do 1945* (Ljubljana, 1987), pp.6-19; Moritsch, 'Deutsche und Slovenen', pp.240-1; Rogel, *Yugoslavism*, chapters 3-5; Arnold Suppan, 'Zwischen Assimilation und nationalpolitischer Emanzipation', *Österreichische Osteheft*, no. 1 (1978), pp.305-8; Barker, *The Slovene Minority in Carinthia* pp.78-80.

[34] Walter Lukan and Andreas Moritsch, *Geschichte der Kärnten Slowenen von 1918 bis zur Gegenwart. Der gesamtslowenischen Geschichte* (Klagenfurt, 1988), p.67.

that this justified an intensified germanisation of Carinthia. For several years afterwards the Slovene intelligentsia in Carinthia (e.g. teachers) lost many of its members, e.g. through emigration to Yugoslavia. And once the conservative, German-oriented parties acceded to the Cabinet Offices and the Ministries in Vienna, the position of the Carinthia-Slovenes became ever more contingent on Austrian–Yugoslav relations and Belgrade's attitude to its German minorities.

The situation became still more difficult for the Carinthia Slovenes after the Second World War, because German national propaganda depicted the Slovenes as 'Titoists'. Since the 1960s the Austrian government has actively sought reconciliation with the Carinthia Slovenes, but the German national activists around the *Heimatbund* have never fully recognised the existence of a parallel Slovene culture in Carinthia, as symbolised primarily by the *Zvezna gimnazija za Slovence v Celovcu* (the Slovene upper secondary school) which has existed since 1957. The so-called *Ortstafelstreit* (the conflict over bilingual street signs) continued into the 1970s, and although there have been bomb attacks since then, the German national opposition has successively subsided.[35]

The post-referendum era in Carinthia may have seen much ethnic-linguistic antagonism, mainly caused by the German element, but in contrast to other ethnic minorities in this part of Europe, the Slovene population had freedom of action, with the right of association and political organisation. They also founded a number of other economic and cultural associations, including a Slovene academic society in Vienna which sought South Slavic cultural unity but expressed absolute loyalty to the Austrian state. And the weekly magazine *Koroški Slovence* was published in Vienna. For Belgrade and Ljubljana Carinthia remained *terra irredenta*, as became clear during the Second World War. However, Yugoslavia's demands for revision of the referendum resolution of 1920 were not conceded.

Both the emerging Cold War and Tito's break with Moscow affected the life of the Slovenes in Carinthia. Two separate factions

---

[35] See Barker, *The Slovene Minority in Carinthia*, chapters 6–8. For a Carinthia Slovene interpretation of 'the official Carinthian' view on the Slovene population, see Klub slowenischer Studenten in Wien, *Kärnten bleibt deutsch. Zur Tradition und Gegenwart der Feiern zum 10. Oktober* (Vienna and Klagenfurt, 1980).

developed, among them a smaller one oriented towards Moscow, and larger groups made up of Yugoslav loyalists. But the clerical group remained the largest, and in 1949 was organised into the National Council of Carinthia Slovenes (Narodni svet koroskih Slovencev). That year, the clerical faction obtained over 4,600 votes, and the Yugoslavists only about 2,000 — which suggests that many Carinthia Slovenes now supported 'German' parties. Carinthia Slovenes loyal to Vienna were behind the often vociferous German national propaganda about 'Slovene Titoists'. This loyalty was linked largely to Carinthian identity: the idea that they were more at home in the Carinthian ambience than they would be in Tito's Yugoslavia. The welfare society of the Second Republic re-asserted this view.[36]

That non-national Carinthian unity had survived was exemplified in the Social Democratic election campaign of 1984 when the 'duke's seat' appeared on the party's billboards. The idea was to highlight the 'common heritage of Carinthia' (*Skupna Koroska*), and undermine the Catholic Church's ethnic reconciliation programme in Carinthia. History and tradition had come full-circle.[37]

From Comitate to Bundesland: Burgenland

No historical-territorial entity named Burgenland existed before 1918, nor had the area been incorporated in Cisleithania. Instead, it had been a part of the Hungarian kingdom since its very inception and during the Hungarian period was generally known as West

---

[36] See Barker, *The Slovene Minority in Carinthia*, chapters 6–8.

[37] E. Bruckmüller, ' "Zentrum" und "Provinz" in der Entwicklung des österreichischen Nationalbewusstseins' in Walter Buchebner–Gesellschaft (eds), *Gespräche regionale Identität* (Vienna, Cologne, Graz, 1987), p.36. The Catholic Church's 'reconciliation programme' has not been successful on all fronts, especially since it has often been perceived by the German national element as involving a strong Slovene bias. It should be noted that several German national activists, including Jörg Haider, have actually been Protestant. See Anton Pelinka, *Zur österreichischen Identität. Zwischen deutscher Vereinigung und Mitteleuropa* (Vienna, 1990), pp.114-23. On the Catholic Church and the ethnic situation in Carinthia, see Josef Marketz, *Interkulturelle Verständigung im christlichen Kontext. Der Beitrag der Kirche zum Zusammenleben der slowenischen und deutschen Volksgruppe in Kärnten* (Klagenfurt, 1994).

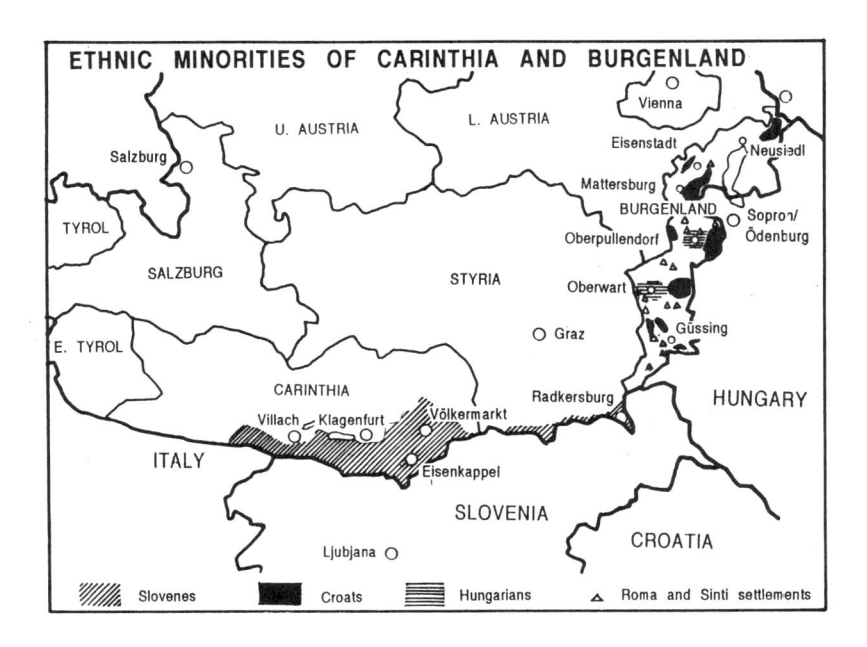

```
┌─────────────────────────────────────────────────────────┐
│ ETHNIC MINORITIES OF CARINTHIA AND BURGENLAND           │
│                                     Vienna              │
│              U. AUSTRIA    L. AUSTRIA                   │
│    Salzburg                       Eisenstadt  Neusiedl  │
│                                  Mattersburg            │
│                                   BURGENLAND   Sopron/  │
│  TYROL                          Oberpullendorf Ödenburg │
│         SALZBURG        STYRIA                          │
│                                  Oberwart               │
│                             ○ Graz    Güssing           │
│  E. TYROL                                               │
│                CARINTHIA      Radkersburg    HUNGARY    │
│              Villach Klagenfurt Völkermarkt             │
│   ITALY                  Eisenkappel                    │
│                         SLOVENIA                        │
│                                          CROATIA        │
│                   Ljubljana ○                           │
│     Slovenes        Croats      Hungarians  △ Roma and Sinti settlements │
└─────────────────────────────────────────────────────────┘
```

Hungary. However, the area was not a cohesive administrative entity, and West Hungary was a collective designation for the four *comitates* (countships), Pozsony (Pressburg/Bratislava), Vas (Eisenburg), Moson (Wieselburg) and Sopron (Ödenburg).[38]

Ethnic-linguistically, the area, ever since the early eleventh century, has represented a typical heterogeneous Central European borderland. German peasants were invited by the new Christian Hungarian dynasty to serve as 'Christian models' in order to impose its control over the peripheral border-areas, and the German nobility was likewise invited to settle in western Hungary. The intention was to create a loyal borderland between the German and Magyar settlements – one of many examples demonstrating that aristocratic loyalty did not depend on an ethnic-cultural identity.

---

[38] In recent Austrian writings the territory is commonly labelled the 'Burgenland–West Hungarian area'. See August Ernst, *Geschichte des Burgenlandes* (Munich, 1987).

The Primacy of the Nation and Regional Identity 167

After the Battle of Mohacs in 1526 and the subsequent Ottoman occupation of much of Hungary, the aristocracy was dominated by Magyars. Notable Magyar families such as the Batthyany, Erdödy and Esterházy moved west and enlarged their domains in western Hungary, where in 1920 a quarter of the land was still under the control of mainly Magyar landowners. Whole border communities also developed there in the Middle Ages, because of the systematic influx of free Magyar peasants (*nobiles unius sessionis*). This border-peasantry was a distinct legal entity in the area (*Communitas nobilis*), a privileged lesser nobility.

The Ottoman invasion in the first half of the sixteenth century had triggered a flow of Croat refugees, leading to the setting up of Croat communities. The Croats of Spitzzicken (Hrvatski Cikljin) in southern Burgenland outside Oberwart gained special privileges in the form of so-called 'Vallakian liberties'[39] Western Hungary has therefore been the scene of multi-ethnic and multilingual contact. This was revealed for instance, in the population census of 1920 (excluding the Comitate Pozsony), in which 75 per cent of the respondents listed German as their mother-tongue, 15 per cent Croatian, and 8.5 per cent (primarily) Hungarian. An indeterminate number of Gypsies must be added to these figures.[40] In 1910 the German segment was estimated to be 27 per cent of the total population. The Germans were the majority (55 per cent) in the Comitate Moson (Wieselburg), and 51 per cent in the city of Sopron.[41]

In the traditional Comitate system, which the nobility directed,

---

[39] Ernst, *Geschichte des Burgenlandes* pp.24-32 and 132-3; Lajos Kerekes, *Von St. Germain bis Genf: Österreich und seine Nachbarn, 1918-1922* (Vienna, Cologne Graz, 1979), p.144; Gerhard Baumgartner, 'Der nationale Differenzierungsprozess in den ländlichen Gemeinden des südlichen Burgenlandes'; Andreas Moritsch (ed.), *Vom Ethnos zur Nationalität. Der nationale Differenzierungsprozess am Beispiel ausgewählter Orte in Kärnten und im Burgenland* (Vienna,1991), pp.99-101. The oldest frontier guard areas can still today be recognised by *'Wart'* in their names, e.g. Oberwart, Siget i.d. Wart.

[40] The statistics do not seem to have included the Comitate Pozsony/Bratislava, which would have reduced the proportion of German-speakers. See Kerekes, *Von St. Germain bis Genf*, p.143. These figures do not cover the referendum area around Sopron, which made up only a small part of western Hungary.

[41] Friedrich Gottas, 'Die Deutschen in Ungarn', in, vol.III of A. Wandruszka and P. Urbanitsch (eds), *Die Habsburger Monarchie 1848-1918*, pp.346-9.

ethnicity and language were not decisive social elements. Through the sophisticated stratified system of privileges and local self-rule, the local community – the village – became the natural reference-point. In the Magyar and Croatian villages, Magyar and Croatian dialects remained the main spoken languages till the 1960s. Regarding the spatial-mental dimension, the population turned primarily to the West.

The most significant market for the Magyar landed nobility was Vienna, and hence western Hungary was important to Vienna as a food supplier. Western Hungarian craftsmen, and after the abolition of serfdom, peasants made seasonal labour migrations to Vienna and at times to western Austria.[42]

The traditional order for Hungarian land holdings was shattered by the *Ausgleich* of 1867. With rising Hungarian state-nationalism, ethnicity and language became ever more important. The striving for Magyar homogeneity was most clearly manifested in West Hungarian schools, which became efficient factories for linguistic assimilation. A decision of 1898 stipulated that every place in Hungary should be given an official Magyar name, which created great changes in multilingual West Hungary. The Hungarian state ideology did not allow for the development of non-Magyar political activity as in Cisleithania. Also, while the Germans in Hungary organised in 1906 as the Hungarian German Popular Party (Die Ungarnländische Deutsche Volkspartei), which had a distinctly national character, the party's main achievement was to mobilise urban German populations in southern Hungary (the Swabians in the Banat and Backa) and the Saxons in Transylvania. The overwhelmingly agrarian western Hungarian Germans remained indifferent to this activity, and the greatest involvement for the German population in western Hungary came from the outside, as plans for an *Anschluss*, unifying 'German West Hungary' (Deutschwestungarn) with the German-Austria core land in Cisleithania. Those ambitions found expression especially in Josef Patry, an elementary school teacher in Vienna who published an article entitled 'Westungarn zu Deutschösterreich' in 1906. The

---

[42] George Barany, 'Ungarns Verwaltung' in vol. II of A. Wandruszka and P. Urbanitsch (eds), *Die Habsburger Monarchie, 1848-1918* (Vienna, 1975), pp. 314-24; Péter Hanák, *History of Hungary* (Budapest, 1991), pp. 13-44; Baumgartner, 'Der nationale Differenzierungsprozess', pp. 102-3.

The Primacy of the Nation and Regional Identity

following year, he founded the Verein zur Erhaltung des Deutschtums in Ungarn (the Association for the preservation of German Hungary), which met with little sympathy in western Hungary, although it was welcomed in both Transylvania and the Banat.[43]

Since the principle of nationality was now regarded as the chief instrument for restructuring the European state system, it was not surprising that the new German-Austrian state, whose main objective was to dissolve itself and be quickly incorporated into Germany, demanded the revision of the Leitha boundary. However, Hungary assumed that the traditional border, which had functioned as its external state border since 1867, would remain. In late January 1919 Budapest proposed that the Germans in western Hungary be granted cultural autonomy – a proposal which especially pleased the Germans living east of the Neusiedler See.[44] Bela Kun seized power in March, after which the Allied victors were more positive towards Austrian demands for territory to the west, not least because these could be presented as a compensation for the provinces which Vienna would lose, such as South Tyrol and the German areas in Bohemia and Moravia.

Also, as compensation for such losses, Austria steadily requested that western Hungary be joined to Austria only after a plebiscite, since the Austrian government would thereby have established a precedent indicating the way other territorial conflicts concerning the country should be resolved. However, in the final peace treaty Austria acquired western Hungary without the plebiscite, and without the consultation of the Bolshevik government in Budapest. When the Treaty of Saint-Germain was signed on 10 September, the Bela Kun government had already been toppled (in August), and Hungary now began to protest vociferously against the decision reached without its participation.

---

[43] Thomas Spira, *German-Hungarian Relations and the Swabian Problem* (New York, 1977), pp.10-14; Gerald Schlag, 'Die Angliederung des Burgenlandes an Österreich', in *Österreich in Geschichte und Literatur* (1971), pp.433-4; Gottas, 'Die Deutschen in Ungarn', pp.353-4, 380-81, and 386-99; Baumgartner 'Der nationaler Differenzierungsprozess', p.107; Kerekes, *Von St. Germain bis Genf*, p.145. Concerning the plans for a union with western Hungary, see August Ernst, *Geschichte des Burgenlandes*, p.186.

[44] Charlotte Heidrich, *Burgenländische Politik in der Ersten Republik. Deutschnationale Parteien und Verbände im Burgenland vom Zerfall der Habsburgmonarchie bis zum autoritären Regimes, 1918-1933* (Munich, 1982), p.36.

Aggressive Magyar opposition in western Hungary by so-called 'paramilitaries', supported by the government, prevented Austria from taking over as stipulated in the peace treaty. The western Hungary question had grown into a Central European diplomatic dilemma that would last for several years, and not be resolved until Italy acted as intermediary in October 1921. Both governments were anxious to solve the problem, but not at the cost of losing face at home. They were able to agree on a plebiscite to be held in the small area around Sopron. The remaining areas of western Hungary covered in the Saint-Germain document would be directly transferred to Austria.[45]

The Austrification of Western Hungary

It was important for the new Austrian nation-state to distance itself from western Hungary's history, as well as legitimising its sovereignty over the region in accordance with nation-state terms. The alternative, not implemented in the incorporation process but realised during the 'Ostmark' period, would have been to join the newly-acquired territories with older Austrian entities, i.e. Lower Austria and Styria. It was not until the leaders began working on the constitution, made necessary by the transformation from monarchy to a republic, that the name 'Burgenland' emerged.

---

[45] The complicated diplomatic process that led to this decision is outside our scope here. The question was linked to the Italian–Yugoslav conflict over the eastern Adriatic. As early as May 1919 a secret Yugoslav–Czechoslovak pact was signed, stipulating that the Czechoslovak army would use Hungary as a corridor for troop movements in return for support to Yugoslavia should Italy press its territorial demands. The background to this exchange was the traditional notion of a Slavic corridor between the western and southern Slavs, a notion that was justified on the basis of the presence of a Croatian population in western Hungary. In an agreement of January 1920 between Austria and Czechoslovakia, the latter pledged to support all the provisions of the treaty of Saint-Germain. This was clearly hostile to Hungary, and Rome became increasingly anxious over this 'entente' and, indirectly, over enhanced French influence in Central Europe. Italy's attempt to act as a mediator owes something to this larger context and was backed up by indications of assistance in the task from Prague. See Kerekes, *Von St. Germain bis Genf,* pp.146-70, 253-71 and 297-316; see also Francis Deak, *Hungary at the Peace Conference* (New York, 1942), pp.85-90, 190-99, 213-15, 221-3, 239-42 and 320-29; Katalin Gyula, 'Die Westungarische Frage nach dem Ersten Weltkrieg. Das Burgenland und die Politik der ungarischen Regierung, 1918-1921', *Österreichische Osthefte,* no.2 (1966), pp.89-99.

As late as in August 1919 the authority at the ministry for domestic and educational affairs was called *Verwaltungsstelle für die Anschluss Deutschwestungarns* (Administration for the Incorporation of German West Hungary).[46] So, in contrast to Carinthia, it is possible in this case to follow closely the construction of a central factor in the symbolic systems of regions: the name. In June 1919 certain elements in Austria still hoped that at least parts of the Pressburg Comitate (though not the city of Bratislava itself) would be granted to Austria, and the name 'Vierburgenland' was thus launched as a collective label for the four *Burg-Komitaten*. In August 1919, after all such plans had been abandoned, the Austrian President Karl Renner himself used the term 'Dreiburgenland'. The name finally adopted is attributed to the West Hungarian *Anschluss* activist George Meidlinger, who suggested 'Burgenland' to Renner in September 1919: this was used officially for the first time in the first constitutional proposal, in 1920, and the establishment of the independent *Bundesland* was finally approved on 25 January 1921. However, its territorial demarcation would later be revised.[47]

Thus an entirely new politico-territorial entity was formed in 1920–2. The new *Bundesland* was composed of three independent and divergent Comitates, each with its own judicial, administrative and cultural sphere. In addition, all the previous chief towns remained in Hungary.[48] This reality was not strictly a technical matter, and had important repercussions on the politico-territorial identity. In Austrian, Hungarian and international historiography, however, the distinction between western Hungary and Burgenland is rarely alluded to, although the two terms actually have different territorial, as well as symbolic, connotations. A common misinterpretation, also an anachronistic one, maintains that the referendum was arranged to determine 'the fate of Burgenland' whereas in reality it was to determine the fate of only a minor portion of the territory that would become the *Bundesland* of Burgenland.[49]

[46] Ernst, *Geschichte des Burgenlandes*, p.199.

[47] Ibid., pp.201-2.

[48] Heidrich, *Burgenländische Politik*, pp.57-60.

[49] For a prime example of this, see F.L. Carsten, *The First Austrian Republic, 1918-1938: A Study Based on British and American Documents* (Cambridge, 1986), p.89; see also Arnold Suppan, *Die österreichischen Volksgruppen. Tendenzen ihrer gesellschaftlichen Entwicklung im 20. Jahrhundert* (Vienna, 1983), p.81.

In Burgenland's own historiography, there has been an effort to emphasise the denied continuity in the territorial-social organisation, resulting in the contemplated chief town, Ödenburg, with its key position in West Hungarian history, being expunged through deliberate forgetfulness. However, the loss of Ödenburg was seen as a division of Burgenland, as is shown by the fact that the new chief town, Eisenstadt, once the centre for the Esterhazy family, was not granted formal status as *Landeshauptstadt* or capital of Burgenland till 1965, although the *Bundesland* government had convened there since 1925. Furthermore, the new entity was plagued by a series of notable difficulties regarding both adaptation and consolidation. When the ties to the Hungarian central authority were cut off, Burgenland for some time lacked trained officials, jurists and educators. Thus administrative personnel as well as party political structure were imported from Vienna, resulting in several noteworthy clashes between *bodenständige Burgenländer* (inhabitants born in Burgenland) and *Nichtburgenländer* (immigrants from Austria) in the 1920s which were generally resolved to the benefit of the former. In consequence, there was no thorough 'Austrification' process, and no German national activities on the Carinthian model developed during the First Republic.[50]

Between the World Wars life in Burgenland showed remarkable continuity. The Hungarian administrative structure at the village and municipal levels largely remained intact. The ordinance for the constitutional transformation (*Verfassungsübergangsverordnung*) of 29 August 1921 stipulated that all Hungarian regulations were to remain until the Provincial Assembly had determined otherwise. Thus Magyar and Croatian schools controlled by the Church under a decree of 1868 were not transformed into state schools with German as the medium of instruction till 1938. Given a shortage of German-speaking lawyers familiar with the Hungarian legal system, efforts were made to recruit Saxons from Transylvania – who, however, were generally better paid in Romania and had no interest in depriving the German settlements in their native land of their skills in order to work in a German-language state.[51]

Another example of 'West Hungarian continuity' was that the Magyar mayor in Oberwart was able to hold on to his position

---

[50] Heidrich, *Burgenländische Politik*, pp.94-106.

[51] See ibid., p.62.

till the *Anschluss*. This was partly due to concerns in Vienna that Burgenland would become an object of Hungarian irredentism, and that Vienna could not safely intervene against the remaining Magyars; and partly because no German, Magyar or Croatian groups which emerged operated on the basis of an ethnic-national rhetoric as in Carinthia. Although the conflict over Burgenland had been conducted in national terms at the state level, the West Hungarian tradition of cohabitation was brought to Burgenland – invisibly but deliberately.[52]

However, it appeared that the new territorial entity of Burgenland would be no more than a brief stop-gap in Central European history. After the *Anschluss*, Berlin decided to merge the smallest Austrian *Bundesländer*, Vorarlberg and Burgenland, with larger entities. In the *Ostmarkgesetz* (Ostmark law) 14 April 1939, Burgenland no longer appeared as an independent area, but was divided between Lower Austria (District of Lower Donau) and Styria. After the Second World War, the relevant actors, particularly those in Graz and the Lower Austrian leaders in Vienna, did not see re-establishment of Burgenland as inevitable. However, Burgenland's main parties agreed that they wanted their land once again to be an independent entity, and following pressure from the *Provisorische Landeskomitee*, it was decided that Burgenland would be a *Bundesland* from 1 October 1945. As a reminder of its distinctive features, the Croat Lorenz Karall, of the *Österreichische Volkspartei* (ÖVP), successor to the Christian Social Party, became the first *Landeshauptmann*. Since the Soviet occupying forces had laid claim to the Landhaus in Eisenstadt, Burgenland's leadership moved into the Esterhazy palace.[53]

An Austrian Necessity

Identification with Burgenland had thus proved too strong for this *Bundesland* to be effaced. It was an 'Austrian necessity' – particularly for the non-German-speaking population, although the German population also did not view affiliation with the Austrian state as related to German national notions. What was

---

[52] Ernst, *Geschichte des Burgenlandes*, pp.205-15; Suppan, *Die österreichische Volksgruppen*, pp.85-7; Baumgartner, 'Der nationale Differenzierungsprozess', pp.111 and 154-5.

[53] Ernst, *Geschichte des Burgenlandes*, pp.215-27.

most important for the German, as for the Magyar and Croatian Burgenlanders, was that the particular social structure of Burgenland should survive. Its particular character is best demonstrated by the effects of Hungarian politics between 1867 and 1918, which brought about a certain western Hungarian social structure; this contributed to the fact that a conservative Croat could direct an Austrian *Bundesland* in the late 1940s. Western Hungarian indifference to the national-political dimension had been transferred to Burgenland, which as the result had somehow 'skipped' the nationalisation phase.

In an overwhelmingly agrarian society, where only a fraction of the people could be politicised and had undergone national-political mobilisation, and ethnic-social relations had been regulated for several centuries, modern national-political notions had not taken hold. At least till the 1960s Burgenland identity was defined by local identities: it meant having the right to speak one's own Croatian, Magyar or German 'village dialect' (*Dorfsprache*). However, in the 1960s there were profound changes in the economic structure, and this network of local identities was progressively eradicated. The decline in the agrarian sector combined with rapid industrialisation resulted in increased social mobility, which in recent decades has broken up the traditional western Hungarian structure.[54]

Thus Burgenland's position as a *Bundesland* within the Austrian nation-state can not be explained on the basis of national arguments. However, Austria has been able to create a perception of Burgenland as an integrated part of the nation-state by capitalising on – or

[54] Andreas Moritsch and Gerhard Baumgartner, 'Vergleichende Zusammenfassung der Ergebnisse der Dorfuntersuchungen in Kärnten und im Burgenland' in Moritsch (ed.), *Vom Ethnos zur Nationalität*, pp.156-62; Suppan, *Die österreichischen Volksgruppen*, pp.87-90, and 122-8. One issue was that the descendants of the Sopron/Ödenburg residents who had opted for Hungary to escape 'Austrian Bolshevism' ended up living in one of Europe's most rigidly governed socialist dictatorships. It could also be argued that the post-war Hungarian regime strengthened Burgenland's ties to Vienna, and thus made Vienna's ambitions to 'Austrify' Burgenland easier to accomplish. The parallels to the Carinthia Slovenes' position on the Socialist Slovene Republic within Yugoslavia are clear. On the role of Marxism in Burgenland, see Andrew Burghardt, 'Marxism and self-determination: the case of Burgenland, 1919' in R. Johnston, David B. Knight and Eleonore Kofman (eds), *Nationalism, Self-Determination and Political Geography* (London, 1987).

The Primacy of the Nation and Regional Identity

perhaps simply by being forced to accept – the presence of historically evolved structures.

Regional Identities and the Nation-state

After the First World War, it appears that the actors who might have restructured state territories did not understand identities other than the national ones. Thus they learned to their great surprise that the majority of Carinthia Slovenes opted for Austria, and that the Germans of the Sopron area chose Hungary rather than joining Austria within the newly-created Burgenland.

The examples of Carinthia and Burgenland both demonstrate how much more complex the European reality was than what the political rhetoric or the established notions of the times might have suggested. We have attempted to show that the populations in both Carinthia and Burgenland were significantly influenced by older identities rooted in the historical region. Indeed they were far more influenced by these than by the national slogans of the day, although this was not apparent to those who saw the world in terms of nation-states. This reality is manifested most clearly in the case of Carinthia.

A Carinthian system of symbols had been evolving over a long period, and in 1920 the Carinthian population was clearly well aware of this. The name 'Kärnten' had been institutionalised as early as in 976 and was to project a Carinthian consciousness at a time when the spatial-social organisation of the region was not yet established. The long and independent history of the region has been critical in the emergence of a Carinthian consciousness. Both ethnic groups have been able to identify with the history of the Carinthian duchy which, in two languages, has been presented as a shared historical memory, and which forms a solid foundation for regional identity at the symbolic level. A prolonged common history and the fact that the modernisation process took place within Austria combined to create structures that successively bound the southern Slovene areas and the northern German ones ever closer together.

Nationalist German and Slovene historiography has exaggerated the importance of the respective populations to the history of Carinthia. The Slovenes maintain that the use of their language at inaugural ceremonies for new rulers at Zollfeld demonstrated

Slovene dominance. Germans in turn launched the *windisch* theory, arguing that Carinthian Slovenes were not truly Slovenes at all. If German national speculations (e.g. the assertion that the Winds did not speak Slovene) are discounted, the Carinthian *Landesgeschichte* school's description of the Winds as Carinthians loyal to their native community comes closer to reality than many nationalist historians would admit. Beyond the national rhetoric lay an older, historical identity that the Carinthians perceived as more significant than a new state-formation based on national identity. Whether they would have viewed the matter differently if the alternative had been a Slovene state was not a topical subject and indeed at the time had not even been formulated.

Burgenland does not exhibit as old a system of symbols as Carinthia. The name of the new *Bundesland* was determined in connection with the incorporation of the Hungarian territories with Austria. Moreover, since Burgenland was quite a new territorial entity, it did not have a distinct, uniform history of its own. Burgenland could thus be described as a political-administrative construction, like Nordrhein-Westfalen. The leadership of the nation-state has striven to depict such regions as 'natural' entities with long politico-historical continuity, particularly where the region is in a border area like Burgenland, thus legitimising the territorial sovereignty of the nation-state. Despite efforts to give it an 'Austrian identity' and to erase the Hungarian past, Burgenland is a classic example of the way in which older structures are transferred to new constructions, either as a part of the deliberate legitimising strategy, or by less obvious means.

Burgenland is unique insofar as few attempts have been made to encroach on the older West Hungarian structures; thus a new Burgenland identity, founded on these older traditions, has emerged. It was not a historical region in 1921, but through the preservation of western Hungarian traditions, a Burgenland regional identity already existed by 1945, as was revealed during the Second World War. Although the identity itself was projected to the interwar period, it was actually based on much older notions and realities. Vienna could observe with satisfaction that its policy in Burgenland had made loyal Austrians of Magyars and Croats, who had struggled to keep the area inside Hungary after the First World War. This development was reinforced by the escalation of the Cold War and by Austria's rise in economic terms. In other words, Burgenland became an Austrian region by being more distinctly West Hungarian than those parts of western Hungary that remained in Hungary after Trianon.

The examples we have discussed show that a critical approach to accepted notions of the nation-state, the principle of nationality and national identity is valid. Such political developments as the restructuring of the European state system after the collapse of the great empires operate on several levels, of which high politics is only one – even if it is the most decisive. The national argument has not always coincided with the affected population's own political understanding of identity. The political-territorial identity is never as simple as national rhetoric would have it. This is especially true of areas that have historically been points of ethnic-cultural confluence and that have thus witnessed several shifts regarding sovereignty and political-territorial organisation. When a population takes a negative view of a nation-state construction to which it is expected to be positive, we have to examine the strata of older historical identities which do not disappear from the consciousness of a people merely because a new state-territorial identity is acclaimed as the universally prevailing political orthodoxy.

In addition, the Austrian cases we have seen suggest that there is no direct opposition between the nation-state construction and the older, regional historical layer. In some instances the regional historical dimension can be incorporated as a key component in the nation-state ideology. For instance, an important element in being Austrian is also being a Burgenlander. Similarly the Austrian nation-state has succeeded in bringing the Carinthian identity into the broader Austrian one, although it is true that a nationalistic struggle for Carinthian identity is still being fought out below the surface. We can also conclude, on the basis of our examples, that the kind of relationship that exists between the nation-state identity and the regional historical identity largely depends on the activities of the nation-state's elite. Older Habsburg territories such as Transylvania, Bohemia and Galicia are all of interest in this context. In short, such theoretical perspectives may be valuable also in analysing cases where the regional historical identity has come to be perceived as an antagonist of, rather than as a complement to, the nation-state.

PART FOUR

REGIONS IN CENTRAL EUROPE UNDER COMMUNISM
A PALIMPSEST

Kristian Gerner

'At least for some regions of Europe, one of which is Upper Silesia, nationalism has brought much suffering.'[1]

The Concept of Region

At the dissolution of the Soviet bloc, the problem, or task, facing the Central European states was seen as follows. They were to depart from the parenthesis that was the Soviet era, and from an anomalous societal condition, and return to Europe, which was defined as that which was 'normal'. The mass media, politicians and social scientists in the West were generally agreed that these states and their peoples had been oppressed, and prevented from realising their inherent potential by the Soviet overlordship and Communist party rule under which they had lived for nearly half a century.

In the post-war era, when the Central European states were constituent parts of a hierarchically structured monolithic bloc, Western Europe underwent profound changes. These included not only evolution toward a European Union (EU), but also the growing importance of the regional level both in political rhetoric and at times also in political reality. When these states rejoined the family, the question that naturally arose was whether their self-fulfilment and welfare would best be served by participation

---

[1] Ingeborg K. Helling, ' "Spätaussiedler" from Poland: Lifeworld and biography', in R. Grathoff and A. Kloskowska (eds), *The Neighbourhood of Cultures* (Warsaw, 1994), p.112.

in the EU, as well as by decentralisation and the strengthening of regions.

Approaching regions as problematic phenomena itself implies that one understands territory – in this case, Europe – as being divided into hierarchically arranged territorial entities, of which some are independent states, others are permitted limited self-rule while yet others exist only as names and contain no independent political institutions. Names themselves have shifting status, some being anchored in a historical context and others merely designations for development projects. Is there such a thing as a Baltic region, a Lake Mälar region and a Barents Sea region? Do they compare with, for example, Sweden, Switzerland and Scania? In which instances are we observing fact, and in which are we rather dealing with constructions and projections that do not correspond to any political reality? Or is there no clear boundary between these two dimensions? How important are issues such as the context and *Zeitgeist*?

In his discussion of the region as a political and territorial concept, Anssi Paasi has noted that it refers to a social construction which needs to be approached from a historical perspective. His definition is a good basis for studying regions in Central Europe during the Soviet era:

Regions are not 'organisms' that develop and have a life-span or evolution in the manner that some biological metaphors – so typical in Western political thought – would suggest. Rather, following Dear and Wolch, regions and localities are understood in this framework as being a complex synthesis or manifestation of objects, patterns, processes, social practices and inherent power relations that are derived from simultaneous interaction between different levels of social processes.[...] Through the institutionalization process and the struggles inherent in it, the territorial units in question 'receive' their boundaries and their symbols which distinguish them from other regions.[2]

Paasi argues that a region's name is its most significant symbol. It 'converges' historical development, great events, episodes and recollections into one, thus engendering in individuals an experience of collective identity linked to the region.[3] In this context

---

[2] Anssi Paasi, *Territories, Boundaries and Consciousness: The Changing Geographies of the Finnish–Russian Border* (Chichester, England, 1995), pp.32-3.

[3] Ibid., p.35.

the question of continuity in the collective consciousness comes to the fore. Can a region which has a historically manifested identity disappear? Can it slumber and reawaken? Can actors on the historical stage construct a 'historical' region which did not in fact exist as such, and thereby endow such a region with legitimacy so it will gain acceptance in the eyes of other actors?

A region can be defined as a structure. Referring to Fernand Braudel, Stein Rokkan and Charles Tilly, Daniel-Louis Seiler gives the concept this meaning:

By structures I mean long-run unvariant systems of relations which subsume social facts and which influence both actors and organizations in an unconscious way.[...] Most of the structures to be dealt with link political power and territory, but also territory and the economy.[4]

According to Seiler, time is an important factor in the reification of regions as structures, at least when it comes to perception and interpretation. Even a newly constructed region such as the Barents Sea region must be given retroactive historical value in order to acquire political legitimacy in the eyes of its own spokesmen. This chapter stipulates that regions do exist in the form of historical concepts. For example, the regions called Silesia and Karelia, although they have never been states (certainly not in the period we are considering here), have been ascribed a particular identity and specific location on the map by both the internal populations and outside observers. However, our assumption here is that the concept of region is problematic from the actor-perspective, because of an ambivalence in its definition between territory and people and because region exists as a political notion only if people act in its name.

The term 'region', as used today, is directly linked to the concepts of boundaries and territorial demarcation, and of political actors. A region is not a statistical compilation of parameters, but rather a reified delimitation that is assigned an identity, either by reference to history or in association with a particular project. In today's Europe a region is a political-geographical realm that has a specific name but no specific citizenship. Accordingly, the core

---

[4] Daniel Louis-Seiler, 'Inter-ethnic relations in East Central Europe: the quest for a pattern of accommodation', *Communist and Post-Communist Studies*, vol.26, no.4 (1993), p.352.

of the problem lies in the impossibility of an individual being a citizen of a region; one can be a citizen only of a state or in certain instances of two states.

As was implied earlier, the concept of region became legitimate in the political discourse of Western Europe after the Second World War, and has acquired political significance as a platform for action also in post-Communist Central Europe. This is in contrast with the aftermath of the First World War and the interwar period, when the nation-state was the central political subject according to the topical theme of the national right to self-determination. In the political language established by the League of Nations, national or ethnic minorities were recognised beneath the level of the state. The political concept 'national minorities' pertained to groups of people rather than to strictly delimited territories; those minorities themselves were granted collective rights but territories were not granted autonomy.

Parallel to the evolution of the European Economic Community into the European Community, and ultimately the European Union, the notion of regions has been forged at the substate and interstate levels. Historical provinces such as Wales and Catalonia began to be represented by politicians who viewed them as actors. In certain cases, e.g. Catalonia, this idea was accepted by the central government. So-called 'Euroregions' were created in the areas bordering the Federal Republic of Germany such as Saar-Lor-Lux based on purely pragmatic or on historical and economic arguments. This devolution occurred within the framework of democracy, market economy and a well-developed legal system.

One way to illustrate what is meant by the concept of region, as well as other historical terms that pertain to corresponding concepts, such as province, is to highlight the relationship between the central power and its border-areas in three major imperial projects in European history – the Roman Empire, the Soviet Union and the EU. From the viewpoints of those in power, order and control over the citizens are critical, since they make the outcome of political decisions predictable. Disorder around the state boundary is thus extremely undesirable; hence this boundary is extended in order to integrate ever new provinces into a hierarchical system.[5] Because of limited resources and/or political

---

[5] See Jochen Martin, 'The Roman Empire: domination and integration', *Journal*

or geographical impediments, a fixed border (*limes*, the Iron Curtain, the external boundary of the Schengen Agreement) is drawn, cutting off the outside world.

An important distinction between the Roman Empire on the one hand and Soviet rule in Central Europe and the EU on the other is that the latter came into being at a time when the system of nation-states had long been prevalent in Europe. Moreover, both the Warsaw Pact and the EU were constructed around the principle that the units which together constituted the system were the individual states. The Roman approach involved integrating the new provinces into the state by granting Roman citizenship to the political elites, while with Soviet rule and the EU the states were integrated in their existing forms. The provinces of the Roman Empire ultimately became part of the state, while in the modern cases the relationship between the whole and its components is problematic, in terms both of the relations among the states and of the political status of the regions within them.

The EU, quite unlike the Roman model, is moving towards political decentralisation in accordance with the so-called subsidiarity principle. This principle requests that any given question should be determined by those who will be most directly affected by its outcome. Macro-economic decisions and large-scale environmental problems are in the hands of the central authority, but matters like local transport, education and health care are dealt with at a lower level.

The actors within the EU all belong to a nation-state, while also cooperating in a supranational organisation. They are thus accustomed to a hierarchical approach to spheres of authority, so it is natural to view the nation-state as constructed in the same way, i.e. by regions. Whether these regions are administrative entities created by the central power like the counties (*län*) in Sweden, or communities established in the Middle Ages like the Swedish provinces (*landskap*) is politically important. As a rule, the older, historically evolved structures have a standardising influence on the formation of the new, administratively conceived regions.

The structure of the Roman Empire resembled a pyramid, with the imperial cult serving as a unifying rite for the towns and provinces, and the Emperor functioning as both the principal

---

of Institutional and Theoretical Economics, vol.151, no.4 (1995), pp.714-24.

authority and the symbol of this unity. The EU in its turn resembles a temple whose columns – states – support the overarching entity and are linked by horizontal functional bonds. Without unifying rites, sacred rituals or a personified deity, the EU is symbolised by an abstract ring of stars. Between Rome and the EU lie the Enlightenment, rationalism and modernisation, which are critical to the configuration of the relationship between state and citizen.

Between Rome and the EU, cultural and ethnic nationalism and 'the modern project' have emerged. Nationalism has often been a more potent source of political mobilisation than the democratic principle of citizenship. Territorial and ethnic identity can either coincide or diverge. Within geographical regions in each of the European states there are populations whose forefathers autochthonously resided in the same historical region for many generations, as well as individuals or groups who are immigrants in the country or the offspring of immigrants. The latter tend to identify not only with the region of settlement, but also with the area from which they arrived, the 'region of origin'. Furthermore, several generations have been reared in ethno-nationalism, and the result is that individuals identify not only with the region but also, in some instances, with the state where those who share their language or faith are state-sustaining/state-defining.

Because of the multidimensional character of 'region' its relations to both territory and people and its blend of historical tradition and political construction, the concept is quite dynamic. Different aspects of its definition are relevant depending on the context in which a particular region is discussed. A political-historical analysis requires more than a purely topological and chronological perspective; it must be contextual.

Parameters for Regions in Central Europe

During the Communist era the states of Central Europe were highly centralised. Local authority was invariably an extension of the central state administration, which in its turn was controlled by the rigidly hierarchically organised and centralised Communist party. It was like a patron–client relationship between individuals, who represented themselves, their own physical security and material gain.[6] During nearly fifty years of Soviet rule there was no integration of the provinces through an expansion of the notion of citizenship as there was under Rome. The leaders of the Warsaw Pact states were not Soviet citizens, who represented their province of origin in Moscow, the centre of the empire; those who showed an inclination to place the interest of their own state above that of the Soviet Union were either forced to back down or removed. Within the Sovietised states, the local administrators did not represent the local population but the central power – and incidentally they used their position in the hierarchy for personal gain. Inside the Soviet bloc there was little room for regional actor-identity or cooperation among the peripheries across state frontiers on the Euroregional model. Each central power made sure that the significance of the border was preserved, and local contacts across the state frontiers were discouraged.

During the Soviet era demographic changes had a profound impact on the historical regions in Central and Eastern Europe. The redrawing of state boundaries affected Germany, Poland, Czechoslovakia and also Hungary, which had to relinquish to Slovakia an area across the Danube from Bratislava. Historical regions such as Carpatho-Ruthenia, Silesia and the Vilna area partly or completely switched their state affiliations. A great number of people were displaced, with the result that the ethnic make-up of the population was radically altered in many historical regions. In 1945 several million former Polish citizens, who had fallen under Soviet rule in 1939, were moved from eastern Galicia, Volynia and Polesia to East Prussia, Pomerania, the Poznan area and Silesia, and once again became Polish citizens. Millions of German-speakers were expelled from Poland, the Sudetenland, Slovakia and Hungary and became German citizens, the majority within the Federal Republic. These developments had important political consequences, given that individuals identified with a particular ethnic group and a given territory. The expelled Germans continued to identify with the Silesia, East Prussia or Sudetenland of the past, and the presence of these *Heimatvertriebene* was one factor which determined the Federal Republic's initially restrictive

---

[6] See Andrew Coulson, 'From democratic centralism to local democracy' in A. Coulson (ed.), *Local Government in Eastern Europe: Establishing Democracy at the Grassroots* (Aldershot, 1995), pp.7-9.

Ostpolitik. In Poland and Czechoslovakia the Communist leadership sought to enhance its tenuous political legitimacy by conjuring up the image of a revanchist and irredentist Germany, from which they would protect the people with the help of the Soviets. The political legitimacy of this leadership remained weak, as the eruption of various crises showed, but the message conveyed to the rising generation was that the Germans had been present in Poland and Czechoslovakia only during the war period of 1939-45. This also influenced naturally the rising generation's views of the regions of Silesia and Erzgebirge, affirming the notion that these were historically geographic designations that had been ethnic Polish and ethnic Czech areas from time immemorial.

Thus the revision of state boundaries and the interstate migrations of the time affected the ethnic identity and social make-up of these historical regions. However, other phenomena also had important consequences in this context. The Communist state's industrialisation and urbanisation policies were critical developments: by 1989 the historical regions harboured the Soviet legacy of large cities with obsolete industries and an immigrant labour force from various rural areas, and of a backward rural society of peasants originating from quite different territories.[7] Communications and the infrastructure in general were severely neglected. Regions had been isolated and thus become provinces in the negative sense: the Socialist states were largely focused on the capitals. In addition, the rigidly hierarchical governing method of the Communist system sought to destroy local collaboration at all levels.[8] Both material and spiritual conditions prevented the evolution of collective consciousness – a regional 'we-feeling' *vis-à-vis* the central state power – and of political organisation within the historical regions.

If the concept 'region' signifies an empirically observable entity with a special identity and distinct boundaries, an independent cultural, political and economic configuration below the state level, it must be affirmed that the existence of regions was not permitted in Communist Europe. However, after 1989 political actors invoked ethno-territorial identities as grounds for special treatment politically,

---

[7] See Ivan Volgyes, 'The legacies of Communism: an introductory essay', in Zoltan Barany and Ivan Volgyes (eds), *The Legacies of Communism in Eastern Europe* (Baltimore, 1995), pp.1-19.

[8] Ibid., p.52.

economically and culturally *vis-à-vis* the titular nation of the state and not necessarily in harmony with the economic policies conducted by this state. Efforts have also been made to forge cross-boundary Euroregions in the former Soviet bloc. Thus the political map of Central and Eastern Europe is beginning to resemble a palimpsest. When political actors in Germany, Hungary, Poland, the Czech Republic and Slovakia invoke history to gain legitimacy, older political-geographic patterns appear under the Communist surface layer. The territorial and ethnic aspects of the region concept are both brought to life.

The Soviet Imprint

During the Soviet era the problem was two-sided. On the one hand, there was a certain continuity insofar as throughout the period there were actors with a preserved regional identity and regional awareness. On the other hand, certain developments in some areas both before 1939 and after 1989 showed evidence of regional identity, although they were not actors between 1945 and 1989. However, it is important above all to estimate how far the Soviet period generated changes in the regional identities.

In Hungary, the county system was reorganised in 1950, and central rule was strengthened. One observer commented concerning the county capitals: '...placed there by the central apparatus and playing a secondary role in redistribution, they had nothing to do with the forming of regions, or even an intermediary form of self-government.'[9] Hungary has a system rooted in the Middle Ages of division into counties *(megye)*. In the Soviet period, these were governed by centrally-appointed administrators who approved the local budget, monitored the collection of taxes and allocated state funds. These counties can be understood as historically established regions, although they were unable to function as actors during this period because the local leadership exclusively represented the central power.[10]

---

[9] József Tóth, 'Historical and today's socio-economic conditions of regionalism in Hungary', manuscript (Pécs: Hungarian Academy of Sciences, Research Centre for Regional Studies, 1990).

[10] Kenneth Davey, 'Local Government in Hungary' in Coulson (ed.) *Local Government in Eastern Europe*, p.73.

In the German Democratic Republic (GDR) former *Länder* were transformed into *Bezirken* with boundaries that did not build upon tradition. In 1975 Poland was partitioned into forty-nine counties without historical foundations. This represented the furthest extent of a deregionalisation process begun in 1945.[11]

States that were labelled federations in no way corresponded to the functional, decentralised structures existing in say the United States or the Federal Republic of Germany. National minorities were largely unable to assert themselves in their home areas, even ones where they were formally recognised as minorities. The notion of a homogeneous nation-state was realised under Communism. In 1967 the situation was described as follows:

In the USSR, as in Yugoslavia, and as in Czechoslovakia ... the federal powers have been gradually reduced.[...] The functional authority of the centre was progressively reasserted and re-imposed. The same is true also of the other European Communist states which are not federal: East Germany, which transformed its initial *Länder* into *Bezirken* (provinces); Rumania, where the Magyar Autonomous Region was slowly, after 1956, de-autonomized, etc.[12]

Czechoslovakia was administered through National Committees at the regional, district and county levels. These were funded out of the state budget, but could retain certain revenues from enterprise, although this too was regulated by the central state power. This was intended not to promote regional independence but rather to lessen economic discrepancies among the regions: the regional administrative level was abolished by the first post-Communist regime.[13] In the Czech case, analysis of possible regional identity must begin with discovering traces of the historical provinces of Bohemia, Moravia and Silesia from the Communist period. In Slovakia the area of greatest interest is Carpatho-Ruthenia.

---

[11] See Anna Cielecka and John Gibson, 'Local government in Poland', in Coulson (ed.), *Local Government in Eastern Europe*, p.23.

[12] Ghita Ionescu, *The Politics of the European Communist States* (London, 1969), pp.122-3.

[13] Kenneth Davey, 'The Czech and Slovak republics' in Coulson (ed.), *Local Government in Eastern Europe*, p.43; Sona Capkova, 'Local authorities and economic development in Slovakia', ibid., p.199.

Historical Parameters

The character of regions in the Central and South-East European context is most closely comparable to the three regions of Belgium – Flanders, Wallonia and Eupen-Malmédy – rather than with regions in countries such as Sweden, France and Britain where today's regionalism involves the artificial resuscitation of older administrative designations, with the territorial definition being wholly decisive. The Belgium regions also entail older administrative entities, but they are defined ethnically insofar as language – French, Dutch or German – represents the principal identity-marker for each group. In accordance with the principles adopted after 1918, the identity of the ethnic group, rather than of the region, forms the basis.

Czechoslovakia and Yugoslavia, like Belgium nearly a century earlier, emerged long after the feudal territorial states in Western Europe had been defined as nation-states, and Bretons, Gaelic Scots and Jämtlanders had ceased to be more than exotic local colour. The historical territorial states such as Bohemia-Moravia and Croatia, which became parts of Czechoslovakia and Yugoslavia respectively, were perceived by most actors as 'belonging' to the ethnic groups of Czechs and Croats and thus as being ethnically defined. This prevented a development of Czechoslovakia and Yugoslavia along 'French' or 'British' assimilationist lines. The result was ethno-regionalism within those states and – after 1968 and 1945 respectively – within the federations, not only among Czechs and Croats but also among Slovaks, Serbs and other peoples.

Poland had been divided between three empires after the ascendancy of the modern nation-state began, and governing was becoming increasingly centralised in Russia, Germany and to a lesser extent Austria. This development was manifested on the symbolic level by *inter alia*, the system of railway lines with strong emphasis on the capitals, and on the practical level by the language policy, Russification or Germanisation. The difference between the diffuse eastern area in the Polish republic, *kresy* and the well-organized western expanse towards Germany, *pogranicze*, was further accentuated.[14] Behind the illusion of a unified Polish identity in

---

[14] Anne Applebaum, *Between East and West: Across the Borderlands of Europe* (New York, 1994), p.47.

the state established in 1918 lay profound economic and mental differences that were to prove important after 1989.

Hungary's identity as a state was linked from the early Middle Ages onwards not only to Pannonia, with Visegrád and Buda as the centres for royal power, but also to Transylvania and Slovakia. During the Ottoman occupation of central Hungary in 1541–1686, Pozsony (Bratislava) was the capital, with a Habsburg as king, while Transylvania was governed as a duchy in vassalage to the Ottoman Sultan, though with significant freedom of action even in foreign policy. Hungary lost the historic provinces of Transylvania and Slovakia through the Treaty of Trianon in 1920.

Romania was constructed in 1919-20 from the old Regate consisting of Wallachia and Moldavia, which during the period after the the end of the Crimean War and the Congress of Berlin in 1878 came to resemble a Romanian nation-state; Transylvania with its large ethno-nationally mobilised Hungarian population; and the multinational regions of Bukovina and Bessarabia – the latter three regions were incorporated into Romania as a result of the First World War. Ethno-regionalism was brought into domestic politics as an explosive ingredient, and as a reason for the irredentist policies pursued in 1940 by neighbouring Hungary and the USSR.

No one has yet determined how many generations need to elapse before the descendants of immigrants see themselves, and are seen by others, as 'natives'. In Transylvania Hungarian and Romanian nationalists alike describe each other as 'immigrants' with less 'historical right' to the province. During the Middle Ages the sparsely-populated duchy of Bohemia, inhabited by Czech-speaking people, received as immigrants German-speaking burghers and entrepreneurs in the mining industry. When Czechoslovakia was formed in 1918 as the state of the 'Czechoslovak nation' president Tomás G. Masaryk described the residing German population as 'colonisers', i.e. no more than a temporary presence. It was thus that the term 'Sudeten German' evolved as the designation for the German-speaking population in the 'Sudeten'. Those who had merely been Germans within Austria – the Habsburg Empire – now became a specific ethnic group.

The evolution of Sudeten German history is well known. The majority identified with Nazi Germany both in the 1930s and during the Occupation, and were collectively penalised for this by being deported in 1945. Most of the deportees came to Bavaria, where they were eventually recognised as a fourth 'tribe' alongside Bavarians, Swabians and Franconians.

If the Germans in Czechoslovakia had not been defined as 'Sudeten Germans' in 1918, and these had not become a 'tribe' in Bavaria, they would have remained merely Germans. The specific group had become as illusory as the Cheshire Cat in *Alice in Wonderland* behind its smile. In order to highlight the subjectivity of the construction further we may consider the regional versus the ethnic identity of the German-speakers in Prague in 1918. They were not 'Sudeten Germans', but the circumstances obliged them to identify with this ethno-territorially defined group. The option of being a Bohemian, i.e. territorially identified with all of Bohemia-Moravia and without ethnic affiliation, did not exist. The only alternative was to become Czech. In Czech, Bohemia is 'Čechy', and Moravian is viewed as a dialect. In other words, the name that denotes the region is also the name of the people.

Traces in the Palimpsest

As we have implied above, the regional question in Central Europe underwent extensive ethnicisation in the twentieth century. The notion of common territorial identity for citizens with different mother-tongues was suppressed by state propaganda, which presented the historical regions as 'actually' ancient Polish, Czech, Hungarian or Romanian areas. Modern ethno-nationalism was projected back into history. In addition, the leadership endorsed the thesis that the ethnic group which had left the earliest traces in the region still had an exclusive claim on the area. Historians, archaeologists and philologists were all made to serve the ethno-national propaganda of the state.

Because the relationship between territory and ethnicity was presented in a one-dimensional way, and because of the socialist state's hierarchical centralism, the historical regions did not evolve into collective actors. Instead they became, explicitly or implicitly, battlefields for ethnically-motivated conflicts. Ethnic groups in regions such as Transylvania and the Vilna area struggled against each other rather than asserting the interests of the region *vis-à-vis* the central power.

In the exposition below we focus on a limited number of

historical regions in Central Europe. Both the previous history and post-1989 development in these areas warrant an investigation of the socialist period to determine whether they can be said to have existed as self-conscious entities during this era. The regions in question are Transylvania, Moravia-Silesia, Silesia, the Vilna area, Carpatho-Ruthenia and the Kaliningrad district. Of these we devote the most attention to Transylvania: the question of its status in Romania and the open political struggle among the ethnic groups imply that it was indeed a region of its own during the Socialist period.

TRANSYLVANIA

Under the leadership of Petru Groza, who was from Transylvania and spoke both Romanian and Hungarian, the popular front government that took power in Romania after the Second World

War conducted a liberal policy towards minorities. MNSz, the Organization of the Hungarian People, functioned as a political party and participated in the popular front government. A substantial number of the Romanian Communist Party's leaders were Hungarian-speaking Jews from Transylvania.

In 1948 the Communists unilaterally assumed power in Romania, and on 13 April the country had a new constitution and became a 'Popular Democracy'. Industry and agriculture were socialised in accordance with the Soviet model. The trial of László Rájk in Hungary in 1949, resulting in his execution, had repercussions in Transylvania, since Rájk was from this region and had maintained contacts across the border. From the Stalinist angle, the Hungarians in Romania were 'Titoists' and traitors. The MNSz leaders were arrested and the organisation broke up. Groza was removed as prime minister in 1952, which confirmed for the Hungarians that things were not going in the right direction.

In 1952 Romania was administratively redivided. A Hungarian Autonomous Region was established in Transylvania. The authorities dissolved the MNSz in 1953, which they justified with the argument that no Hungarian political organisation was necessary since the Romanian Communist Party protected minorities. Also in that year, the party leader Gheorghe Gheorghiu-Dej declared that the nationality question in Romania was resolved. It now became impossible to discuss the status of minorities openly.

During the Communist period there was significant social and geographic mobility, and this served to alter inter-ethnic relations in Transylvania. In 1977, 35 per cent of the population were living in areas outside their native communities. The cities in Transylvania were Romanianised, and previously Hungarian centres such as Satu Mare (Szatmár), Oradea (Nagyvarad) and Cluj (Kolozsvár) now had a Romanian majority.

The 1956 revolution in Hungary aroused expressions of sympathy among Hungarians in Transylvania, and thus led to arrests. In that year the Romanian Communist party adopted a manifestly Romanian-nationalist line. The myth of Daco-Romanian continuity has long been an essential component in Romanian consciousness of historical identity. The theory, according to which Romanians have lived in the area since antiquity and thus 1,000 years before the Hungarians arrived in 895, first appeared as a historical-political argument in the writings of Inochentie Micu-

Klein (1692-1778).[15] Ceaușescu, who assumed the post of First Party Secretary in 1965, further emphasised Romanian nationalism. A new constitution was drafted, its stipulations securing individual human rights while also affirming collective cultural rights for the 'coexisting nationalities'. These groups were granted the right to use their own language in public life within their administrative area. In 1968 the designation 'areas populated by Hungarians' was substituted for 'areas with mixed populations'. The Hungarian Autonomous Region was dissolved in 1967.

Under Ceaușescu, Romania was a rigid Communist dictatorship plagued by a disastrous economic policy, the effects of which struck at all citizens without regard to nationality. The regime sought to prevent all its subjects from forging contacts with the outside world, and thus made any contact across borders difficult, including the exchange of books and journals. Hungarian acquaintances visiting Romania were classified as 'foreign tourists', and so were not allowed to stay at the homes of their friends. In 1979 a decree was passed stipulating that foreigners could purchase petrol only with Western currency; obviously this would have been difficult for visitors from socialist Hungary. These restrictions denied Hungarians the right to visit their kin on the other side of the border. The repressive policies were understood as deliberate ethnic discrimination. Because the Hungarians in Transylvania not only contrasted their circumstances with the relative prosperity of Hungary, but could identify with the Hungarian state, dissatisfaction with the government became explosive.

In 1957 a reorganisation of the school system was initiated in Transylvania. Hungarian schools became subsections of Romanian schools and thereafter were successively weakened. The Hungarian university in Cluj was included in the Romanian one. In some specialist colleges, all instruction in Hungarian was stopped. In 1973 a new law was introduced stipulating that there had to be a minimum of twenty-five students at secondary school level and thirty-six at the lyceum level for instruction in a minority language to be possible. If one Romanian-speaking student was present, a Romanian-medium class would be set up.

---

[15] Sándor Vogel, 'Transylvania: Myth and Reality' in André Gerrits and Nanci Adler (eds), *Vampires Unstaked: National Images, Stereotypes and Myths in East Central Europe* (Amsterdam, 1995), pp.78-9.

As for what was actually taught, Transylvania's history was utterly ignored, except for how it served the continuity theory, as during the Hungarian period in 1940-4. However, the national overtones were reversed. In 1977 one observer wrote: 'From the description of Transylvanian history, no one could guess that Hungarian politicians and noblemen, together with the German Saxons, ruled the province for almost a millennium. Not even the anti-social estate holders and nobles are described as Hungarians, lest the reader be told that Hungarians ruled the province.'[16]

Hungarian cultural institutions, such as the society of writers, the theatres and the opera in Cluj were fused with Romanian ones and became sections within them. The Romanian language generally prevailed. Hungarian-language books were published in smaller editions in proportion to the population than Romanian-language texts and were often translations of Romanian works. Locally published Hungarian books and journals were more widely sold outside Transylvania than within its borders. The greatest blow to the cultural tradition of the Hungarian minority came in 1974 with a law which though not overtly directed against minorities, had severe repercussions on them:

In accordance with laws 63 and 207/1974, all books, archives and in essence all objects older than thirty years were nationalised. These laws were implemented in order to 'preserve the national cultural heritage'. In reality, the development proceeded in precisely the opposite direction. The archives and document collections of the Hungarian Catholic and Reformed churches were seized. Material that had previously been accessible to scholars and the public was removed and stored in various places with no consideration for classification. The archives of the Roman-Catholic bishopric in Oradea were transferred from a building put up in the 18th century for the specific purpose of storing this material, to a warehouse in an old castle that was utterly ill-suited for its preservation and for research. The archives in the bishopric of Satu-Mare have been virtually destroyed in this same way. Moreover, there has been no training of librarians and archivists in Romania since 1957, which makes the consequences of these new laws even worse. Material that is unique not only to Hungary, but to all of Central Europe is about to go to waste.[17]

---

[16] Michael Z. Szaz, *East European Quarterly*, vol. II, no.4 (1977), p.499, cited in Gellért Tamás, 'Ungrare i Transsylvanien' in *Ungrarna i Transsylvanien* (Stockholm, 1988).

[17] *Ungrarna i Transsylvanien*, pp.41-2.

In 1978 the Hungarian minority in Transylvania attracted international attention: one of its leaders, Károly Király, who had held a high position in the Communist party, released to the foreign press three letters which had been sent to the Romanian party leadership the previous year thoroughly criticising the national discrimination suffered by Hungarians in the area. Király was punished with a brief internal exile, but Ceauşescu visited Transylvania and put in motion a campaign intended to gain the sympathy of the minorities, while he simultaneously branded 'decadent persons' (read Király) who had conspired with foreign forces (read Hungary). In 1981 Hungarian intellectuals in Transylvania launched an underground journal, *Counterpoints*, and the September 1982 issue appealed to the CSCE conference in Madrid to draw up a treaty on collective rights for nationalities and found an international committee to review the situation in Transylvania. From 1984 reports on the state of affairs in this region were regularly sent to the outside world. From the mid-1970s to the fall of Ceauşescu in 1989 ample testimony exists to show that the representatives of the Hungarian minorities in Transylvania felt that they were subjected to discrimination.

Relations between Hungary and Romania deteriorated further after Ion Lancranjan, a Ceauşescu aide, published a book in 1982 which portrayed an eternally Romanian Transylvania, to which the Hungarians came as intruders. This produced an intense reaction in Hungary. In 1984, in conjunction with its congress, the Hungarian Communist Party asserted the right of the minority to develop its own culture. The point was conveyed to the Romanian party congress the same year by the Hungarian delegation but the statement was censored by the Romanian press, which wrote of 'revanchist currents' in Hungary. Romania closed its consulate in the Hungarian border town of Debrecen, and the Hungarian consulate in Cluj was closed in 1988.

The situation went from bad to worse in 1986, when the Hungarian Academy of Sciences published its three volume *History of Transylvania*, edited by the minister for cultural affairs, Bela Köpeczi. This work accorded the Hungarians an important place in Transylvania's history and was met with a vehement Romanian campaign in which Kádár's Hungary was compared to Miklós Horthy's authoritarian interwar regime, called Fascist by the Romanians.

Hungary was accused of making irredentist claims on Transylvania.[18]

Because of Ceauşescu's economic policy, Romania by the late 1980s had a backward economic structure, severe supply problems and widespread petty crime. The whole of society was in a state of dissolution. Ceauşescu attempted to create legitimacy of a pseudo-Byzantine sort for his regime through a zealous cult of personality and of Romanian nationalism. This made life still more difficult for the Hungarian minority, which was now subjected to forced assimilation. The method in this process consisted of population transfers in connection with the so-called 'systematisation' of the countryside, where the old villages were to be eradicated and the populations thrown together in barracks in 'agro-towns'. This 'systematisation' was an obvious threat to Hungarian culture, with further encroachments on Hungarian-language instruction, the closing of cultural institutions, and harassment of the churches.

In March 1988 the Romanian government announced that 'socialist evolution' required the razing of 8,000 villages, to be replaced by urbanised 'agro-industrial complexes'. This policy was not to follow any particular ethnic considerations, but it was clearly well-suited to wreck the material foundations of the old peasant culture among the Hungarian and German peoples of Transylvania. In addition, the government's declaration was made at a time when tens of thousands of Hungarians had gone to Hungary fleeing ethnic persecution.

In his speech to the Romanian Communist Party Congress in November 1989 in Bucharest, Ceauşescu rejected all notions of liberalisation, but by this time the tide that was bringing down the regimes of Central Europe was about to reach him.

During 16-18 December thousands demonstrated in Timisoara (Temesvár in Hungarian) in the Banat, a town of some 300,000 inhabitants, many from the Hungarian or German minorities. The demonstration of 16 December was triggered by a rumour that László Tökes, a priest of the Hungarian Reformist Church and a champion of civil rights, was to be seized by the police. Hungarians and Romanians demonstrated together against the authorities. Many youths were severely injured when Securitate troops violently

---

[18] George Schöpflin, 'The role of Transylvania in Hungarian politics', *Radio Free Europe Research*, vol.13, no.48, Part I (1988).

broke up the demonstrations on the 17th and 18th in an event that became known as the Timisoara Massacre.

Despite this bloody repression, the protests continued both in Transylvania, where the Hungarian minority resided, and elsewhere in Romania. The regime tried in vain to depict the incidents in Transylvania as being caused by provocations by Hungary and attempts to recover Transylvania as it had done in 1940. On 21 December, Ceauşescu organised a rally in Bucharest as he often did, to address the people and be hailed by them. He was interrupted by angry calls, whereupon the security forces fired on the demonstrators, claiming still more lives. Ceauşescu fled with his wife, and on 22 December, the defence authorities aligned themselves with the popular rebellion. A National Salvation Front consisting mainly of prominent Communists who had fallen out of favour with Ceauşescu a few years earlier formed a provisional government. Ceauşescu and his wife were executed. Subsequent developments revealed that Ceauşescu had been overthrown by men who belonged to the ruling caste. However, it was not possible to determine whether the demonstration and repression at Timisoara had actively been manipulated by the coup instigators, or whether the latter merely recognised the opportunity that was presenting itself and thus sprang into action when it became clear that the people were ready to part company with Ceauşescu.

The arrest of the Hungarian László Tökes was the spark that ignited the revolution in Romania. The revolt began with an ethnic minority that Ceauşescu had actively persecuted and which was influenced by the liberalisation process going on at the same time in Hungary. This minority suffered from the oppression more strongly than any other group, and also had an alternative – life in Hungary – in its field of vision. Although Transylvania with the Banat did not appear as a collective actor, it was still this region, the battlefield between the central government and the ethnic Hungarians, that finally caused the political upset in Romania in the fall of 1989. The region still had an identity.

MORAVIA-SILESIA

Between 1945 and 1989 the Sudeten area was simply the border area of Bohemia-Moravia, sparsely populated, with dilapidated villages whose former German inhabitants had been superseded by Gypsies from Slovakia. But the 'tribe' had settled in Bavaria and cultivated the myth of its origins – in the Sudetenland. According to their own view, the 'colonisers' had brought civilisation to Bohemia, and thus the area was their land. When the Communist surface layer was erased from Bohemia and Moravia-Silesia in 1989, the prewar pattern of mixed German and Czech settlements re-emerged – not as a reality, but as a retrieved and, in the eyes of many political actors, re-legitimised recollection.

Under a law passed in 1968 and effective from 1969, Czechoslovakia became a dual federation in which Slovakia had some autonomy. To the extent that one can speak of regionalism in the Soviet period, the exact status of Slovakia was the issue. Historically, the Czech portion comprised three entities or regions. Those were Bohemia, Moravia and Silesia, and Bohemia (*Čechy*) was identified with the entire portion. After 1969 Slovakia was a part of equal standing; but Czech and Slovak were distinct languages, and the religious differences were likewise so marked that there was a veritable cultural boundary between the two peoples. Thus Moravia and Silesia are of special interest in the context of regions.

During the Prague Spring of 1968, in Brno, the National Committee for Moravia, i.e. a Communist administrative structure, put forward a project for a three-part federation in which Moravia-Silesia would become an entity equal to Bohemia and Slovakia. In late May a Society for Moravia and Silesia was established in Brno to promote the project, and by its own account it soon had 200,000 members. The project met with resistance, both in many cities in the Brno area and in northern Moravia, from those who wished for greater autonomy for districts and municipalities rather than federalisation; and in Silesia from local forces who wished to see their region become the fourth in a federalised state.

The Moravian and Silesian projects encountered massive opposition from the Slovak leaders, who balked at any idea of granting the Czech people still more regions to pit against Slovakia in a federation. Czech leaders in Prague were likewise against the project.[19] Requests for a plebiscite, presented by the Association for Moravia

---

[19] H. Gordon Skilling, *Czechoslovakia's Interrupted Revolution* (Princeton, NJ, 1976), pp.470-47.

and Silesia, were rejected. The 'Moravian patriots' wished to vote on a number of issues, including official recognition of a specific Moravian tradition, and the removal of anti-Moravian Czech senior officials from their posts.[20]

After 1989 the Moravian-Silesian question once again became topical in Czechoslovakia. In the parliamentary elections of 1990 the Movement for a Self-Governing Democracy and the Association for Moravia and Silesia received 8 per cent of the votes in the Czech Republic. The movement was territorially defined but was soon faced with an ethnically-oriented contender, the Moravian National Party. The Czech constitution, adopted in November 1992, is informed by the notion of a civic state rather than an ethnically demarcated state. In its preamble, the constitution defines the population as 'the citizens of the Czech Republic in Bohemia, Moravia and Silesia'. Although this formulation can be understood as acknowledging the existence of historical regions, respect for pertinent regional identities had no place in the policies of the government headed by Václav Klaus. In 1993 a proposal was drafted for the division of the Republic into thirteen regions, and in 1994 a similar plan proposed division into seventeen regions not based on any historical boundaries. Klaus expressly refuted all arguments that invoked history for the determination of regions. In 1993, in a speech in conjunction with Brno's 750th anniversary celebrations, President Václav Havel appealed to his listeners to 'think of the destiny of the entire people', and urged Brno to refrain from demanding a separate government and parliament for Moravia, and to become instead a symbol of cooperation and cohesion in Central Europe.[21]

Moravian regionalism had apparently become no stronger in the period after 1968, and Prague's position on greater independence for Moravia and Silesia was as reserved after 1989 as it had been during the Communist era.

---

[20] Otto Ulc, *Politics in Czechoslovakia* (San Francisco, 1974), p.68.

[21] Matthew Rhodes, 'National identity and minority rights in the constitutions of the Czech Republic and Slovakia', *East European Quarterly*, vol.29, no.3 (1995), pp.353-7.

SILESIA

A destiny comparable to that of the Sudeten Germans befell the Polish-speaking people from the interwar Polish Republic's *kresy*, the eastern areas which were incorporated into the Soviet Union after 1945. The Polish-speaking groups were moved to the formerly German Silesia, Pomerania and East Prussia – areas from which the Germans had either fled or been expelled, or where they had escaped attention by allowing themselves to be Polonised.

Silesia experienced a distinctive displacement in relation to Eastern Galicia, which Poland was forced to relinquish to Soviet Ukraine in 1939. The process can be illustrated by name-changes: for example Lwów, became L'viv and Breslau became Wroclaw – and by the fact that intellectual and academic Lwów lived on in Wroclaw after 1945, with the traditions of the Polish university in Lwów being transferred to the former German university in Breslau. Polish schoolchildren learned that the German influence was a legacy from the time when the western part of Poland belonged to Prussia after 1772, not of medieval settlement. The Instytut Slaski in Opole propagated the thesis of Silesia's quintessentially Polish character. Correspondingly, Germans learned little of the situation in Silesia after 1945: their history ended with the expulsion.[22]

In the interwar period, the autochthons in Silesia were known as Slonzaks (with differing spellings in German, Polish and Czech). They spoke a West Slavic language or a dialect of Polish or Czech. German elements maintained that this was a corrupted form of German, so-called '*Wasserpolnisch*'. Silesia was not a state during the interwar years, having then been divided between Germany, Poland and Czechoslovakia. Inhabitants who later migrated to the area identified themselves and each other as Czechs, Poles and Germans, not as Silesians, and viewed Slonzaks as Polonised Czechs or Germans, Czechised or Germanised Poles, or Germanised Czechs and Poles. The specific ethno-regional identity of the original population was completely disregarded in political and cultural affairs.

With Poland's resurrection as a state in 1918, one great dilemma was the question of how the boundary with Germany (and with

---

[22] Mariusz Urbanek, 'Slask Polaków i Niemców', *Polityka*, no.44 (1995), pp.68-70.

Czechoslovakia) was to be drawn in Silesia. It seemed self-evident that Silesia should not become an independent state; however, the area was perceived by the majority of the actors involved, including the victorious Allied powers, as a historically-given region. Was the region to be divided, or should it fall entirely within one or other of the states? Following a plebiscite which left Polish nationalists aggrieved, and a revolt led by the Polish plebiscite commissioner Wojciech Korfanty, the area was partitioned in 1922 under supervision by the League of Nations. In a preparatory study the Allied Control Commission had written that it would be impossible to draw boundaries on the basis of ethnic criteria both because the 'races' lived intermingled with one another and because the 'industrial triangle' could not be broken up for geographical and economic reasons.[23] The victorious powers determined that Silesia would be divided on the basis of a combination of ethnic and economic factors. The partitioning of Silesia between Germany and Poland meant that three-quarters of the coal-producing areas and two-thirds of the steelworks went to Poland, while 625,000 Polish-speakers found themselves in Germany and 260,000 German-speakers in Poland.[24]

From 1919 up till the plebiscite in 1921, a lively propaganda war raged in and around Silesia. The newspaper *Der Oberschlesier* in Oppeln, which had close ties to the Catholic *Zentrum* Party in Germany, promoted the notion of a specific Silesian identity, as did the *Oberschlesische Zeitung* in Bytom, organ of the Democratic Party, and the *Oberschlesischer Kurier* in Königshütte and *Ratiborer Rundschau*, both also associated with *Zentrum*. It is noteworthy that the assertion of Silesian particularity was identified with the assertion that the region should belong to Germany. The argument implied that the area was historically German, that it was a geographical and economic entity, and that it also manifested the German people's cultural mission in Central Europe.[25] From this angle Silesia appears as a region in the German nation-state.

In 1939 Germany seized the whole of Silesia and incorporated

---

[23] Peter Wozniak, "*Blut, Erz, Kohle*": a thematic examination of German propaganda on the Silesian question during the interwar years', *East European Quarterly*, vol.28, no.3 (1994), p.321.

[24] Ibid.

[25] Ibid., pp.326-7.

the region into the *Reich*. It fell to Poland in 1945, whereupon the majority of German-speakers were expelled. Those who remained, including the allegedly indispensable experts in the mining industry and the so-called autochthonous border population, were subjected to Polonisation. After 1989, autochthonous individuals appeared in Silesia, who defined themselves partly as Germans, and partly as Slonzaks. With the return of the latter group, the region began to retrieve its ethno-territorial identity.[26]

The newly-awoken regional identity in Silesia is primarily linked to the German element in the population, which for opportunistic reasons increased a hundredfold after 1989, and in early 1996 was estimated at between half and three-quarters of a million – 90 per cent of the entire 'German' population in Poland. About 150 German organisations were created after 1989, which suggests that efforts to revive a German cultural identity have been largely successful, despite the absence of a local German intelligentsia after 1945, and despite the fact that German-language instruction was non-existent before 1989.[27] Miners had been a materially privileged group in Communist Poland, and under the government of Gierek (1970-80), who was of Silesian origin, the province received a large new steelworks, Huta Katowice. This does not imply that the region asserted itself as an actor before 1989; it was the state's ideology and the personal preferences of the party leadership that gave the commitment to heavy industry in Silesia such importance. The region's inhabitants did not conduct policy.

Yet the post-1989 German 'revival' in Silesia was accompanied by manifestations of Polish regionalism, in the form of local protests against the possibility that the Warsaw government would treat the area unfairly. The background to this was the relative deprivation faced by the Silesian population with high unemployment and a decreased standard of living – developments that resulted from the country now operating as a free market economy and no longer being focused on heavy industry.[28]

---

[26] See Kristian Gerner, 'Östeuropa sju år efter vändningen' in Klas-Göran Karlsson (ed.), *Östeuropa vid skiljevägen* (Moheda, 1995), pp.50-2.

[27] Tomasz Kamusella, 'Asserting minority rights in Poland', *Transition*, vol.2, no.3 (1996), pp.15-18.

[28] See Gerner, 'Östeuropa'.

THE VILNA AREA

By Poland's north-eastern border lies another historical region, the Vilna area (Wileńszczyzna), where a shift in ethno-regional identity took place during the Soviet period. The area, of which the city of Vilna (today, as Vilnius capital of the independent state of Lithuania) was the centre, had been a centre of Polish and Jewish culture since the Middle Ages. During the National Romantic period, Vilna and its surrounding area came to occupy a key place in Polish mythology; the national poet, Adam Mickiewicz (1798-1855), was from there. In 1920-39 Vilna belonged to Poland, while Lithuanian peasants lived in the countryside and there were substantial Polish and Jewish communities. The Jews were murdered by the Nazis and only a negligible Jewish minority remains today. As for the Poles the Nazi Occupation and Stalin's purges in the late 1940s combined to eradicate all that remained of the intelligentsia. The most renowned of those who were able to avoid this fate was Czeszlaw Milosz, who received the Nobel Prize for literature in 1980.

As a result of the interwar Polish–Lithuanian conflict concerning Vilna's state affiliation, the few hundred thousand Poles who remained after 1945 saw Lithuanians and the Lithuanian Soviet government as their antagonists. The poorly-educated Polish rural population thus turned instead to Moscow and the local Russians. For instance, schoolchildren were taught Russian rather than Lithuanian. This was made easier by the Soviet authorities effectively preventing the population of Lithuania from making contact with or learning about Poland. This alienation was reinforced by the Communist regime in Warsaw which, out of consideration for Moscow, repressed Poland's historic bonds with Lithuania, White Russia and Ukraine, i.e. the history of the Polish–Lithuanian commonwealth.[29] However, nostalgia over Vilna persisted among the Polish intelligentsia, who were critical of the government. A manifestation of this was Andrej Wajda's film *A Chronicle of Love*, based on a script by Tadeusz Konwicki, which was set in Vilna during the summer before the outbreak of the Second World War.

A collective regional identity remained among the Polish-speaking

[29] Stephen R. Burant and Voytek Zubek, 'Eastern Europe's memories and new realities: resurrecting the Polish–Lithuanian Union', *East European Politics and Societies*, vol.7, no.2 (1993), p.375.

population in Vilna during the Soviet era, but this was not oriented towards Poland or the values associated with democracy and civil rights. Such values were disseminated in Poland in the 1970s and culminated in the Solidarity Movement in 1980 and the change of government in 1989. In assuming a pro-Soviet position hostile to the Lithuanian popular front, Sajudis, in 1988-91, the Polish-speaking population demonstrated a Soviet mentality and identification with the Soviet Union. In extended form this standpoint indicates a link to White Russia and Moscow, and further alienation from both Lithuania and Poland. During the Soviet period the Vilna region was transformed, politically and culturally, from a Polish cultural centre facing east into a Soviet outpost facing west.

CARPATHO-RUTHENIA

Carpatho-Ruthenia, or Zakarpatska, exemplifies an emerging ethno-region that was a potential actor during the Soviet era. This area belonged to Hungary up to 1918, to Czechoslovakia after 1920 and to Soviet Ukraine after 1945. In 1991 it became part of the republic of Ukraine. Alongside those who consider themselves Russian, Ukrainian, Slovakian or Hungarian, there exists an autochthonous group calling itself '*Ruskie*', or 'Ruthenian' in Western languages, with subgroups with other names. The Ruthenians in Carpatho-Ruthenia and eastern Slovakia have politically mobilised themselves since 1989-91 with a distinct ethno-territorial profile.[30]

Alexander Duleba, a Ruthenian scholar from Presov in Slovakia, has claimed that Carpatho-Ruthenia is a region with a specific character due not only to ethnic but also to geopolitical conditions.[31] He argues that the ancient identity in this area survived the Soviet period; moreover he finds a precedent for self-rule in Carpatho-Ruthenia's autonomous status during the period of Czechoslovakia's dissolution between October 1938 and March 1939. Duleba also asserts that since the state affiliation and status of Carpatho-Ruthenia changed six times during the twentieth century, those who speak

---

[30] Ivan Pop and Volodymyr Halas, 'Ukrajina a Zakarpatsko: dilemma spolocenskej a geopolitickej stratégie', *Medzinárodné Otázky*, no.4 (1993), pp.79-92.

[31] Alexander Duleba, 'Zákládné geopolitické characteristiky Zakarpatska', manuscript, n.d.

the Rusin language have maintained their sense of cohesion and identity as a border-country despite profound international changes. As for belonging to independent Ukraine after 1991, it has been said that Zakarpatska is 'as far from Kiev as it is from God'. This quip also hints that the population does not want Kiev to interfere in the region's internal affairs. Meanwhile, the Ruthenians have come to recognise that the region's ability to assert its own identity is wholly dependent on external factors, especially great power relations in Europe. It was hardly possible to develop an independent identity during the period of Moscow's rule (1945–91), but in the last Soviet years under Gorbachev, these conditions changed.

Soviet domination implied that the Ruthenian political elite were subjected to Russification and central rule, and were approached as a 'provincial' part of the Ukrainian elite – according to Duleba, 'emerging from their shadow only during the early years of the Gorbachev regime in the late 1980s'. In 1987 Ruthenian politicians drafted a project geared toward the regional development of Carpatho-Ruthenia, with the aim of achieving a 'special free economic zone'. In 1989, a commission was set up with the authorities' approval to draft a plan for an economic free zone, as well as for a recreational zone for the citizens of the Ukrainian SSR.

The ethno-regional political mobilisation in Carpatho-Ruthenia was already under way during the the Soviet years. The region's relations to the outside world possess an independent dynamic that already existed before Ukraine's independence in 1991.

THE KALININGRAD OBLAST

Northern East Prussia, the Kaliningrad *Oblast*, constitutes a region in the strictly cartographic sense, but one that lacked both a territorial and an ethnoterritorial identity during the Communist period. The region was long part of Prussia, and belonged to Germany till 1945. The overwhelming majority of the population of approximately 1 million had a distinct ethno-regional identity. These Germans disappeared in 1945 and were succeeded by Russians and other Soviet citizens from various parts of the empire. The bulk of this contingent consisted of military professionals, a group who tend not to strike roots in the areas where they are stationed. Other categories of Russians, such as university staff, likewise tended to view Kaliningrad (former Königsberg), as a temporary stopping-place on their career path. Indeed it is impossible to discern any particular identity in this area during the entire period 1945-91. After spending a total of five months in the Kaliningrad district between 1990 and 1993, the West German journalist Ulla Lachauer concluded:[32]

Nothing more than a waterlogged skeleton is left of the cultural landscape. Only a rough outline of Gumbinnen remains – a few abstract lines, no face... "The Murdered Echo" is the name of a song by Vladimir Vysotskii. This is the most dreadful of all his songs. The singer describes a situation which, *mutatis mutandis*, reminds one very much of the Kaliningrad Oblast. Somewhere in the mountains there lived a strange echo that answered the cries of people. Only the echo and nothing else answered their calls for help and sent them back loud and exactly as they had been uttered. One night, unknown persons – presumably drunk – killed the echo, choked it and trampled on it. The next morning they stowed away the already silent echo. The Kaliningrad district is a place without an echo – and still today it is all too clearly more akin to a madhouse than to a republic.... Looking for a role of its own, the region could emancipate itself to become a prostitute.

The Soviet residents in Kaliningrad were told nothing about the area's history, but were given the impression that it was a Baltic and Russian territory temporarily occupied by the Germans in 1941-5. The Soviet authorities attempted to eradicate every trace of German culture from the area: the ruins of the royal palace in Königsberg were blown up, the statue of Immanuel Kant was demolished (it was re-erected in 1992), estates and arable land were allowed to fall into decay. Only after 1989 was the German history in the area officially acknowledged, and that for economic reasons. The objective was to attract hardworking Germans from other parts of the Soviet Union – after 1991 from Russia and Kazakhstan – by inviting them to settle in a 'German' area, and use the presence of a German-speaking citizenry to encourage banks and large-scale enterprises in the Federal Republic of Germany to invest in the area and extend subsidies.[33] Kaliningrad's

---

[32] Ulla Lachauer, *Die Brücke von Tilsit. Begegnungen mit Preussens Osten und Russlands Westen* (Reinbeck bei Hamburg, 1994), pp.63, 242, 383, 385.

[33] Alvydas Nikzentaitis, 'Das Kaliningrader Gebiet im Spannungsfeld internationaler Interessen', *Osteuropa*, no.10 (1995), pp.327-35.

tendency to function as a regional actor was wholly a product of post-Soviet uncertainties. It was not based on any particular dynamic rooted in the Soviet period.

Conclusions

The notion of regions emerged in Central Europe late in the Soviet era and took on new significance after it ended. This indicated that local politicians, economic actors and cultural officials estimated that their home community stood to gain if it could create a positive image of itself *vis-à-vis* the rest of 'grey and drab' former Communist Europe. It is not a question of an uninterrupted tradition dating from the interwar period, since there were not regions that operated as collective actors in Central and Eastern Europe under Communist rule. Today, when politicians in Poland and Kaliningrad wish to bolster their regions, they try to convey that the territory has become the bearer of ethnically determined characteristics, that the German element remains despite the absence of any German people, and that an area once dominated by Germans should act as a magnet for German capital. In Transylvania the ethnic struggle is the critical issue: the Hungarians seek to enhance their status by making their situation known to Western Europe and the Council of Europe.

The question of a region's socio-cultural character, and the way in which it is 'handed over' and transformed is a complex one. It involves the effect of psychological processes such as socialisation, perceptions and projection. In a conversation on the future prospects of his area, a Polish politician from the Polish section of old East Prussia claimed that in Elbląg county only the native-born pay their taxes and display financial integrity, 'although they no longer speak German'. Conversely, the Polish immigrants evaded taxes.[34] This suggests that it is the socialisation of the individual into inherited traditions that determines individual behaviour, rather than affiliation with a territory and given social norms. Those with German roots acted in certain ways, and immigrants did not adopt those ways. Christian Graf von Krockow, who visited Polish Pomerania and specifically the county of Slupsk in the mid-1980s,

---

[34] Conversation with Marek Sitnicki, member of the town council of Kwidzyn, at Karlskrona, 19 September 1995.

provides a contrasting view. The infrastructure in Slupsk made a different impression from that in other parts of Poland:[35]

> Are the burdens of tradition lighter in the recently-acquired territories, where almost everything had to start from the beginning? Do people turn to the future more energetically here than in the old and central parts of Poland? There, says our interpreter who is from Warsaw, the main roads are in a worse state than in Pomerania.

Regions are constructions. In this chapter we have examined a few that have in common their location within the formerly socialist Central Europe, as well as relatively long histories under their own names and without independent statehood. In everyday language they are generally accepted and recognised as concepts.

In the early Communist era Transylvania did enjoy autonomy, but under Ceauşescu it was transformed into an arena for political struggle between the Hungarian population and an increasingly Romanian-nationalist state government. Towards the end of the period, the already much-depleted German element (Saxons and Swabians) began emigrating in large numbers, with the result that little remained subsequently of the region's heritage as a Hungarian and German outpost in Orthodox South-East Europe. The name itself, Transylvania, has retained a major symbolic function in Hungarian historical consciousness: still today Hungarians perceive not only the ethnic Hungarians living in the area but the territory itself as essential to their sense of identity.

During the Communist period Silesia consisted of approximately ten counties in Poland. An inconspicuous German population continued to exist in the area and reactivated itself and greatly increased in numbers after 1989. As it became economically advantageous to assert a German ethnicity the Germans ceased to be social undesirables. It was good sense to associate with German symbols rather than cling to specifically Silesian ones. For instance, place names linked to the time of German occupation were chosen over Germanised versions of older Slavic names, although the right to local self-rule was also asserted in the name of one's *Heimat*. In the process of reconstructing a Silesian identity, a living Silesian tradition could be invoked, but the new political and economic situation after 1989 was a necessary precondition for

---

[35] Christian Graf von Krockow, *Die Reise nach Pommern* (Stuttgart, 1985), p.240.

it. It was not a question of unbroken continuity from 1944 to 1989.

Like the *kresy* for the intellectuals in Poland, the Vilna area existed as a region in historical Poland, but a shift of identity took place there. The Polish-speaking people were Sovietised and allied themselves with Belarussians and Russians in an effort to counter Lithuanisation. Polish tradition ultimately died out in a population that lacked an intellectual stratum of its own. Those who rose in social class were Russified. To some extent the area preserved its ethnic distinctiveness *vis-à-vis* Lithuania, but it was nonetheless de-Polonised as effectively as Scania was de-Danified between 1658 (the peace of Roskilde) and 1710 (the Battle of Helsingborg).

The Kaliningrad district, once a part of East Prussia, was thoroughly Sovietised and Russified. No specific regional identity evolved in this area, partly because the Russian intellectuals, those who sustain culture, viewed their residence there as no more than a step in their career path. This was true also of the substantial body of officers in the area. When the Soviet Union was near to disintegration, the local elite began referring to a special 'Königsbergian' identity in an effort to attract German funds. The attempt largely failed, and the region has yet to carve out an identity of its own in the post-Soviet Baltic.

Between 1945 and 1985 Carpatho-Ruthenia led a rather obscure existence on the outskirts of Ukraine. However, the centrifugal consequences of Gorbachev's *perestroika* and *glasnost* gave rise to manifestations of a specific Ruthenian regional identity. This identity comprised an ethnic core, but was oriented towards the entire administrative entity. This development had a spill-over effect into eastern Slovakia. The course of events in Carpatho-Ruthenia indicates a certain 'geopolitical determinism' behind tenacious regional identities, as has been highlighted by Ruthenian intellectuals such as Ivan Pop in Ukraine and Alexander Duleba in Slovakia. This region's cross-border position makes it of particular interest.

Moravia and Silesia in Czechoslovakia (after 1992 the Czech Republic) provide examples of repeatedly failed attempts to forge a specific identity through references to historic names. In retrospect, it seems more than a coincidence that Tomás G. Masaryk, the main figure in Czech democratic nationalism and president of the republic from 1918 to 1935, was from Moravia. The historical entity and linguistic unity of Bohemia-Moravia served as unifying factors outweighing the separatist potential, although Moravia is somewhat more agrarian and less secularised than Czech society. People in Moravian Silesia apparently also identify with the Czech state.

The emergence of ethno-regional movements in Silesia and Carpatho-Ruthenia, and the regional image conveyed by the leadership in Kaliningrad, are mainly indications of the desire to attract Western capital for economic growth. In both Carpatho-Ruthenia and Kaliningrad there has been talk of establishing an economic 'free zone'. Once historical arguments have been mobilised, they can assume their own dynamic and may persuade even outside actors to perceive the reconstructed or constructed region as 'real'. Thus we may tentatively conclude that the Soviet era did not result in the total eradication of the potential for regional identity.

Silesia, with its links to Germany, and Carpatho-Ruthenia, with its cross-border character, appear to have the greatest potential for becoming regions in the West European sense. The Kaliningrad area seems likely to remain a province closely supervised by Moscow, without the possibility of acting independently. In Moravia-Silesia the distinction from the Czech people has been so slight that regionally oriented actors have not gained sufficient ground among the population to assert themselves in relation to Prague. In the years up to 1991 the Poles in Lithuania were definitively Sovietised and alienated from Polish culture. An enduring consequence of the Soviet era is that the Vilna area, so prominent in Polish national mythology, has forever ceased to be a Polish region.

VIADRINA TO THE ODER–NEISSE LINE
HISTORICAL EVOLUTION AND THE PROSPECTS OF REGIONAL COOPERATION

Hans-Åke Persson

On 17 June 1991 the Federal Republic of Germany (FRG) signed a friendship treaty with Poland. It emphasised the need for cross-border cooperation in an ever more integrated Europe, to promote closer relations between regions, cities and organisations on either side of the Oder–Neisse line. The frontier-area between Poland and Germany, from the Baltic Sea to the Czech border, was divided into four regions; Pomerania, Pro-Europe-Viadrina,[1] Spree-Neisse-Bober and Neisse-Nisa-Nysa. The collective designation for this new zone of cooperation was Oderraum.[2]

There were many reasons for the introduction of regional cooperation in Oderraum. First, throughout the post-war era the border had symbolised the undefined relationship between Poland and Germany, as well as between the German Democratic Republic (GDR) and the FRG. The border was legally fixed after 3 October 1990, when the GDR formally became part of the FRG. Oderraum thus represents an effort to forge a stable peace between two countries with a long history of mutual conflict. Moreover, the Oder–Neisse line symbolises the separation of a Western Europe that is increasingly integrated both politically and economically from a Central and Eastern Europe experiencing dissolution and revolutionary changes.

However, the implementation of the Oderraum project has been plagued by problems, which have proved more difficult to overcome than could be foreseen in the initial euphoria following the Soviet collapse. This is partly because Germany and Poland represent two essentially different political cultures. In Oderraum, the federatively constructed Germany has encountered a neighbour

---

[1] Viadrina was the Latin name for the Oder.
[2] *Zeitschrift für kommunale Selbstverwaltung*, G4416e (Nov 1994), p.487.

ruled by a strong central authority. For Poland an integration and modernisation process in the form of regional cooperation may act as a challenge to its established state tradition.

This chapter has two aims: first, to examine the development of cross-border cooperation as a political notion, as it was formulated and as it evolved in Western Europe under the guidance of the European Union (EU), and secondly to address the sluggish historical processes that have been a characteristic of this part of Europe. Common belief systems and institutions are formed over long periods of time, and the alteration and eradication of structures is also a lengthy process. The possibility of creating a region or of initiating regional cooperation rests upon the similarities and differences between the political, economic, social and cultural structures that are to be linked.

To appreciate the difficulties of the Oderraum project, we must consider the way in which the generations of people who have inhabited the Oder-Neisse border area – Vandals, Slavs, Germanic peoples, Brandenburgers, Prussian Germans and Poles – have been affected by the events of history. The central authority – whether in Berlin, Warsaw, Moscow or Brussels – has been the final arbiter shaping the lives of those residing there. Meanwhile, networks, collaboration and channels of contact have developed among people, implying a certain continuity at the local level.

The Region as Project

As a result of European integration and the building of supranational institutions, the national central authorities have faced a challenge from two directions. First, the situation in Western Europe continues to proceed towards greater unity and supranational decision-making within the framework of the EU. Secondly – in reaction to this development, this 'centralism of Brussels bureaucrats' – the EU member-states have introduced the so-called subsidiarity principle. The main tenet behind this decentralisation principle is that decisions should be made as close to the affected population as possible. The signing of the Maastricht Treaty agreed in December 1994 may entail a boost for the regions, a division of power between them and the EU at the expense of the state. At the same time, regional entities, together with the nation-states and Brussels, enhance the integrative dynamic of the EU.[3]

So far, however, great variations are still to be found among the regional entities, which therefore cannot compete effectively with either the central power or the supranational sphere. The political notion of a 'Europe of the regions' has not yet materialised, but there are regions in Europe that have been granted executive power in the form of self-rule without formally being granted statehood, and thus constitute political realities. It is thus important to distinguish between different types of regions, not least if we are to consider the Oderraum project's chances for success.

For the sake of brevity, only two conceptions of region will be presented here, namely the *historical region* and the *transnational region*. The historical region is defined on the basis of the historical, cultural roots and traditions of the population. The historical process whereby the region emerges, involving historically and culturally given notions of affinity, often plays a significant role. Most importantly, history often fosters a regional identity that subsists long after the region has been stripped of its political and administrative relevance.[4] Older identities and regions can be revitalised for political purposes. This may be exemplified by the GDR's incorporation into West Germany. In autumn 1990, in an effort to neutralise the differences between the two German societies, the Kohl government reconstructed the earlier *Länder*-division of East Germany. This division had been abolished in the GDR in 1952, since it was perceived as an impediment to the realisation of socialist society. The government was now resuscitating the historical regions. Saxons were once again Saxons, and an ancient identity was thus restored. This deliberate activation of a historical region as a basis for identity represented an attempt to bridge the differences between the two German states that had developed in such markedly divergent directions for almost a half a century.[5]

The Oderraum project has no such foundations to mobilise – quite the contrary. Transboundary regional cooperation is here

---

[3] Franz H.U. Borkenhagen, 'Regions in Europe', *Aussenpolitik*, no.2 (1994).

[4] Rune Johansson, Ralf Rönnquist and Sven Tägil, 'Territorialstaten i kris' in Sven Tägil (ed.), *Europa – historiens återkomst* (Hedemora, 1993), pp.16-17.

[5] Hans-Åke Persson, 'Soweit die deutsche Zunge klingt' in Tägil (ed.), *Europa*, p.296.

intended to raze a barrier between two countries, to revitalise the border-area and to secure long-term friendly relations between the states.[6] Oderraum can thus be described as a transnational region.

A transnational region can in some cases have a historical identity founded on either the fact that it has been partitioned by nation-states, or has switched between nation-states during the course of history, as is the case for Tyrol and Alsace. Up to the Second World War, the population of the Oder region, for instance, had been homogeneous, since the area was a part of Germany. However, the Germans were expelled from the land east of the Oder–Neisse line at the end of the war, and Poland was pushed further west towards Oder–Neisse. The river thus became a distinct partition between two separate cultures.

The success of this cross-border collaboration rests on two factors: first, a free market implies that state boundaries are of diminished relevance, and secondly, decision-making is decentralised. The region must be able to resolve questions without the interference of either Warsaw or Bonn. Accordingly, hierarchies within both politics and industry must be broken. Thereafter, on the basis of the Western European experience with cross-border cooperation, so-called functional regions and networks will proliferate across state boundaries.[7]

THE WEST EUROPEAN MODEL

The post-war years saw the rise of cross-border cooperation and integration in various parts of Western Europe. Border conflicts of the traditional, interstate kind have been virtually eliminated. Regionalism has become the instrument used, enhancing dynamic interaction in an ever more united Europe. The region as a notion is seen as a significant means for enhancing cooperation between Western Europe and Central, Eastern and South-eastern Europe. The model for this type of cross-border cooperation, Euregio, has been borrowed from Western Europe.[8]

Euregio was first conceived to express the idea of a Europe

---

[6] *Zeitschrift für kommunale Selbstverwaltung*, G4416E (Nov 1994), p.487.

[7] Borkenhagen, 'Regions in Europe', pp.186-7.

[8] *Zeitschrift für kommunale Selbstverwaltung*, G4416E (Nov 1994), pp.491-4.

united at the local level, and thus it is not surprising that it was first developed in the European Community's core area where West Germany, France and Benelux meet. The nation-state has approved Western Europe's cross-border cooperation in the form of Euroregions, thus imparting legitimacy to regional and local collaborative efforts. The German–Dutch cooperation over the border region has been particularly successful, and after some thirty years of progress, has come to symbolise West European cross-border collaboration, and been studied to determine how future transnational regions should be forged.[9]

The cities of Gronau and Enschede were the first to begin cooperation across the German-Dutch border. The initiative was taken by the German side and had been preceded by consultations between representatives of the German and Dutch governments. In 1965 the collaboration was formalised under the label Euregio, and today it consists of four interwoven regions along the German–Dutch border with a total population of 1.9 million. In 1978 a Euregio Parliament was established, in which counties, cities and villages on both sides of the frontier were represented. The Parliament exercises no political power, its primary function being to expand and coordinate the cooperation within the region. Euregio has its own budget but is also subsidised by both the EU and the two governments.[10]

In the framework of this cooperation, great importance was originally attached to cultural and educational matters. This was in order to increase understanding between the German and Dutch peoples and by extension to make possible the mobilisation of the population around a distinctive identity of its own, which would be conducive to the internal resolution of regional problems. Measures intended to improve the infrastructure and environment of the region followed. The region's appeals to both the then European Community and the respective national governments were effective: the German–Dutch border was classified as a 'crisis area', and funds thus allotted for the restructuring and monitoring of its industry. The result was a fall in unemployment. This early

---

[9] James Scott, 'Dutch–German Euroregions: a model for transboundary cooperation?', Paper, Institute for Regional Development and Structural Planning, Berlin, 1995.

[10] Borkenhagen, 'Regions in Europe', p.185. See also Scott, 'Dutch–German Euroregions', p.18.

success vindicated the existence of the region as a unit.

However important social, economic and cultural matters may be, the region must also function as a forum in which questions relevant to the region itself can be formulated, discussed and resolved. For instance, the region must be able, in a joint effort, to argue its own case with the central authority through lobbying or other means. It has thus been possible to counterbalance the area's peripheral position in relation to central governments.

Regional cooperation in Euregio has developed because West European collaboration has prioritised the regions, and because the central governments have resolved to allow the regions more decision-making powers. There are three fundamental elements in the Euregio model: integration, subsidiarity and synergy.[11] *Integration* stands for the importance of the transnational region in bringing the nation-states closer together: it is to be viewed as an area of mutual understanding, a microcosm of international collaboration. *Subsidiarity* means decentralisation, nearness and the constant interaction between different decision-making levels.[12] The combination of these elements results in *synergy*.

The EU's more comprehensive regional policies are handled by Interreg, an interregional organ founded after the dissolution of the Soviet Union and the reunification of Germany. One of Interreg's main functions is to give financial support to the regions along the EU's external frontiers. The West European experience of continued integration is adopted as a frame of reference for establishing transnational regions between Germany and Poland. Transnational cooperation between these two countries has been initiated by Brussels in the Oder region which, if it is to succeed, must somehow defeat the historically evolved suspicions between the peoples living on either side of the border.

The River System in the Borderland during the Age of Nationalism

Over time the names Odra and Lausitzer Neisse have had various negative connotations including expulsion, ethnic cleansing and

---

[11] Scott, 'Dutch–German Euroregions', p.21.

[12] See Bo Stråth, *Folkhemmet mot Europa. Ett historiskt perspektiv på 90-talet* (Falun, 1993), pp.300ff.

the Cold War. However, this was not always so. There was a time, early in the nineteenth century, when steamships carried both cargo and tourists on the river.

Before the First World War Oder-Neisse debouched from land that was wholly German. The river originates in the Carpathians, which at the time were within the Dual Monarchy of Austria-Hungary. On its way to the Baltic it flowed only through German cities, including Frankfurt-an-der-Oder – also through Pomerania, Brandenburg and Silesia, all parts of Prussia which after 1871 was the dominant state in the German empire.

In his *Journeys through the Mark of Brandenburg* the German author Theodor Fontane (1819-98), who wrote of Prussian society in the nineteenth century, described passenger and cargo steamers leaving Frankfurt-an-der-Oder regularly twice a week. On Sundays and Wednesdays they would sail from the docks of this old city, arriving ten hours later in Stettin. On the way they docked at Küstrin and Schwedt to pick up and drop off passengers, and to load and unload agricultural produce and other cargo:[13]

It is Saturday and 5 o'clock in the morning. Alongside the broad quay in the old city of Frankfurt, under the shadow of tall houses and churches – all more or less resembling the Kölner Quai between the Schiffsbrücke and the Eisenbahnbrücke – the steamship lies spluttering and puffing. It is the time for departure. We are hardly on board when the gangway is pulled up. Without more ado, the steamer pulls away from the bank and sets off downstream. On our left the city vanishes in the dawn mist; on the right, through poplars and willows, we see this hilly country with a name that, after all, has a historical ring to it – Kunersdorf. During our journey we will often be reminded of this name.

During the nineteenth century, the Oder and its tributaries formed one of many river systems in Germany, and part of a network that included railways and roads. This infrastructure was part of a cultural terrain that included estates, small and large villages and expanding cities. The area was predominantly agricultural and managed by the large landowners, 'Junkers' who had been the land's social power-base since the sixteenth century.

The Oder–Neisse area cannot be described as a region, if region implies a specific identity that would give the riparian

[13] Theodor Fontane, *Wanderungen durch die Mark Brandenburg* (Leipzig, 1980), p.14.

population a sense of internal solidarity and affinity. However, the particular character of the river area did create the basis for local networks among peasants and townspeople. At the turn of the century the mainly rural and sleepy environment surrounding an expanding Berlin experienced economic and social changes. During the nineteenth century the ethnic composition of the population by and to the east of the river was relatively homogeneous. The main language was German, or various dialects of German, but several Polish dialects, including *Wasserpolnisch* were also spoken.

Due to migrations, wars and the revision of political boundaries the area ultimately acquired the character of a buffer zone and a demarcation between Germanic and Slavic peoples. Over time, the Germans had come to dominate and colonise the expanse east of Oder–Neisse. From the consolidation of the German state in 1871 up to the outbreak of the First World War, Germany's eastern sections were subjected to extensive Germanisation campaigns. In 1885 Polish-speaking Russian and Austrian citizens were expelled, and in 1886 the central power initiated a programme intended to buy out the property of the Polish nobility, and spent 150 million German marks on such purchases. Between 1886 and 1915, 22,000 Germans settled in Prussian Poland under the auspices of a settlement programme launched by the Prussian state.[14]

The so-called *Kulturkampf*[15] had particularly dire repercussions for the Poles. Before the establishment of the state, those in Prussia's eastern provinces had been subjects in a Prussia that was dynastically defined. After 1871 they became a minority in a nationally defined Germany that was becoming increasingly hostile to all non-German groups. The nation-building process brought a dual pressure on the Poles, since they were both Catholic and ethnically distinct. From 1873 German was the only language of instruction allowed in elementary schools.[16]

---

[14] James Harold, *A German Identity* (London, 1989), p.90. See also Elizabeth Wiskemann, *Germany's Eastern Neighbours* (London, 1956), p.11.

[15] The *Kulturkampf* was the struggle in the 1870s between the German state and the Catholic Church.

[16] Richard Blanke, *Prussian Poland in the German Empire, 1871–1900* (New York, 1981), pp.17-37. See also Finn Mygind, 'Demokrati på preussisk. Det tyske kejserrige, 1866/71–1918', *Den jyske Historiker*, nos 43-4 (1988), p.94.

In Posen the Polish nobility had been able to induce a Polish national consciousness in all levels of society. Friction in the borderland increased when Prussian patriotism became ever more closely associated with German nationalism, as occurred throughout the nineteenth century but especially after 1871. The situation in Posen was linked to the question of a Polish nation and state, while simultaneously accentuating and questioning Germany's future position in Europe.[17]

History had favoured the German element in Silesia, which was an ethnically heterogeneous area, but numerous non-German industrial workers recruited from the countryside began to recognise that they were ethnic Poles. The industrialisation and urbanisation process of the nineteenth century radically altered the existing structures. Industrialisation and the rapidly growing mining industry in the Ruhr required a substantial increase in labour over a few decades, triggering a westbound migration of Germans and Poles from the borderland and the Oder–Neisse region. The prospect of better housing, higher wages, shorter working hours and enhanced status persuaded many to abandon the Junker estates in East Prussia and embark on a 1,000-km journey to a better future in the Ruhr.[18]

The westbound migrations within the German Empire began early in tandem with the establishment of the state, but did not gain momentum until the 1890s. By the start of the First World War some 2 million people had moved from the eastern to the western parts of Germany spurred by the relative overpopulation in the eastern parts, and the rapid expansion of mining in the Ruhr. The labour-intensive coal and other heavy industries had quickly exhausted the available labour force, leading to recruitment in the older Junker areas east of the Elbe. The targeted group were the agricultural workers who faced a shortage of work and were easily persuaded to move west. One such group was that of the so-called *Ruhrpolen*.[19]

---

[17] Werner Conze, *Die deutsche Nation* (Göttingen, 1963), pp.50ff.

[18] Hans-Ulrich Wehler, 'Die Polen im Ruhrgebiet bis 1918' in *Moderne deutsche Sozialgeschichte* (Berlin, 1966).

[19] Christopher Klessman, 'Long-distance migration in industrial Germany: the case of the "Ruhr Poles"' in Klaus Bade (ed.), *Population, Labour and Migration in 19th and 20th-Century Germany* (Leamington Spa, 1987), pp.102-5.

The Borderland and the Resurrected Polish State

During Prussian expansion in the nineteenth century, the Oder–Neisse population witnessed major changes that affected state and society, such as nationalisation policy, the rationalisation of large-landed property, labour migrations westward, and the processes of modernisation and industrialisation. In the course of the First World War, both rural and urban centres were virtually drained of their young men who were sent to fight for the Fatherland. Ethnic Poles, who lacked such a Fatherland and came from areas under Prussian control, were forcibly mobilised to serve the German war effort. In the aftermath of the war Germany's eastern boundary was pushed westward. Meanwhile, Poland's new western boundary lay closer to the Oder–Neisse, and the result of this was that a million Germans moved west. Thus, after several centuries of German expansion, the east-west pendulum swung back in favour of the Slavs.

The borderland became the focus of extensive deliberations at Versailles. Germany lost to Poland both the territories inhabited by the ethnic Poles and those with mixed populations. However, it was understood that the Oder–Neisse and its vicinity would continue to lie within Prussia, while Posen and parts of Silesia would be transferred to Poland. The German–Polish boundary question was put before the people in referendums, several of which demonstrated the presence of serious social tensions. The one planned to take place in Teschen (Těšín, Cieszyn) between Poland and Czechoslovakia had to be cancelled, although the international commission was already in place. That in Oberschlesien (Gorny Sląsk) between Poland and Germany was preceded by violent riots. Both regions were important for mining and national and social antagonisms were rife.[20]

The referendums forced individuals in the borderland to take a position over the area to which they wished to belong; they had to choose between Germany and Poland, i.e. between two competing nation-state projects. The new boundary was to traverse historically evolved regions such as Silesia, and thus cut through cohesive local communities.

[20] Tom Gullberg, ' "Folket har bestämt...", Folkomröstningar och det europeiska statssystemets omstrukturering' in Max Engman (ed.), *När imperier faller. Studier kring riksupplösningar och nya stater* (Stockholm, 1994).

SILESIA: A HISTORICAL REGION

The comprehensive river area, stretching from the Baltic to the Carpathians and from Berlin to Warsaw, can best be described as an unstable buffer zone, with the exception of one area: Silesia (Slask), which was a historically evolved region with a heterogeneous population. The Versailles Treaty stipulated that this region should be divided into two parts.

Many of the inhabitants of this region saw themselves primarily as Silesians. Their view was rooted in the notion that a territorial identity existed, which implied that, whether one was mono- or bilingual, one was first and foremost a Silesian. Silesia was understood as a historical region with a specific dynamic and evolution.

Lower and Upper Silesia lie in the long valley on either side of the Oder's southernmost fork. The labels 'Lower' and 'Upper' are strictly topographical terms, and refer to the river's lower and upper reaches. The principalities of Oberschlesien and Niederschlesien were founded in 1163. Subsequent divisions brought new principalities, and the bonds to Poland became successively weaker in the Middle Ages. In the thirteenth century, under the Polish duke Henry I, a German immigration to Silesia began. This also comprised Walloon, Flemish and Italian merchants, craftsmen, monks and priests. The Polish influence was weakened, and was superseded by a powerful German influence in the form of colonisation, state-formation and political dependence on the kingdom of Bohemia.[21]

During the fifteenth, sixteenth and seventeenth centuries, Silesia was plagued by the wars of religion in Central Europe. The conflict between Hussites and Catholics had repercussions on Silesia in the fifteenth century, and both Calvinism and Lutheranism gained ground following the Reformation. Silesia was incorporated into the Habsburg Empire in the sixteenth century, and in the context of the Counter-Reformation this favoured the Catholics. The mainly German-speaking town of Breslau (Wroclaw) remained Catholic and was subordinated to the Polish archbishop in Gnesen (Gniezno), which ensured a certain Polish influence in that area. Frederick II of Prussia made inheritance claims on Silesia in 1740. The region was partitioned in 1742, following the Austrian War

---

[21] Kaziemirz Piwarski, 'The Historical Development of the Polish Western Territories' in *Polish Western Territories* (Poznan' Instytut Zachodni, 1959).

of Succession: Lower Silesia and the main part of Upper Silesia was incorporated into Prussia, while the Habsburgs received a smaller section in the south, which included the towns of Teschen and Troppau.

The link between religious and national affiliation was not as uniform in Silesia as in other parts of the border area. In certain instances, mainly in the Habsburg past, Poles converted to Protestantism in order to assert their distinctiveness from the German Catholics. Conversely, in Prussian Silesia they asserted their Catholic identity for similar purposes.[22] However, language and religious affiliation were not the only factors that distinguished Polish- and German-speaking Silesians from each other. In the nineteenth century, Silesia went through rapid industrialisation and intensive expansion, and the Germans were soon associated with both technical progress and capitalism, while Poles were over-represented in the working class. It could be argued that events in Silesia were fostering greater congruence between class and ethnicity, but the population generally saw itself not as Polish or German but as Silesian, which may have been because since the Middle Ages the region had lain outside Polish state-constructions. It may also be that the region's inhabitants had become interdependent through social relations evolved over centuries, and that some form of regional identity existed which lessened the relevance of ethno-national distinctions.

Around the turn of the century structural changes in both the political and economic realms were increasingly relevant to the ethno-national composition of Silesia. The rapidly increasing exploitation of Silesia's resources proceeded parallel with a notable process of Germanisation. The sense of regional affinity was challenged primarily by German nationalism and German politics. At first the Polish reaction was slight, but it gained strength in the ensuing decades.

Following unification in 1871 Germany, as it expanded and developed, became increasingly attractive in comparison with Poland, whose future remained uncertain. Integration and assimilation into the German-speaking communities could bring the Poles social and economic security. German was a universal language, and knowledge of it could open the door to education, not least

[22] Wiskemann, *Germany's Eastern Neighbours*, p.23.

in technical subjects. German was after 1872 in fact the sole language of instruction. At general elections German industrialists urged the Polish labour force to vote in accordance with the wishes of the former.[23]

The *Kulturkampf* launched by Bismarck concerned domestic issues, yet it had repercussions on the self-perception of the Poles, as well as on the quest for a Polish nation-state. The Catholic Polish population suffered tangible oppression in the borderland of Posen and Pomerania; conditions were somewhat more comfortable for the Catholic Church in Silesia, since it included a German as well as Polish congregation. Many Silesians were bilingual and over several generations had acquired both German and Polish roots.

By the turn of the century it was estimated that the national campaign had achieved its objectives in Germany's eastern parts. Meanwhile, Polish nationalism had gained ground among ethnic Poles in the border area. The same was true in Silesia. The development was well exemplified by the case of Wojciech Korfanty, a well-known Polish nationalist in Silesia who was elected to the German Parliament in 1903 to represent the Katowice constituency. His principal task, he said, was to make Polish national interests an issue in the *Reichstag*. He thus broke with a tradition promoted by the Polish Catholic clergy, who desired consensus and strove mainly for greater local self-rule in Silesia and, to a lesser extent, increased rights for ethnic Poles.[24]

Korfanty was to play an important role in the referendums and the inflamed national conflicts after 1918. A notion prevalent among both German and Polish nationals was that Upper Silesia should remain intact, since it was quite prosperous and was seen as an economic unit. Both groups were prepared to grant autonomy to the area. Up to this point the national groups were in agreement, yet they became unyielding when Upper Silesia's state affiliation was to be determined.[25] The historical region was to be preserved, while the decisive question was whether Silesia should answer to Berlin or Warsaw. The Allies resolved the issue through a popular

---

[23] Blanke, *Prussian Poland*, p.22.

[24] Thomas Urban, *Deutsche in Polen Geschichte und Gegenwart einer Minderheit* (Munich, 1993), pp.32-7. See also Blanke, *Prussian Poland*, p.222.

[25] Wiskemann, *Germany's Eastern Neighbours*, p.29.

referendum held on 20 May 1921. 707,393 Upper Silesians voted in favour of Germany, while 479,365 chose Poland – a devastating outcome for the latter since some 300,000 Polish-speaking Silesians had voted for incorporation into Germany.[26]

The results of this referendum have been interpreted in various ways. Some claim that the boundary demarcations of the referendum had favoured Germany, since Germany had been able to mobilise its emigrants, and others that Polish-speaking Silesians felt obliged to vote for incorporation into Germany. These are only partial explanations; indeed there is much to suggest that national identity had little part in the referendum. When it was held some time had passed since the end of the war, and it is quite credible that 300,000 Polish-speaking Silesians should have put personal benefit before some diffuse notion of nationalism. In other words, the German alternative offered the possibility of a secure future and greater opportunities.[27]

The drawing of the new boundary became highly complicated because Polish and German dwellings were intermingled. After the referendum the Allies drew it directly through Upper Silesia, thus fracturing the region's social, cultural and political continuity that had existed for centuries. The popular vote therefore shattered and divided this historical region with its distinct regional identity.[28]

The consequence was that 250,000 Germans and 500,000 Poles[29] ended up on the 'wrong' side of the border, becoming minorities in their new homelands. The Allies determined that Upper Silesia would be preserved as an economic zone for a transitional phase of fifteen years, or up to 1937. In another referendum in September 1922, the population of German Silesia voted against granting the area autonomy. Meanwhile, Polish Silesia would be the only place in Poland to have an organ of self-government, which would also administer the Polish section of Teschen. As the central power in Poland tightened its grip over the country, Silesia successively

---

[26] Ibid., p.28.

[27] Gullberg, ' "Folket har bestämt..."', p.59.

[28] Janusz Ziolkowski, 'The population of the Western Territories' in *Polish Western Territories* (Poznan' Instytut Zachodni), 1959, pp.128-9.

[29] The majority of this Polish group had voted for incorporation into Germany.

lost its autonomy, and Korfanty, one of its main representatives, was gaoled in 1930.[30]

War, Migration and Territorial Revisions

Between the World Wars, ethno-national tensions increased on both sides of the border. A great number of people had suddenly become citizens of a different country in which they were minorities. Many emigrated, while others decided to remain in the hope that their rights would be safeguarded by the various conventions on minority rights. Some 800,000 Germans are said to have moved out of Poland up to 1923.[31] But the Poles in Germany did not have the option of invoking the League of Nations, since they had not been recognised as a minority; the Allies feared that recognition of such a large minority group would imply a similar acknowledgment of say, the Scots and the Welsh, and this was a risk the Allies were unwilling to take.[32]

Successor-states such as Poland and Czechoslovakia urged both German and other minorities to disregard their distinctiveness, and to assimilate totally into the new state – to different reactions among the German minorities. Immigration was one option, and it was not uncommon for these immigrants to be actively involved in the existing revisionist movement in the Fatherland. Those who did not move to Germany were divided into those who were mobilised into militant groups with the primary goal of combating the state-sponsored de-Germanisation policy, and those who chose to cooperate and arrive at some sort of *modus vivendi* with the majority population.[33]

In October–November 1939 Germany reached an agreement with the Baltic states, Italy and the Soviet Union, stipulating that

---

[30] Wiskemann, *Germany's Eastern Neighbours*, pp.32-3.

[31] Richard Blanke, 'The German minority in inter-war Poland and German foreign policy', *Journal of Contemporary History*, XXV/I (1990).

[32] Allan Sharp, 'Britain and the protection of minorities at the Paris Peace Conference, 1919' in A. C. Hepburn (ed.), *Minorities in History* (London, 1978), p.183.

[33] Anthony Komjathy and Rebecca Stockwell, *German Minorities and the Third Reich: Ethnic Germans of East Central Europe between the Wars* (New York, 1980), p.2.

Germany had the right to 'bring home' all Germans threatened with de-Germanisation. This German *Umsiedlung* (resettlement) would not be compulsory; people who so wished could thus say 'no' to Hitler's *Heim ins Reich* policy. Although many hundreds of thousands of *Volksdeutsche* did move into the Third Reich, there continued to be German minorities scattered throughout Central and Eastern Europe.[34] Only after Germany's borders had been secured did the government activate its *Lebensraum* policy, in which the *Volksdeutsche* played a pivotal role.[35]

The first stream of immigrants was relatively modest, but a much larger influx followed it – prompted by the pact between Hitler and Stalin signed in August 1939, with a secret protocol added in September. The agreement concerned spheres of interest and was related largely to the division of Poland. The German occupation of Poland resulted in 2 million Polish residents of German descent being absorbed into the Third Reich.[36]

With the outbreak of the Second World War, Germany's migration policy could either remain 'voluntary' or be replaced by an expansionism which would ultimately incorporate all ethnic Germans living outside of Germany into a greater German *Reich*. Hitler's conception of *Lebensraum* was critical in this context, since its fundamental element was the Germanisation of Eastern Europe. The Slavic peoples were to be Germanised, expelled to Siberia or exterminated. The operational phase of this project was called *Generalplan Ost*, and contained detailed stipulations on how this Germanisation process was to be implemented.

Poland became the foremost victim of Nazi Germany's race-biological political notion of *Volkstum*. Shortly after the pact between Hitler and Stalin, Poles would be deported eastward and replaced by ethnic Germans from the Baltic states, Bessarabia and Bukovina. The Nazis partitioned Poland into two sections, which included a number of *Reichsgau* areas that were subjected to violent Germanisation, and the so-called *Generalgouvernement* under the

---

[34] Alfred M. de Zayas, 'A historical survey of twentieth-century expulsions' in Anna C. Bramwell (ed.), *Refugees in the Age of Total War*, (London, 1981), pp.21ff.

[35] Komjathy and Stockwell, *German Minorities*, pp.4-5.

[36] Agnis Balodis, *Sovjets och Nazitysklands uppgörelse om de baltiska staterna*, (Stockholm, 1978), p.44.

leadership of Hans Frank, whose task was to supply the Third Reich with a labour force to satisfy its rapidly escalating requirements. The area thus became a colossal labour camp.[37]

An early stage in the Nazi demographic programme entailed the forced transfer of 600,000 Jews to the *Generalgouvernement*, but Hans Frank objected to this measure, insisting that the *Generalgouvernement* should not become a 'dumping ground'. However, his protests could not prevent the area from ultimately acquiring the greatest concentration of Jews in all the territory controlled by Nazi Germany.[38]

Between 1939 and 1945 the population transfers conducted under the RKFDV system *(Reichskommissariat für die Festigung deutschen Volkstums)* affected 1.5 million ethnic Germans. Less than half of these ended up in Poland, where they were to participate in a Nazi-sponsored agricultural programme – while the remainder, 350,000 from the Soviet Union and 500,000 from Hungary, Slovakia, Romania and Yugoslavia – shifted back and forth between different camps, due to constant revisions in the plans of the RKFDV.[39]

The Third Reich's search for a labour force began in Poland. This recruitment project was both voluntary and coercive, and was directed by a German control apparatus unmatched anywhere else in Europe. The programme affected millions both during the war and for several years afterwards.[40] Shortly before the outbreak of war, the German military had indicated that the country's expansionist policy required generous access to both labour and natural resources. The bottleneck in German calculations was not resources but labour. A highly efficient organisation was therefore set up with the express purpose of forcibly recruiting workers

---

[37] Wolfgang Benz, 'Der Generalplan Ost. Zur Germanisierungspolitik des NS-Regimes in den besetzen Ostgebieten, 1939-1945' in Wolfgang Benz (ed.), *Die Vertreibung der Deutschen aus dem Osten. Ursache, Ereignisse, Folgen* (Frankfurt am Main, 1985). See also Michael Marrus, *The Unwanted: European Refugees in the Twentieth Century* (New York, 1985), pp.219ff.

[38] Michael Marrus, *The Holocaust in History* (London, 1988), pp.62-3.

[39] Robert Koehl, *RKFVD: German Resettlement and Population Policy, 1939: A History of the Reich Commission for Strengthening of Germandom* (Cambridge, MA, 1957), pp.210ff.

[40] Malcolm Proudfoot, *European Refugees, 1939-1952: A Study in Forced Population Movement* (London, 1957).

outside the German heartland: 115 recruitment offices were opened in Poland alone, administered by the SS, the Gestapo and other German bodies. The programme resulted in 1.8 to 2 million Polish workers being brought into the German armaments industry. Botched military undertakings, such as the effort on the eastern front in which the Germans lost both human and material capital, led to intensified recruitment of foreign labour, which became ever more brutal as the war progressed.[41]

By actively conducting population transfers, Germany had launched a migration process, the most intensive phase of which occurred at the end of the war and in its immediate aftermath. *Lebensraum, Umsiedlung, Germanisierung, Entgermanisierung* were all terms linked to a political dream of great power status; when implemented, this vision brought lasting consequences for the Germans who for many generations had lived in Central and Eastern Europe. Between 1939 and 1945 the political evolution of Germany brought about population transfers, expulsion, flight and extermination on a scale unparalleled in modern history. The Oder–Neisse area and the adjacent territitory were to experience these phenomena more profoundly than any other part of Europe.

SOVIET SECURITY POLICY, POLAND'S WESTERN BOUNDARY AND ETHNIC CLEANSING

With the end and immediate aftermath of Second World War almost all Germans fled or were otherwise removed from East Prussia, Pomerania, Silesia and East Brandenburg. The Allies wished to ensure that no ethnic Germans remained east of the Oder–Neisse line, which would act as both an ethnic and a state frontier.

There were two principal factors at the root of this development. First, the Western Allies tended to give sympathetic consideration to the security concerns of the Soviet Union.[42] Secondly, the principle of the homogeneous state became paramount. The expulsion of the Germans was implemented in order to obliterate

---

[41] Ulrich Herbert, *Europa und der 'Reichseinsatz'. Ausländische Zivilarbeiter, Kriegsgefangene und KZ-Häftlinge in Deutschland, 1938-1945* (Essen, 1991), pp.8-9.

[42] This section is based primarily on Hans-Åke Persson, *Rhetorik und Realpolitik. Grossbritannien, die Oder-Neisse Grenze und die Vertreibung der Deutschen nach dem Zweiten Weltkrieg* (Potsdam, 1997).

for ever the problem of German minorities in Central and Eastern Europe, which could always be exploited as a justification for German expansionism, as it had been by Hitler. Although the presence of German minorities was certainly not the sole reason for Hitler's aggressive foreign policy, ethno-territorial tensions in Poland and Czechoslovakia could easily be used to legitimise his actions, and thus helped to trigger the great power conflict in Europe.

At the Teheran Conference in 1943, the Allies reached secret agreements on Poland's future frontiers. Although these mainly concerned the eastern side of the country, they also involved Poland being moved westward, with obvious consequences for German territory. More precisely, the Polish–Soviet border was to follow the Curzon Line, but the question of Poland's western boundary was at first uncertain.[43] The issue of expulsion was likewise dealt with, although no specific decisions were made here either.

Because of their military advances, the Russians were able to discuss Poland's future from a position of strength, and the western Allies were inclined to concede that Soviet security interests in Europe extended further west than previously. Outside the circle of the Allied great powers, the Czechoslovak government-in-exile was the main actor pressing for action on the question of the German minorities in Central and Eastern Europe. Because actions by the German minority had helped to undermine the existence of their state, the Czechoslovaks now demanded that its members be banished from the country.

In the Polish case the conditions were different. While the expulsion of *Volksdeutsche* from Czechoslovakia could be viewed as a collective sentence passed on an ethnic minority, the expulsion of *Reichsdeutsche* from the areas east of the Oder–Neisse line was the direct consequence of the new boundary. The Polish government-in-exile in London could not effectively influence Allied proposals for redrawn boundaries and population transfers within Poland's eastern and western border-areas; this became evident in the autumn of 1944 during the negotiations on the future demarcation of Poland, in which the Soviets, Britain and the Polish government-in-exile in London took part. The power-base

---

[43] The Curzon line, which moved the Polish-Soviet boundary 160 km. to the west, was named after Lord Curzon, who as British Foreign Secretary proposed the demarcation between Poland and Russia in July 1920.

of the Polish representatives had been greatly eroded by the stance of the Soviet-controlled Lublin government which had established itself in Poland.

The representative for the Polish government-in-exile, Stanislaw Mikolajcyk, opposed this new Polish–Soviet boundary (the Curzon Line), pointing at the complications involved in pushing Poland westward: millions of people, both German and Polish, would be expelled, and Poland would be forced to sacrifice crucial Polish cultural areas in exchange for territories that might have been Polish 700 years earlier. However, the government-in-exile's position was swiftly overridden; as the Red Army made headway, the views of the Lublin government prevailed.[44]

The altered Polish–Soviet boundary and the subsequent extensive population transfers were not discussed at the Yalta conference.[45] The issue was seen as a bilateral affair to be handled separately by the Soviet Union and Poland. However, negotiations became entangled over the question of Poland's western boundary and the population transfers. The Allies were beginning to understand that the supply situation in occupied Germany could be negatively affected by the territorial revision of Poland. When the negotiations closed, no agreement had been reached either on this issue or on the nature of Poland's future political system.

The Western Allies arrived at Potsdam with little room to manoeuvre. The stream of Germans that had been moving westward for six months showed no signs of abating and indeed seemed to be swelling. Washington's main contribution to the Potsdam negotiations was to propose a compromise, which became the final document of the conference. The parties agreed, among other things, to defer decision on the status of the Oder–Neisse line to a future conference. Article XIII, which regulated the expulsion of the Germans, was largely a formality since it stipulated an already ongoing process. However, the meeting did produce an agreement on organised expulsion. After the Potsdam Conference

---

[44] Hugh Thomas, *Armed Truce: The Beginnings of the Cold War, 1945-1946* (London, 1986), pp.246ff.

[45] Joseph B. Schechtman, *Postwar Population Transfers in Europe, 1945-1955* (Philadelphia, PA, 1962), pp.172-3. Schechtman notes that some 2 million people east of the Curzon line opted for repatriation. Many of these were directed to the areas which Germany relinquished to Poland.

of the Polish representatives had been greatly eroded by the stance of the Soviet-controlled Lublin government which had established itself in Poland.

The representative for the Polish government-in-exile, Stanislaw Mikolajcyk, opposed this new Polish–Soviet boundary (the Curzon Line), pointing at the complications involved in pushing Poland westward: millions of people, both German and Polish, would be expelled, and Poland would be forced to sacrifice crucial Polish cultural areas in exchange for territories that might have been Polish 700 years earlier. However, the government-in-exile's position was swiftly overridden; as the Red Army made headway, the views of the Lublin government prevailed.[44]

The altered Polish–Soviet boundary and the subsequent extensive population transfers were not discussed at the Yalta conference.[45] The issue was seen as a bilateral affair to be handled separately by the Soviet Union and Poland. However, negotiations became entangled over the question of Poland's western boundary and the population transfers. The Allies were beginning to understand that the supply situation in occupied Germany could be negatively affected by the territorial revision of Poland. When the negotiations closed, no agreement had been reached either on this issue or on the nature of Poland's future political system.

The Western Allies arrived at Potsdam with little room to manoeuvre. The stream of Germans that had been moving westward for six months showed no signs of abating and indeed seemed to be swelling. Washington's main contribution to the Potsdam negotiations was to propose a compromise, which became the final document of the conference. The parties agreed, among other things, to defer decision on the status of the Oder–Neisse line to a future conference. Article XIII, which regulated the expulsion of the Germans, was largely a formality since it stipulated an already ongoing process. However, the meeting did produce an agreement on organised expulsion. After the Potsdam Conference

---

[44] Hugh Thomas, *Armed Truce: The Beginnings of the Cold War, 1945-1946* (London, 1986), pp.246 ff.

[45] Joseph B. Schechtman, *Postwar Population Transfers in Europe, 1945-1955* (Philadelphia, PA, 1962), pp.172-3. Schechtman notes that some 2 million people east of the Curzon line opted for repatriation. Many of these were directed to the areas which Germany relinquished to Poland.

TERRITORIES CEDED TO POLAND AND THE USSR IN 1945

the previously haphazard expulsions assumed a more organised and coordinated character.

In the Soviet view Poland's adjustment westward meant that Polish–German relations now had the potential for future conflict. With Germany neutralised and Poland significantly weakened, the Soviet Union could play a decisive role in East European politics. Thus it openly supported the Lublin government's extensive demands on German territory. Furthermore, the expulsion of Germans would serve as an argument for the construction of a Polish state. The ethnic homogenisation of Poland was one of the few issues on which the various government factions in Poland agreed.

Had the Soviet Union not been in a position of strength, Poland's western boundary could not have been moved to the Oder–Neisse line. The Western Allies would have preferred to establish the border in a way that would satisfy two demands, both linked to occupied Germany: namely that Germany retain important parts of its traditional agricultural areas in the east, and that the number of Germans to be expelled be kept to the minimum.

The Oder Region, Pax Sovietica and the 'Peace Frontier': the First Post-war Transformation Process

While making the GDR's first governmental statement in October 1949, the Prime Minister, Otto Grotewohl, said the following concerning the East German position over the Oder–Neisse line:

'For us the Oder-Neisse frontier is a peace frontier (*Friedensgrenze*) which makes friendly relations with the Polish people a possibility. It is criminal even to consider the possibility of the German people, who have expended so much blood, being plunged yet again into war and catastrophe.'[46]

Despite Grotewohl's description of Oder–Neisse as a '*Friedensgrenze*', this border between the GDR and Poland was heavily patrolled. It also demarcated a country with a strong nation-state tradition, namely Poland, from a one that was undergoing the very first phases of state-formation, namely the GDR.

---

[46] Cited in Hans Georg Lehmann, *Der Oder–Neisse Konflikt* (Munich, 1979), p.168.

Meanwhile, both of these states were within the socialist bloc under Soviet hegemony.

The boundary proved significant in the self-perception of both Poland and the GDR. For the Sozialistische Einheitspartei Deutschlands (SED), the monopoly ruling party in East Germany, defence of the border became inseparable from the protection of the national interest. Likewise, the official rhetoric in Poland asserted that through the Oder–Neisse line the nation had successfully recovered areas that had previously been Polish;[47] also that the new border would guard against a potentially revanchist German Federal Republic. Within the socialist bloc, the Soviet Union fixed the geographical boundaries of both Poland and East Germany. The Oder–Neisse line came to function as a state boundary between two socialist states, as a cultural boundary between two peoples, and as a symbolic factor in the Cold War.[48]

Moreover the revision of the boundary would dramatically affect the population living in the border region. Because of the outcome of the war and the influx of several hundred thousand expelled Germans, the German population on the western side was overlaid by German arrivals from Neumark, Silesia, Pomerania and West and East Prussia.[49] Developments on the eastern side of the border brought still greater upheavals, with the void created by the expulsion of the Germans being filled by Poles from central Poland and areas east of the Curzon Line.[50]

ETHNO-DEMOGRAPHIC CHANGES AND THE SETTLERS

Despite the conflict-ridden history of the borderland, Germans and Poles had for centuries interacted on an everyday basis, both in business and socially. The new boundary brought all such

---

[47] Anthony Polonsky (ed.), *The Great Powers and the Polish Question, 1941-1945: A Documentary Study in Cold War Origins* (London, 1976), pp.220 ff. See also Alfred M. de Zayas, *Nemesis at Potsdam: The Anglo-Americans and the Expulsion of the Germans* (London, 1979), pp.47 ff.

[48] Helga Schulz, *Wirtschaftliche und kulturelle Transformationen in der deutsch–polnischen Grenzregion an der Oder, 1945 bis 1990* (Frankfurt-an-der-Oder, 1995), p.9.

[49] Ibid.

[50] Wiskemann, *Germany's Eastern Neighbours*, pp.95 ff.

activities to an end. Flight, expulsion and repatriation brought a break in continuity more drastic than any other in modern European history. Agriculture, commerce and social life would now be regulated according to a political and economic ideology foreign to the area. The mental and cultural effects of such changes on the population are difficult to measure materially and have hereto been little analysed.

In 1945 the Polish state leadership was faced with the complex and difficult task of drafting immigrant Poles into towns, villages and individual farms covering one third of the new Poland's total area. The first Poles arrived in the spring of 1945 when the expulsion of Germans had only just begun. Demographic Polonisation was to proceed rapidly, since the incorporation of the western areas into Communist Poland was a government priority. As has been mentioned, it was claimed that Poland had recovered former Polish territories. However, it was necessary actively to Polonise the areas, thus achieving a *fait accompli* in advance of the post-war negotiations on the Polish–German frontier. When these former German areas had been stripped of their whole population, over 6 million Germans had been forced abandon their homes and resettle in occupied Germany (i.e. the territory of the present-day reunified Germany).

For Poland the recovery of lands east of the Oder–Neisse entailed a massive colonisation project, in an area where half of the cities and one-third of the villages were literally in ruins. Both demographically and politically the Polish population that remained in the recovered areas now came to occupy a crucial position. This group had previously been a minority of approximately 1 million people, making up one-seventh of the total population in the ceded areas. In Poland's post-war ethno-national propaganda, this group was hailed as an 'autochthonous population' that had survived and preserved its identity in a mainly German environment. The demographic Polonisation process of the recovered areas based itself precisely on this autochthonous people. Moreover, by their sheer presence these autochthons legitimised Poland's historically motivated claims to the areas east of the Oder–Neisse line. They were politically indispensable in the nationalisation process, which to 5.5 million, or 65 per cent of the total population in 1939.[55]

The migrants were of varying backgrounds, vocational skills and family patterns. They had migrated west either voluntarily or under coercion and left their old lives behind to begin a new existence in the borderland. For individuals the encounter with the new environment was difficult. At the highest level, the future status of the recovered areas remained undetermined; formally, they continued to belong to Germany and the adjusted boundary was not ratified till 1991. At the most basic level the newly-arrived Poles were forced to share accommodation temporarily with Germans who were being expelled.

The adversities faced by the Polish migrants are best exemplified by the situation in Breslau (Wroclaw) in the early post-war years. When the first Poles arrived there in the summer of 1945, there remained 200,000 Germans to be expelled. Some years later, the number of Poles had risen to half a million, while only 3,000 Germans still lived in the area. Most of the Poles came from the countryside, and this was their first experience of a sizable city. Although many parts of the city were in ruins, those that had been spared were aesthetically alien to the newcomers and quite different from what they had known. The city's new residents did all they could to erase traces of the former population. The churches had the greatest symbolic value, and the first to be rebuilt and stripped of all that recalled the German period was that in Oder-Bahnhof. Numerous German churches were likewise reconstructed, and their neo-Gothic style was replaced by a Gothic form associated with the churches in eastern Poland. It was argued that the medieval churches were in fact a Polish legacy, and that their neo-Gothic decoration was a later German accretion. German cemeteries and all German monuments were likewise destroyed. As late as in the early 1970s bulldozers were still crushing gravestones and sculptures in German cemeteries as the city's traffic system was being reconstructed. A later proposal to build a monument commemorating a German cemetery met with vehement protests from the local population.[56]

---

[55] Schechtman, *Postwar Population Transfer*, p.227. By 1959 this number rose to 83 per cent of the prewar figure.

[56] Wlodzimierz Kalicki, 'Als es hiess: "Jeder Pole hat seinen Deutschen"', *Frankfurter Allgemeine Zeitung* (23 Nov. 1996).

However, several circumstances held back the integration of the new settlements in western Poland. First, the settlers were in no way a homogeneous group. Friction between the newcomers and the autochthons was unavoidable – the autochthons were sometimes even accused of being Germans. Secondly, adaptation was hampered by Polish settlers being constantly reminded of the German cultural legacy in the former eastern German areas. Thirdly, uncertainties over the constitutional status of the area presented an ever-present threat, with psychological effects on the local population. And fourthly, the integration of the new territory into Communist Poland bore the the stamp of Soviet influence.

The 'peace frontier' was highly significant to the evolution of the borderland. It was securely fortified and regularly patrolled, and local residents could not move about freely in the area. Certain zones were entirely closed to civilians, and military garrisons were permanently stationed in most villages. All those who lived in the border zone were under an obligation to report anything unusual.[57] Fear and uncertainly over the future were more acute here than anywhere else in Poland.

EXPELLED PERSONS, INTEGRATION INTO THE GERMAN STATES AND THE DREAM OF 'DIE ALTE HEIMAT' EAST OF THE BOUNDARY

The transfer of Poland's western boundary to Oder–Neisse meant that historically evolved cities that had once been important commercial and industrial centres in eastern Germany, like Frankfurt-an-der-Oder, Guben and Görlitz, were divided. The total expulsion of the Germans east of Oder–Neisse meant that the area was vacated and thus ready for the arrival of the new Polish occupants. On the other side of the river, some 12 million Germans from Central and Eastern Europe had to be integrated into a Germany that was overpopulated, occupied by the victorious allies and ravaged by the war.

While the political, cultural and social circumstances that faced the 7.9 million Germans expelled to the Federal Republic have been thoroughly documented and analysed, the situation of the

---

[57] Brencz, 'Die Herausbildung...', p.55.

4 million who entered the GDR has received much less attention.[58] Because of the difficulty of access to primary sources in East Germany it has been difficult to gain a well-founded understanding of the Soviet Union's and the GDR's economic, political and social resolution of the problem. Fifteen years after the end of the war it was officially claimed that there were no refugees within the borders of the country and that the expellees had been fully assimilated and integrated into East German society.

The German refugees in the Soviet zone wished to return to areas administered by Poland, and the Russian authorities quickly acted to prevent this from happening. Within the German administration of the Soviet zone, a so-called 'Central Administration of Resettlers' was opened with the express purpose of managing the integration of the refugees. It monitored refugee camps and was responsible for resettling individuals in different *Länder*. The administration operated with remarkable efficiency during the critical years 1945 and 1946. It was undoubtedly under pressure from the Soviet leadership, for whom rapid integration of the resettlers was important. Since the Soviets refused to grant the East European refugees formal refugee status, the Refugee Administration was soon brought under the auspices of the 'Central Administration for Labour'; the term 'refugee' does not appear in East German documentation. The jurist and historian Leo Schwartz has commented on the Allies' different policies:

> The Soviets immediately erased any distinction and imposed a policy of integration. The Western powers recognised distinction (in their respective zones of occupation) especially of a social and economic character, and left integration to the normal process of assimilation. These contrasting policies are rooted in different concepts of society.[59]

In the Federal Republic the conditions faced by the expellees were exploited for both domestic and foreign policy purposes. The first West German government swiftly opened a Ministry for Expelled Germans *(Bundesministerium für Vertriebene)*. The question of expelled persons had thus been elevated to the state level, and in 1950 it became politically possible for the expellees to

---

[58] Persson, *Rhetorik und Realpolitik*, pp.29-34.

[59] Leo W. Schwartz, *Refugees in Germany Today: Their Legal Status and Integration* (New York, 1957), p.111.

organise at this level. The resulting party was called *Gesamtdeutsche Block-Bund der Heimatvertriebenen und Entrechteten* (BHE), whose primary objective was to promote the right of expellees to fair treatment in their new homeland, and to return to their countries of origin. Predecessors of the BHE included the *Landsmannschaften*, as well as political and cultural organisations with membership based on the refugees' previous place of residence.[60] Indeed, it may be argued that the expellees came to play an important role in the Federal Republic's official *Ostpolitik*. Both Konrad Adenauer and Helmut Kohl capitalised on the issue in their political rhetoric, particularly in discussions concerning recognition of the Oder–Neisse line as the German–Polish boundary. The distinctive political image of the expellees has naturally had consequences for all the postwar Polish governments, as well as for the people who settled in the former German areas east of the Oder–Neisse line. The image of Germany in Poland has been largely coloured by the expellees in the Federal Republic and their political ambition to reclaim their earlier home communities.

Among the 4 million expellees who settled in the GDR, many settled close to the Polish border and thus their former homes. The East German state suppressed anything that could be interpreted as signs of discontent among the expellees. Organisations such as *Landsmannschaften* and *Umsiedlerverbände* were forbidden. In the GDR, despite rapid economic and social recovery and a goal-oriented integration policy (e.g. the land reform of 1946), the social and psychological trauma that expellees experienced was not once publicly discussed. It was up to each individual to sort out the emotions, events and experiences resulting from the expulsion.[61]

The East Berlin government had a dilemma: it had to consider both its own unquestioning loyalty to the Soviet Union and the political demands of the population in general, and the expellees in particular. The existence of the state rested on the Soviet definition of Russian postwar security interests. This legitimacy 'from above' should ideally have been paralleled by a corresponding

---

[60] Hans W. Schoenberg, *The Germans from the East: A Study of their Migration, Settlement and Subsequent Group History since 1945* (The Hague, 1971), p.77.

[61] Alan Nothnagle, 'Die Oder–Neisse Grenze und die Politik der SED' in Schulze and Nothnagle (eds), *Grenze der Hoffnung*, p.28.

legitimacy 'from below', i.e. from the people. This would only have been possible if the expellees' demands and dreams of revising the Oder–Neisse line were pacified.

In the early post-war years the SED recognised the political value of discussing an adjustment of the Oder–Neisse line. Conflicting signals came from the state leadership, and party members with roots in East Prussia or Silesia were thus mobilised, forwarding petitions to the party leadership in Berlin with demands that the boundary be revised. In the summer of 1947, in order to suppress the revisionists, the SED leadership decided that the Oder–Neisse line should be accepted as the boundary between Germany and Poland pending a resolution of the matter at a future peace conference.[62] Three years later in 1950, the GDR and Poland signed an agreement at Görlitz that defined the boundary between them as the Oder-Neisse-*Friedensgrenze*. It acquired a symbolic function and became the basis for stable relations between the GDR, Poland and the Soviet Union.[63]

Following the Görlitz treaty the East German state leadership made various efforts to institutionalise its stable relations with Poland, and in this the demonisation of the Federal Republic was a key component. The entire East German propaganda machinery was activated for this purpose. Journals wrote of Polish culture and folklore, while ignoring the religious life around the Catholic Church in Poland. Various associations were formed, like the *Hellmut-von-Gerlach-Gesellschaft für kulturelle, wirtschaftliche und politische Beziehungen mit dem neuen Polen*, often with the object of neutralising the demands of the expellees for revision, which continued into the 1950s.[64]

However, it was clear that the official policy of proclaimed friendship between the peoples had generally failed. The official rhetoric was nullified by reality, since the government actively suppressed the past and prevented open discussion. Public life was censored, and a consistent falsification of history cemented national prejudices and impeded cross-cultural understanding and contacts. Still today East Germans and Poles know little about the populations that peacefully coexisted in the borderland for long periods of

[62] Nothnagle, 'Die Oder-Neisse Grenze', p.30.
[63] Ibid., p.31.
[64] Ibid., p.33.

history. The only image that has survived is that of a conflict-ridden border.[65]

THE CONSTRUCTION OF SOCIALIST SOCIETY IN THE BORDER AREA

The ethnic homogenisation of Poland, as much as the establishment of a Socialist society, was a cornerstone in the post-war construction of the Polish state.[66] The incorporation of the 'recovered areas' into Poland became one of the *raisons d'être* of the Communist regime. In November 1945 the West Institute in Posen (Instytut Zachodni) came to play a significant role in the integration of western Poland.[67]

The infrastructure and the planning and administrative bodies in the 'recovered areas' were quickly brought under the authority of Warsaw. However, similar measures could not immediately be put into effect in the western areas, since these had not legally been incorporated into Poland. The area on the other side of the border was part of occupied Germany up till the GDR came into existence in 1949. In 1952 the GDR dissolved the *Länder*, which were viewed as barriers to Socialist evolution and fifteen new administrative entities, *Bezirke*, were formed.

The actual reconstruction of the border area did not begin till the early 1950s. Matters had deteriorated since substantial sections of the German industry on both sides of the Oder–Neisse had been dismantled and transferred to the Soviet Union. This badly damaged a border region that was already poorly developed industrially, and had suffered extensive injuries in the final phases of the war.[68]

Land and agricultural reforms became important elements in the integration of rootless people who had for various reason been directed to one side of the Oder–Neisse. Major land reforms were carried out both in Poland and in the GDR. In Poland, a

---

[65] Ludwig Melhorn, 'Die Sprachlosigkeit zwischen Polen und der DDR. Eine Hypothek' in Ewa Kobylinska (ed.), *Deutsche und Polen* (Munich, 1992), pp.526-7.

[66] Mieczyslav Gorski, 'En skiss av en tragedi', *Invandrare och minoriteter*, 1/91.

[67] Lehmann, p.17.

[68] Stanislaw Jankowski, 'Der Zustand der polnischen Industrie in der zweiten Jahreshälfte 1945', *Jahrbuch für Wirtschaftsgeschichte*, no.1 (1991), pp.13-15.

decree of September 1944 stipulated that all land belonging to Germans, war criminals or traitors would be confiscated. One-fifth of this land was taken over by private landowners; 5 million hectares were transferred to an estimated 700,000 families. Of those who arrived in the 'recovered areas' and acquired land from the state half were from Central Poland, 40 per cent from territories now controlled by the Soviet Union, and 10 per cent were demobilised soldiers. Special agricultural cooperatives were set up to assist the settlers. Immigrants from eastern Poland, who were experienced in private agriculture, were particularly apprehensive about these institutions, and by 1947 their membership was only one-sixth of what had been expected.[69]

As in Poland, extensive land reforms were also introduced in the GDR, in the hope that these would foster the integration of the Germans who had been expelled from areas east of the Oder–Neisse line. However, many of them had arrived from urban surroundings, and knew nothing of agriculture. This had repercussions on both the implementation of the reforms and on the individuals themselves. Socialisation and an increase in taxes on productive farms led 5,000 farmers to leave their farms and migrate westwards in the early 1950s. By this time 30 per cent of the settlers had still not been able to establish a functioning agricultural operation. The failed agricultural policy ultimately resulted in a far-reaching process of collectivisation in 1952.[70]

Collectivisation proceeded differently on the two sides of the Oder–Neisse. The process was initiated later in the GDR, yet it became more extensive than in Poland. By 1953, 30 per cent of agricultural holdings had been socialised. At the Fifth Party Congress in 1958, it was announced that a definitive collectivisation of all agriculture would take place, and a great number of peasants began leaving the GDR. The erection of the Berlin Wall in 1961 was a desperate measure to curtail this *Republikflucht*. Large-scale farming, linked to the so-called *Landwirtschaftlichen Produktionsgenossenschaften* (agricultural production societies or LPGs) gained momentum after the building of the Wall, and became the basis

---

[69] Nigel Swain, 'Agriculture in Poland and the former G.D.R.: a research agenda for the Oder region' in Schulz and Nothnagle (eds), *Grenze der Hoffnung*, pp.140-1.

[70] Ibid., p.142.

on which the socialist agricultural system was built. Its ideological significance is reflected in the slogans like, '*Frohe Zukunft*' (joyful future) or '*Neues Leben*' (new life), given to groups such as the LPGs.[71]

In Poland the socialisation of farming was carried out most consistently in the western territories: for instance, in 1956, 40 per cent of the acreage had been collectivised in the counties of Szczecin and Wroclaw. After disturbances in Poland in the summer of 1956, the process was halted and the former ownership conditions had already been restored in the autumn of that year. From 1957 the government introduced a new agricultural policy based on private ownership, with the addition of a socialist sector with state-owned units. Thus after 1956 socialist agriculture was following divergent paths in the border-area.[72]

The incorporation of Silesia was important to Poland's post-war industrialisation and modernisation. With the division of Germany the GDR no longer had access to the Ruhr's natural resources, and accordingly a steelworks in Eisenhüttenstadt and the petrochemical plant in Schwedt were created as the GDR's answer to the Ruhr. The location of the steelworks was determined by the river system which linked it to the coal deposits of Slask/Silesia, to Berlin and to the port of Szczecin.[73]

Establishing the conglomerates at Eisenhüttenstadt and Schwedt was a radical break from the industrial enterprises that had evolved in the region over the centuries. The area had long been a peripheral one, part of Berlin's economic area, with modest industry in the form of lumber and food production. Under the slogan '*Eisen für die Republik*' (iron for the Republic), heavy industry was established on the Oder as one part in the large-scale Soviet planned economy and the lives of those living in the border-area were profoundly altered. Eisenhüttenstadt now provided valuable propaganda as '*die erste sozialistische deutsche Stadt*' (the first socialist German town). Together with the land reforms, it was also a means of integrating at least some of the 4 million expellees who sought residence and subsistence in the GDR. In its early years, settlers from Silesia and other industrial areas in East Germany made up a portion of

---

[71] Helga Schulz, 'Die Oderregion in wirtschafts- und sozialhistorischer Perspektive', in Schulz and Nothnagle (eds), *Grenze der Hoffnung*, p.103.

[72] Swain, 'Agriculture in Poland', pp.142-151.

[73] Schulz, 'Die Oderregion...', p.99.

the labour force, and some became part of the new working-class elite who were to lead the way for socialist Germany.[74]

REGIONAL COOPERATION IN THE BORDERLAND

The economic relations that developed between these two states that were both subordinated to the Soviet planned economy were determined mainly through decrees from Berlin and Warsaw. There was no possibility for spontaneous contact or for local collaboration between the divided border regions. When such contact was allowed, it was primarily for political reasons and had no economic consequences.

The Polish sociologist Stanislaw Lisiecke has distinguished six phases in the evolution of regional cooperation from 1945 to 1989. During the first, 1945-56, the principal function of the boundary was to create a barrier between the People's Republics of Poland and Germany. The second phase, 1956-60, was one of *détente*. At this time cooperation was initiated in the region in a number of fields, and contacts between the populations were developed at the *Land*, county and municipal levels. The third phase was during the 1960s, and the 1967 Treaty of Friendship marked its culmination. At this time existing contacts were expanded, and some cross-border movement began, including commuters and tourists. In the 1970s the boundary was labelled '*Die offene Grenze*' (the open border): the need for visas was abolished in November 1971, and further commercial links and spontaneous travel became possible for all citizens, Germans and Poles alike. In proclaiming the open border, Berlin and Warsaw sought to speed up and deepen integration between the peoples of the Eastern bloc. The fifth phase, spanning the 1980s, began when East Germany unilaterally reintroduced the visa requirement thereby once again limiting and obstructing personal contact between the two sides of the Oder-Neisse line. The sixth phase began after 1990, with the opening of the border between Poland and a reunified Germany, and marks the beginning of a transformation phase involving a free market economy and new political thinking in the border region.[75]

---

[74] Ibid., pp.112ff..

[75] Stanislaw Lisiecke, Introduction to Stanislaw Lisiecke (ed.), *Die Offene Grenze: Forschungsbericht polnisch–deutsche Grenzregion (1991-93)* (Westinstitut Poznan,

Up to 1949 the frontier between Poland and the Soviet zone of occupation in Germany remained closed, and its militarisation prevented contacts between residents of the two sides. After the Görlitz treaty of 1950, such contacts became possible through various agreements regulating boat services, water control and tourism. After 1955 the *Oderbrücke* between Frankfurt-an-der-Oder and Slubice, which had been unusable since 1945, was rebuilt. Between 1952 and 1955 the first talks at different levels were initiated between leading party officials from cities such as Frankfurt-an-der-Oder and Zielona Gora and between Wroclaw and Dresden. This contact was superficial and centrally directed: also events encouraged by the party like jubilees, conventions and youth activities were not particularly conducive to significant transnational communication. A youth festival, the 'Frühjahr [new year] an der Oder und Neisse' was organised annually by the cities on the Oder and Neisse. Collaboration over water regulation and energy supply became possible in the later 1950s, and series of agreements were reached between Polish and German counties in the region.[76]

Up to the early 1960s the regional cooperation that took place was essentially motivated by political and propaganda considerations, but contacts in the next two decades were expanded and modified. Water supply could function better in the borderland after the so-called Berlin accords were signed in March 1965, and in 1966 Berlin and Warsaw reached an agreement regulating the export of Polish labour to the GDR. The East German authorities lacked the necessary workforce for the major industrial complex that had been erected on the western side of the Oder–Neisse, including the plants for the manufacture of precision lenses and for chemical condensation in Görlitz, the synthetic-fibre combine in Guben and the semiconductor plant in Frankfurt-an-der-Oder.[77] Polish workers, mainly women, could now commute across the border, and this resolved the labour problem. In conjunction with the combine at Eisenhüttenstadt, a railway was

---

1995), pp.10-11.

[76] Maria Rutowska, 'Die regionale Zusammenarbeit in der deutsch–polnischen Grenzregion in den Jahren 1945-1989', Schulz and Nothnagle (eds), *Grenze der Hoffnung*, pp.43-4.

[77] Ibid., p.77.

built in 1968 between this city and Frankfurt-an-der-Oder to transport workers. The legal Polish labour migration to the GDR rose consistently from 1971 onwards but by 1984 it had begun to subside, and it came to an end in 1991. Alongside this legal movement there was also an illegal labour force, including Polish seasonal workers.[78]

In the 1970s both East Germans and Poles could cross the border without passport or visa; and the number who did so between 1972 and 1979 is estimated at 100 million. This was the first time since the Second World War that individuals could make that journey freely. For two and a half decades the encounter between Poles and Germans along the 'peace frontier' had been directed by the central authorities and it was now broadened by everyday contact among people. The relaxation of the border also enabled the German expellees to visit their former homes for the first time.[79] Differences in prices and the selection of goods available made shopping trips popular, but these fell off somewhat in the mid-1970s because of the decreased purchasing power of the Polish zloty. While the Poles expanded their infrastructure and built market-places, hotels and car parks to welcome their visitors, the Germans for their part became more restrictive towards Polish tourism.

The democratisation process in Poland began in 1980 with the Solidarity movement, which made the leadership of the GDR reclose the border in October of that year, affecting both tourism and institutionalised cooperation. Given the continuing labour shortage in the GDR, Polish workers could still commute on a daily basis but they were no longer free to buy consumer goods. Thus the relaxation that had resulted from daily personal contacts in the borderland was reversed. During the 1980s the borderland was affected by the climate of conflict between a Poland experiencing popular demands for liberalisation and a GDR striving to the utmost to prevent similar developments on its side of the border. The whole post-war evolution in the borderland represented a dramatic break with all that had a emerged organically

---

[78] Ewa Helias, *Polnische Arbeitnehmer in der DDR und der Bundesrepublik Deutschland* (Berliner Institut für vergleichende Sozialforschung, Berlin, 1992), pp.13-15. The illegal Polish workforce was estimated at 10,000 annually.

[79] Rutowska, 'Die regionale Zusammenarbeit', pp.45-6.

throughout the centuries. There was virtually no possibility for this region to form its own network of contacts and communications: Berlin and Warsaw determined the parameters of all such activity.

The Collapse of Communism and West European Integration: The Second Post-war Transformation Phase

The decline of the Soviet empire was accompanied by both international and national changes. The process first affected the states of Central and Eastern Europe, particularly the Federal Republic. In connection with German reunification the Oder–Neisse line was once again to occupy a critical position. Allied acceptance of German reunification was conditional upon the Federal Republic recognising the Polish–German border.

At the so-called '2 + 4' negotiations in July 1990, which brought together the two German states and the four wartime Allies – Britain, the United States, France and the Soviet Union, the Federal Republic guaranteed that the border question would be resolved via a German–Polish accord as soon as reunification became a fact, and the Poles raised no objections. The border agreement was signed in November 1990 and ratified by the *Bundestag* in October 1991. Germany thereby annulled its claims to former German areas east of the Oder–Neisse Line.[80]

However, the recognition of the boundary was not wholly without complications for Germany. The expellee organisations viewed the accord as a *Grenzdiktatur* that had now legitimised the expulsion of Germans. The older generation of expellees were those least inclined to accept the Oder–Neisse line: 25 per cent of all West Germans over the age of sixty and 15 per cent of East Germans in that age group refused to acknowledge Poland's western frontier. Among the generation that had actually been subjected to the expulsions, 43 per cent were against the government's recognition of Oder–Neisse. This opposition could not be without some bearing on the ensuing negotiations concerning the border.[81]

---

[80] Hanno Drechsler, Wolfgang Hilligen and Franz Neumann, *Gesellschaft und Staat. Lexikon der Politik* (Munich, 1991), pp.532-3.

[81] Peter Merkl, *German Unification in the European Context* (Philadelphia, PA,

Since the days of the first Federal Chancellor, Konrad Adenauer, the CDU/CSU had sympathised with the expellees' wish to return home, and in the spring of 1990 a German right-wing national party, Die Republikaner, made headway, particularly among the expellees. In the domestic debate at this time on Germany's eastern frontier, Chancellor Helmut Kohl appeared to oppose Oder–Neisse as the state frontier. General elections were to be held in December that year, and Kohl was undoubtedly anxious to secure the votes of Germans with East Prussian, Silesian or Pomeranian roots. However it is certain that he did not intend to jeopardise German reunification, dependent as it was on German acceptance of the Oder–Neisse line.[82]

Both the GDR and the Federal Republic had recognised the Oder–Neisse boundary in connection with the Helsinki accords in 1975, but the Polish state continued to require a legally binding accord. Poland also hoped that by merging the two German states, German reunification would once and for all enable claims from the expellees to be evaded. Poland's demands had solid international support, and Kohl's apparent vacillation produced negative reactions in Paris, London, Washington and above all, Warsaw. In the face of this onslaught, Kohl immediately backed down. Before inter-German monetary union was introduced on 1 July 1990, both German parliaments had approved the accord on the external frontiers of the GDR and the Federal Republic.[83]

Simultaneously, voices were raised in favour of regional cooperation across a border that had hitherto symbolised only conflict between Germany and its neighbours. This would bridge mental, economic, political and social divisions, and help to join areas that had been separated for over a half a century. Oderraum became the title of this regional project, and institutions were created to ensure its realisation.

DEUTSCH-POLNISCHER GRENZRAUM: A POST-COMMUNIST MODERNISATION PROJECT

In July 1991 Manfred Stolpe, Minister President of Brandenburg,

---

1993), pp.153-4.

[82] Persson, 'Soweit die deutsche Zunge klingt', p.291.

[83] Nikolaj Petersen, *Tysklands enhed, Europas sikkerhed* (Copenhagen, 1991), pp.70-71.

advised Jan Krzystof Bielecki, Prime Minister of Poland, of his interest in further cooperation in the German–Polish border-area. The so-called Stolpe Plan called for economic and industrial collaboration in a region that had long been neglected. It was to extend 50 km. into Germany and 100km. into Poland, thus affecting some 5 million people, in equal numbers on either side of the border.[84]

In Poland the Stolpe Plan was met with suspicion. Some groups saw it as a smokescreen for German expansionism, and as a zero-sum game in which the Poles would lose and the Germans win rather than as a project that would genuinely stimulate growth. Polish nationalists warned that the implementation of the 'Euregio' in the Polish–German border region was a new device to partition Poland: if Poland was to join the EU, they argued, it must do so as a whole rather than piecemeal.[85]

The West European and German conception of transnational cooperation stirred deep underlying structures in Polish society. On the one hand, ever since the collapse of Communism the Polish government had advocated rapid integration of the country into Western Europe. In a speech to the Polish parliament in July 1995 Kohl said that Poland could well become a full member of the EU by the year 2000, and his statement received rousing applause.[86] On the other hand, Poland's westward orientation has been criticised by groups who perceive the assimilation of the country into Western Europe as a threat to traditional Polish values. The Catholic Church in particular has expressed apprehension over German–Polish regional cooperation, observing that the infiltration of Western influence could ultimately erode fundamental cultural elements in Polish society.[87]

The transnational activity in Oderraum has had to cope with several obstacles. One complication arose even during the introductory stages of the project, when German newspapers called the German-Polish border area '*Oderland*' – to immediate Polish

---

[84] Jan B. Weydenthal, 'German plan for border regions stirs interests in Poland', *RFE/RL Research Report*, vol.1, no.7 (1992), pp.39-42.

[85] Ibid. See also Jan B. Weydenthal, 'Cross-border diplomacy in Eastern Europe', *RFE/RL Research Report* vol.1, no.42 (1992), pp.19-23.

[86] *The Economist* (15 July 1995).

[87] Weydenthal, 'German plan for border regions...', 1992.

THE EUROREGION ALONG THE POLISH-GERMAN BORDER

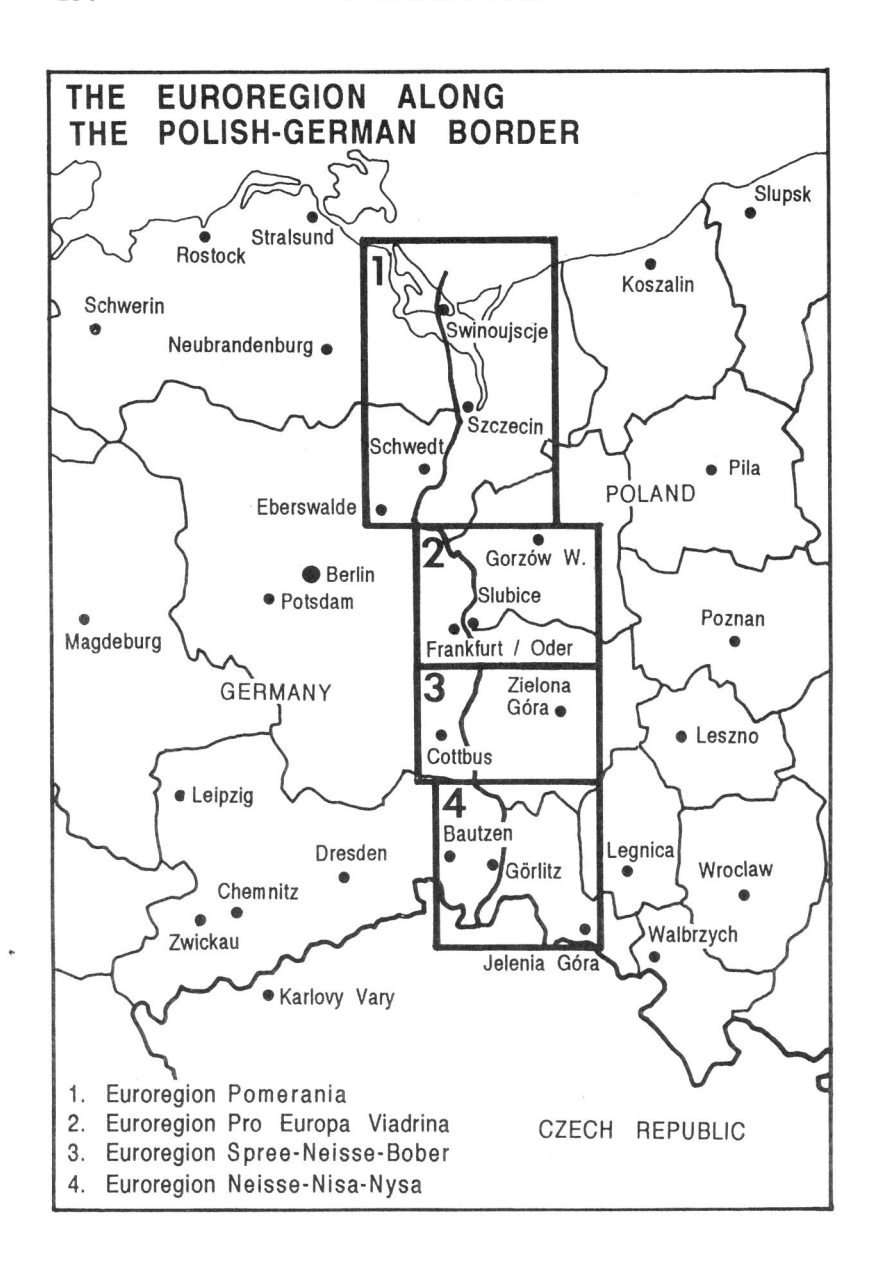

1. Euroregion Pomerania
2. Euroregion Pro Europa Viadrina
3. Euroregion Spree-Neisse-Bober
4. Euroregion Neisse-Nisa-Nysa

objections. Because term 'land' is associated with the German *Länder*, the choice of that name was seem by the Poles as confirming their fears that the collaboration was a smokescreen for German expansionism.

This incident was fairly minor, and *Oderland* was quick replaced by Oderraum, but it drew attention to the asymmetrical relations prevailing between Germany and Poland. German influence in Poland has grown since reunification and the German minority in Poland, thus encouraged, have demanded increased rights. Indeed, during the deliberations leading to the friendship treaty in 1991, the Federal Republic indicated its concerns over the rights of Germans in Poland, suggesting that Germans be allowed to settle in the former German areas of the country, and expressing the hope that villages populated by Germans would be allowed to reclaim their German place-names. These issues became connected to Poland's wish to become an associate member of the EU.

The situation became still more tangled after 1990, when it became clear that many of the Germans living in the borderland had applied for citizenship in the Federal Republic; this is allowed by the Federal German constitution to all Germans living within the boundaries drawn in 1937. Thus numerous Germans domiciled in Central and Eastern Europe have done precisely that in connection with their immigration to Germany, but a not insignificant number of ethnic Germans have thus acquired German citizenship while preferring to remain in Poland.

Despite the Polish parliament's enthusiastic response to Kohl's statement of July 1995, and the expansion of economic and political contacts in the borderland, the legacy of the past has continued to hamper German–Polish relations. Since 1990 the Oder–Neisse has become the meeting-place for three distinct political cultures – rooted in Poland, the GDR and the Federal Republic.

At a conference on the theme '*Grenze der Hoffnung: Geschichte und Perspektiven der Oderregion*' (Border of hope: history and perspectives of the Oderregion) at the University of Frankfurt-an-der-Oder in April 1995, both the Polish and the German participants noted that cultural stereotypes and mental blocks had been reinforced rather than reduced since the start of the cooperative effort.[88]

---

[88] *Berliner Morgenpost* (25 April 1995).

The Borderland: Past, Present and Future

The French cultural geographer Paul Vidal de la Blache was a representative of the so-called regional-geographic school, which maintains that a solid and significant relationship exists between individuals and their regional environment. His *La France de l'est*, written in 1917, examined the history of Alsace-Lorraine over two millennia, and noted that the conditions of people's lives remain remarkably stable over long periods. In essence plagues, wars and cataclysmic political events like the French Revolution had not changed the relationship between man and nature.[89] However, Vidal de la Blache noted that the powerful, dynamic forces of the nineteenth century had pulled Alsace-Lorraine apart and brought dramatic changes in society. An organically and historically evolved stability had been challenged and radically altered.

Inspired by the American-Chinese geographer Yi-fu Tuan, the Swedish sociologist Johan Asplund has developed the concept of topophilia – emotional affinity with a given place. This means that the individual is marked by the physical place, its nature and its neighbourhood; that there is a sense of affinity between man and nature; that those who live and work in a certain area have a unique solidarity with it that only can be understood by its other inhabitants and internally communicated among them; and that a characteristic of the region/place is continuity over time.[90] Historical changes in a borderland, may become clearer if they are stratified into phases or time-periods, but this also makes for difficulty in distinguishing the particularity of a phase or period while simultaneously trying to discern stability and slow-moving change.

The developments in the borderland discussed in this chapter may be periodised in the following way. The first phase extends up to the nineteenth century. Theodor Fontane described the twilight of this epoch, and his portrayal of people in Prussian society, in the border provinces and around the Oder–Neisse are romantic and with a strong implication of consensus. Fontane expresses the spirit of his time as it captures the stable, enduring

[89] See Rune Johansson's chapter above (pp.1-30).

[90] Johan Asplund, *Tid, rum, individ och kollektiv* (Stockholm, 1983); also Eva Österberg, 'Tradition och konstruktion. Svenska regioner i historiskt perspektiv' in Barbro Blomberg and Sven-Olof Lindquist (eds), *Den regionala särarten* (Lund, 1994).

interplay between man and nature, also discussed by Vidal de la Blache.

In the political and economic perspectives, the evolution of the borderland in relation to Western Europe has been plagued by a perpetual syndrome of underdevelopment. In its development West Germany proceeded along the same broad lines as the rest of Western Europe. It was industrialised, urbanised and modernised, and a political pattern emerged that was similar to those of other West European societies. The situation was quite different for East Germany, as for much of Eastern Europe. These societies were marked by a hierarchical structure, repression and a faltering economic dynamic.[91]

The first transformation that challenged the stable, historically evolved structures in the borderland developed in connection with the dissolution of the regional world in the nineteenth century. This introduced the second phase. Regional and local production processes were superseded by industrial production, most prominently in Western Europe. The possibility of transporting goods over great distances between sites of natural resources, factories and consumers was dramatically increased. People moved and settled in new areas.[92] In the border area this was primarily a matter of transporting labour, but in Silesia too there was some expansion of the infrastructure, together with industrialisation and exploitation of natural resources. The German state had recently been consolidated, and an increasingly powerful Berlin overshadowed the Oder region and its principal city, Frankfurt-an-der-Oder, which already in the early nineteenth century had lost its university to Breslau, today's Wroclaw.[93]

Towards the end of the century, there were far-reaching structural changes in German society and local communities were changed as an over arching national identity was being formed. The national integration process was intended to heighten German citizen's consciousness and transform their identity from *Gemeindebürger* to *Staatsbürger*, from regional to state citizen. These national processes affected society in the borderland. Growing

---

[91] Perry Anderson, *Lineages of the Absolutist State* (London, 1974).
[92] Gunnar Törnquist, *Gränsöverskridandets former och villkor* (2nd edn, Malmö, 1996), p.31.
[93] Schulz, 'Die Oderregion...', p.90.

Polish nationalism and demands for a Polish state had repercussions on both Germans and Poles in the area.

The third phase began with the resurrection of Poland as a state. The border between Germany and Poland was adjusted westwards, and the asymmetrical political relationship between the two countries was altered. The revision of the boundary, which divided the historically evolved region of Silesia, was traumatic. State- and nation-building on both sides of the border fractured established economic, cultural and social networks. In both Poland and Germany centralist tendencies combined with national pathos and patriotism.

However, notions of the role of the nation differed. Polish nationalism had for centuries been coloured by the struggle against oppression, epitomised in the poet Adam Mickiewicz's description of Poland as the 'crucified nation'. German nationalism evolved in a quite different direction, becoming ever more aggressive and expansionist. However, despite divergences between Berlin and Warsaw, collaboration between people in the borderland continued right up till the outbreak of the Second World War.[94]

The fourth and most dramatic phase was ushered in by the Second World War. State and territorial changes, combined with population transfers, profoundly affected the borderland. Residents of the two sides of the river underwent a major transformation between 1945 and 1989, and here the concept of topophilia helps to illuminate the effects of major political and economic decisions on those who had lived in the border area for generations. Their way of life changed, and the interaction between man and nature was distorted. For over five decades the settlers east of the Oder–Neisse built no private residences but generally preferred to live in state housing, thus displaying their reluctance to strike roots in the borderland.[95]

Dreams of the 'homeland' – *die alte Heimat* – have been cultivated and communicated by the German expellees in West Germany for five decades, while never being publicly discussed in either the GDR or Poland; in those societies the trauma had to be a private affair. Alienation within the new homeland was to be overcome by adoption of a new vision of man and society. *Pax*

---

[94] Peter Alter, *Nationalism* (Frankfurt am Main, 1985), pp.28-40.

[95] Brencz, 'Die Herausbildung...', p.56.

Sovietica became the credo around which the future was formed in the border-area, and the border itself became a 'peace frontier'.

To a certain extent the border also became a factor in identity-formation – not as a region but as a border between East Germans and Poles, and by extension between Germanic and Slav peoples. For Poland the region was determined primarily by the fact that Oder–Neisse was a border to both German states, and for the GDR its very existence and self-perception were intimately connected with this state boundary.

However, *homo sovieticus* could not be produced either in the borderland or in any other part of the Soviet empire. The five decades of *Pax Sovietica* brought no intensification of contact among the populations of the Oder region. The 'peace frontier' was a dictate and merely caused the inhabitants of the region to remain separated. The lack of contact fostered the development of national stereotypes and prejudices among both the Poles and Germans. For many of the Polish settlers and their successive generations in western Poland, the German artefacts in the area were all that they saw of German culture over a fifty-year period.

Today's encounter between the borderland populations has been remarkable for faltering efforts, mutual suspicion and various other problems. The collapse of *Pax Sovietica*, the new world order and West European integration are the external parameters that define the fifth phase.

During the 1990s new political structures were established in the border region. The population west of Oder–Neisse has been incorporated into the old division into *Länder*, and with the historical region as a basis for identity, it is hoped that this division will bridge the differences between the two German societies that have grown up during five decades of divergent evolution. Structural transformation in the political, economic and social spheres on either side of the boundary, and the launching of the Euregio project by the EU, have combined to create general instability in the border region. Both East Germans and Poles in this area are the heirs to five decades of a failed social experiment and a political culture of coercion and centrally delegated decrees.

Polish–German antagonism is deeply rooted in history and serves as a psychological barrier to further cross-border cooperation. Another complication is the freedom enjoyed by Poles with German origins to obtain German citizenship. Many migrate to the Federal

Republic, while others prefer to stay in Poland. Dual citizenship is not allowed by the Polish government.

In the words of Stanislaw Bieniasz, Silesia may represent the bridge – '*die dritte Option*' (the third option) – linking Poland with Germany – and with Europe. Over time it has gained the experience of local self-rule, and historically has had close economic and cultural ties with Germany. However, the population must somehow recover its historical identity.[96]

Federalism, regionalism, subsidiarity and a higher degree of democracy – these are the main components of the German vision of Europe. In the debate on European integration, it has been argued that Germany's federal structure is a model for the future federalisation of Europe. The German *Länder* also coaxed the German central government to press the question of a 'Europe of the regions' at Maastricht.[97]

This issue is potentially explosive. The states of Central and Eastern Europe, and Poland in particular, may view a 'Europe of the regions' as a German project. Both the Poles and the former East Germans are experiencing difficulties in adapting to the political culture that has emerged in an ever more integrated Western Europe. Moreover, in German–Polish negotiations on cross-border collaboration the West Germans represent decentralised power, the principle of local community, and cross-border consciousness – all matters that were quite alien to the former Soviet satellites.[98]

For results to be achieved and genuine progress made, there is no escaping the need for revisions in political, economic, social, cultural and mental structures. The idyllic riverland described by Theodor Fontane is not the objective. Instead, a dynamic society presupposes that people have the power truly to determine and control their own activities in the local arena.

In their analysis of the democratisation process in the Federal Republic Gabriel Almond and Sidney Verba highlight the concept of 'political culture'.[99] They deal with the evolution of support

[96] Stanislaw Bieniasz, 'Schlesien: die dritte Option', in E. Kobylinska (ed.), *Deutsche und Polen*, (Munich, 1992).
[97] Borkenhagen, 'Regions in Europe', p.184.
[98] Ibid.
[99] Gabriel Almond and Sidney Verba, *The Civic Culture Revisited* (London, 1989).

Viadrina to the Oder-Neisse Line

for democracy among the voters; the sense of being able to affect the decision-making process; and participation in informal political discussions giving a sense of movement. Today East Germans and Poles are undergoing this same democratisation process. In an area seen as a link between East and West, the populations must now cultivate a new mentality – one based on the values of the West European ideal. A historical tradition of political structures, belief systems, metaphors, notions and values must somehow be replaced with a new tradition based on norms that the bulk of the population find alien to them. This 'reprogramming' of Poles and East Germans in the borderland has met with considerable resistance, not least because two or more generations have been brought up amid censorship and falsification of history.[100]

The transnational region of Oderraum cannot make progress until local bodies are able to make pertinent decisions concerning their own communities. A programme geared to the promotion of self-reliance and collective action would surely be helpful to this.[101] The necessary elements must develop organically, within the individual, and cannot simply be interjected as rhetorical formulations, e.g. by Brussels. The setting-up of the University of Viadrina in Frankfurt-an-der-Oder, intended to attract students from both sides of the Oder–Neisse, is of great symbolic significance to continued democratisation and integration. The historical region of Silesia may provide a model for the German–Polish cross-border activity which Brussels treats as a priority. Under good conditions the functional border-area that is Oderraum may evolve into a place where both Germans and Poles will have a sense of cohesion and community.

---

[100] Melhorn, 1992.

[101] Kristian Gerner, 'Centraleuropa – sju år efter "vändningen"' in Klas-Göran Karlsson (ed.), *Östeuropa vid skiljevägen* (Moheda, 1995), p.27.

INDEX

Aachen, 39, 91
Adenauer, Konrad, 239, 248
affinity, 4, 5, 6, 9, 10, 13, 18, 62, 252
Age of Migrations, xiv, 30-1, 33, 36, 37, 41, 46-9
Alemania, 43
Alemanns, 33, 34, 62, 63, 83, 110
Allies, Western (in both World Wars): 223, 224, 225, 228, 229, 230, 247; desire to break up Germany, 83-4
Alsace, 54, 61, 82, 102
Alsace-Lorraine, 77, 252
Althusius, Johannes, 70
Alto Adige, 61
Aquitania, 35
Arabs, 34
Arminius, 32
Ascanians, 50
Assembly of European Regions (AER), 54, 56, 111
assimilation, 115, 225
Association for Moravia and Silesia, 198-9
Association for the Preservation of German Hungary, 169
Augsburg, 68
Ausgleich, 137, 143, 163, 168
Austria: 50, 56, 61, 73, 74, 82, 117, 122-4, 132, 134, 135, 136, 137, 150, 155-6, 170, 174-7; as *Reichskreise*, 68; federalisation, 62; Inner Austria. 156-7: Lower Austria. 156, 170, 173; *see also* Habsburg Monarchy
Austria-Hungary, 117, 139, 217
Austrian Silesia, 120
Austro-Marxists, 148
Avars, 34, 154

Backa, 168

Backnang, 106
Baden: 71-3, 78, 87, 99, 101, 102, 105, 107-12; liberalism, 108-9
Baden-Württemberg: xiv, 51, 56 86, 89, 99-112; *Musterländle*, 101, 109, 111, 112
Baltic states, 225
Baltic, 206, 209, 217
Bamberg, 155
Banat, 168, 169, 196-7
Batthyanys, 167
Battle of Mohacs, 167
Bavaria: xiv, 27, 31, 43, 48, 50, 51, 68, 69, 71, 72, 78, 84, 87, 88, 102, 154, 190; identity, 20
Bavarians, 34, 39, 62, 63
Belgium: 29, 61, 82, 187; federal structures, 53; identity, 8
Belgrade, 164
Benelux, 215
Berbers, 34
Berg, 71
Berlin, 58, 97, 106, 218, 243, 253
Bernhard of Spanheim, 155
Bernath, 143
Besigheim, 106
Bessarabia, 189
Biedenkopf, Kurt, 88n.
bilingualism: Bohemia, 125-6, 130; 159; Silesia, 223; *Wasserpolacken*, 235
Billunger Mark, 46
Bismarck, Otto von, 76, 77, 79, 83, 223
Blaschke, Karlheinz, 98
Blut und Boden, 15, 65, 81
Bodin, Jean, 158
Bohemia, xiv, 17, 24, 26, 47, 48, 50, 61, 118-20, 122, 124-7, 130-7, 145-6, 150, 169, 177, 187, 188,

259

197, 198, 221; Czech-German polarisation, 134; Estates, 130; Germans in, 17, 120, 124-7, 128, 131-7, 145-6, 189; institutionalisation, 129; integration, 125-7, 132; nation, 131, 132, 136; National Committee, 132-3; nobility, 120; pan-Slavic angle, 133; relationship with Moravia, 117, 133; State Rights, 135
Bohemianism, 131, 137
Boii, 47
Bolzano, Bernard, 131
Bonaparte, Jerome, 71
Bonaparte, Napoleon: xi, 71, 76, 104; abolishes Holy Roman Empire, 31, 71
Bonn, 91
Borussianism, 81
boundaries, 2, 41, 180, 181, 182, 185
Boyne, battle of the, 24
Brandenburg, 46, 47, 58, 96-7, 119, 217
Bratislava, 171, 151
Bremen, 84, 88, 98
Breslau/Wroclaw, 200, 221, 236, 253
Britain, 56, 247
Brittany, 54
Brno, 198, 199
Brussels, 212, 213, 216, 257
Buda, 189
Budapest, 138, 139, 140, 149
Bukovina, 134, 139, 189
Bulgaria, 25
Bund, 83
Bundesländer, see Länder
Bundesrat, 77, 79, 83, 89
Bundesstaat, 77
Bundestag (Deutscher Bund), 74
Burgenland: 118, 150, 165-77; coining of name, 170-1; eradicated and restored, 173; historiography, 172; identity, 174, 176
Burgundians, 34
Burgundy, 45-6

Calvinism, 221
Canada, 82

Carinthia: 48, 106, 118, 154-65, 171, 173, 175; bilingualism, 160-2; ducal seat, 157-8, 165; early history, 154-7; Estates, 156-7; French-Illyrian period, 157; *Landesbewusstsein,* 157; *Landesgeschichte,* 158, 176; *Landesrecht,* 155; *Landtag,* 156; Liberal National-Progressive Party, 163; National Council of Carinthia Slovenes, 165; national histories, 158-62; post-war referendum, 150, 152, 160, 163; tradition of independence, 157-8
Carolingian: dynasty, 63; empire, 35, 36, 38, 39, 42, 44; period, 91
Carpathians, 217
Carpatho-Ruthenia, xiv, 184, 187, 204-5, 209, 210
Catalonia, 54, 111, 181
Catholic Church/Catholics, 41, 49, 69, 91, 86, 107, 109, 163, 165, 218, 221, 222, 223, 240, 249
Catholic Liberal Party, 109
Ceauşescu, N. 193, 195, 196, 197, 208
Čechy, 198
Celts, 32, 33, 43, 47, 48
census: Austrian, 137; Bohemia, 126; Burgenland, 167; Carinthia, 159, 160
centralisation, 19, 78, 184
Champagne, 19
Charlemagne, xi, 34, 35, 39, 40, 42, 43, 44, 46, 63, 154
Charles IV, Emperor, 120
Charles V, Emperor, 157
Charles VI, Emperor, 122
Christian Democratic Union (CDU). 109, 111, 248
Church, the, 64
Cisleithania, 165, 168
civic nation, 12, 26
Cluj, 195
Cold War, 84, 217, 233
Cologne, 44, 91
common descent, 14-15, 18, 30
communities, culturally and territorially defined, xiv

Concordat of Worms, 41
conflict, 26
conflicts, territorial, 10
Congress of Vienna, 50, 73, 74
Constantinople, 33
Council of Europe, 54, 56
Counter-Reformation, 221
Court Chancelleries (Habsburg Monarchy), 123
Croatia: 188; regional privileges, 20
Croatia-Slavonia, 139
Croats: 149, 188; in Burgenland/West Hungary, 167, 168, 170, 174, 176
Crown of St Stephen, 121
CSE, 195
cultural: aspects, xiv; communities, 115, 116, 146; identity, 115, 116, 118, 125, 126, 129, 140; nationalism, 183; space, 142, 146
culture, 6, 31
Curzon Line, 229, 230, 233
Czech Republic, 186, 199, 209
Czech: cultural space, 145;-German conflict, 133; historiography, 131; language, 134; national space, 136
Czechoslovakia: 29, 149, 185, 190, 198, 199, 200, 204, 209, 225, 229; boundary changes, 184; Germans as colonists, 189; Soviet era, 187, 188
Czechs, 61, 124, 127, 131, 134, 149-50

Daco-Romanian continuity, 192
Dalecarlia, 13
Dalmatia, 134
Danube, 99
Danube-Alb, 56
Danube-Swabians, 62
de-Germanisation, 225
decentralisation: 84, 27, 28, 38, 107, 182, 216, 256; Baden-Württemberg, 110-11
demographic changes, 184
Deutscher Bund, 73-5
disintegration, xii, 31, 112
Dortmund, 90
Dresden, 245
Druzba sv. Mohorja, 162

Duisburg, 90
dukes: 39, 41, 44, 63, 64; in feudal society, 37-40
Durlach, 106

East Brandenburg: Germans flee, 228
East Francia/East Frankish realm, 37, 38, 42, 43, 48, 49, 60
East Frisia, 92
East Frisians, 83
East Prussia: 184, 199, 205, 207, 209, 219, 233, 240; Germans flee, 228
Ehard, Hans, 82, 87
Eisenach, 94, 95
Eisenhüttenstadt, 243, 245
Eisenkappeln, 162
Eisenstadt, 172
Elblag, 207
Emmanuel, Prince, 96
Emmius, Ubbe, 93
Ems-Dollart region, 92
Enschede, 215
Entzäuberung (disenchantment), 10
Eppensteiners, 155
Erodödys, 167
Erfurt, 94
Erzgebirge, 185
essentialism, 7, 8, 10, 11
Esterházy family, 167
ethnic revival, 27-8
ethnicity, 11-17, 26, 27
ethnies, 15, 21
ethnonation/ethnonationalism, 14, 21, 23-5, 28, 183
ethnoregional conflict, 29
ethnoregionalism: Czechoslovakia, 188; Romania, 189; Yugoslavia, 188
ethnoterritorial: development in Central Europe, 31; identification, xv, 25
Ettlingen, 106
Eupen-Malmédy, 25, 188
Europe 2000+, 53
Europe: xv, 53, 94, 95, 179; as macroregion, xiii; attempts to unite. xi: evolution of states. 30; integration, 212; of the Regions, xii, 27,

53-6, 58, 97, 213, 256; of the States, xii; restructuring of state system, 147, 177
European Commission, 27
European Community (EC), 32, 89
European Union (EU), xi, xii, 5, 6, 28, 53, 87, 89, 97, 178, 181, 182, 183, 212, 213, 215, 216, 249, 251, 255
Europeanisation, 87, 113
'Euregio', 214-16, 249, 255
Euroregions, 181
Evangelical church, 86

federalism: 28, 29, 53, 67, 74, 198; Baden-Württemberg, 110; German, 70, 75-85, 89, 256; Habsburg monarchy, 148
feudalism, 18, 37, 38, 40, 51, 67, 80
Finanzausgleich, 98
Finland: non-functional provinces, 6
First World War, 147, 148, 149
Flanders, 27, 54, 60, 188
Flemish, 8, 221
Fontane, Theodor, 217, 252, 256
Fourteen Points, Wilson's, 149
fragmentation, xi
France: xi, 20, 39, 45, 83, 84, 91, 106, 215, 247, civic nation, 12; identity in Middle Ages, 19; state-nation, 13
Franche-Comté, 45
Francia, 30
Francis I, Emperor, 158
Franco-Prussian War, 76, 77
Franconia, 42, 43, 49, 68, 73, 90
Franconians, 190
Frank, Hans, 227
Frankfurt am Main: 51, 74; German parliament 1848, 75, 131-2, 133
Frankfurt-an-der-Oder, 217, 237, 245, 246, 253, 257
Frankish empire, 34, 35, 44, 94
Frankish tribes, 63
Franks, 34, 39, 42, 46, 62, 63
Franz Ferdinand, Archduke, 139, 144
Frederick II, Emperor, 67, 70
Frederick the Great, 72, 221

Freiburg, 111
French Revolution, 19, 123
Friedrich August, King, 96
Friedrich III, Emperor, 156
Frisia, 31, 43-4, 92-3
Frisians, 33, 34, 63

Gaj, Ljudevit, 15
Galicia, 134, 177, 184, 200
Gascony, 35
Gaul, 32, 34, 49
Gauleiter, 82
Gellner, E., 16, 21, 148
Gemeinde (local community), 56, 103
Gemeindebürger, 253
Generalplan Ost, 226
Genossenschaft, 64
geographical position, 19
German cultural space, 58, 59-62, 79-80, 88
German Democratic Republic (GDR): 51, 69, 87, 88, 211, 231, 248, 253, 255; collectivisation, 242; dissolves *Länder*, 187, 241; refugees/deportees, 237-40, 242-3, 254; regional cooperation with Poland, 244-6; regions, 93-7; regional history, 93-4; restoration of *Länder*, 213
German Empire: 45, 47, 50, 70, 73, 90; (Wilhelmine) 77, 81, 83, 219; *see also* Holy Roman Empire
German language: 36, 40, 128, 134; as criterion for national belonging, 61
German League, 50, 133
German nation, 49
German-Bohemian parties, 132, 134
German-Czech historian's conference, 131
German-Hungarian movement, 140, 144, 145
Germania, 44, 49
Germanic languages, 60
Germanic peoples/tribes: 31, 32-7, 63, 212, 218, 255; and Slavs, 46-8
Germanic world, 44
Germanisation: 218, 228, 235; Poland, 226; Silesia, 222

Germans: Bohemia, 17, 120, 124-7, 128, 131-7, 145-6, 189; Carinthia, 159-65; Central and Eastern Europe, 226-9; expelled, 184, 214; expelled from Poland, 230, 231, 233, 234, 236, 237, 246; Hungary, 121, 128, 138-42, 146; Kaliningrad, 206-7; Poland, 207-8, 225, 251; sense of community with Poles, 257; Silesia, 201-2, 219, 221; Soviet Union, 206; Transylvania, 208; West Hungary, 166-9
Germany: xiii, xiv, xv, 31, 51, 56, 58, 59, 62, 132, 186, 200, 212, 215, 216, 225, 230, 233, 234, 253; 1933-45, 80-2; 19th century, 74-6; boundary changes, 184; early medieval, 39; embryo of, 63; evolution of state system, 70; Federal Republic, 51, 85-9, 93, 97; federalism as model, 256; friendship treaty with Poland, 211; identity in Middle Ages, 19; legacy of decentralisation, 66; medieval fragmentation, 60, 64; Napoleonic reforms, 72; national awareness, 60-1, 76, 78; national movement, 74; nationalism, 254; *Ostpolitik*, 184, 239; post 1945, 82-113; refugees/deportees, 237, 238, 247, 248, 254; regional awareness, 53-4; religious warfare, 69; reunification, 247-8; Silesia, 224; Stolpe Plan, 249; support for democracy, 256-7; territorial revolution, 71, 73; unification, 50, 77; Weimar Republic, 79-80; *see also Länder*, stems, stem duchies
Gesamtdeutsche Block-Bund der Heimatvertriebenen und Entrechteten (BHE), 239
Gestapo, 228
Gheorghiu-Dej, Gheorghe, 192
Gierek, 202
Gierke, Otto von, 64
glasnost, 209
Gleichschaltung, 51, 81

globalisation, 113
Gnesen, 221
Golden Bull, 46
Gorbachev, M., 205, 209
Gorizia, 155
Görlitz treaty, 245
Görlitz, 93, 237, 340, 245
Görtz, house of, 155
Graz, 156, 157, 162
Great German solution, *see Grossdeutsch* solution
Greek Orthodox Church, 129, 142
Gronau, 215
Gronigen, 92
Gross-Hessen, 85
Grossdeutsch solution, 61, 76
Grotewohl, Otto, 231
Groza, Petru, 191, 192
Guben, 237
Gypsies, 167, 198
Gyula, K., 170

Habsburg Monarchy: xiii-xv, 13, 17, 143-4; as buffer zone, 149; break-up, 147-51; Carinthia, 154-7; consolidation of possessions, 122-3; nationality policy, 137; nationality problem, 116; regions, 115-16; regional privileges, 20
Habsburgs, xi, 44, 45, 48, 96, 107, 120, 189, 222
Halas, V., 204
Hälsingburg, battle of, 209
Hamburg, 50, 84, 88, 98
Hannover, 51, 72; identity, 20; separatist activity, 79
Hansa, 5, 68, 88, 91, 95
Havel, Václav, 199
Heidelberg, 111
Heim ins Reich, 226
Heimat: 65-6, 80, 81, 208, 254; Marxist definition, 88
Helsinki accords, 248
Henry I, Duke, 221
Henry the Lion, Duke, 42
Herder, J.G., 15
Hermann I, 106
Herzog, President R., 83

Hesse, 50, 89
Hessen-Darmstadt, 73
Hispanic March, 35
Hitler, Adolf, xi, 87, 79, 82, 91, 226, 229
Hobsbawm, E., 9, 16, 21
Hohenzollerns, 50, 96
Holstein, 51
Holy Roman Empire: 20, 31, 39, 40, 42, 49, 68, 70, 120, 133, 154; as remnant structure, 135; dissolved, 71, 107; Bohemia, 119; *see also* German Empire
Honnigfort, B., 88
Horthy, Miklós, 195
Hugo, Ludolf, 70
Humboldt, Wilhelm von, 74
Hungarian German Popular Party (*Ungarnländische Deutsche Volkspartei*), 139-40, 168
Hungarian(s): 62; in Romania, 208; minorities, 143; nobility, 120-2, 129; repression, 193-7
Hungary: xiv, 48, 118, 128, 137, 139, 141, 142, 143, 144, 145, 148, 167, 169, 174, 176, 189, 192, 195, 204, 227; boundary changes, 184; German migration, 121, 128; Germans in, 138-42, 146; institutionalisation, 130; Nation of the Nobility, 130; nationality policy, 138; reconquest, 121, 122, 128; regional privileges, 20; Soviet era, 186-7; Turkish invasion, 120
Huns, 62
Hussites, 221
Huta Katowice, 202

identification, 5-6; regional, 11
identity: 7-11, 27, 36, 177; construction, 21-6; formation, 255; historical, xv; in early history, 17-21; national, 12; regional, 11-13, 18; religious, 12; structures, xv; territorial, 5-6; territorially bound, 37
imagined communities, 9

Imperial Chancery, 69
Imperial Court Council, 69
indigenisation, 13
institutionalisation: 6, 19, 28, 153, 179; regional, 118-19
institutionalised: regions, 115, 116; space, 117-18, 146-7
Instytut Slaski, 200
integration, xii, 31
Isidorus of Seville, 18
Israel, 89
Istria, 156
Italians, 61, 221
Italy: 26, 42, 49, 170, 225; regional awareness, 54; regionalisation processes, 53

Jarnick, Urban, 160
Jena, 94
Jews, 203, 227
Joseph II, Emperor, 118, 123
July Revolution (1830), 108
Junkers, 217, 219
Jura, 54
Jutland, 61

Kádár, J., 195
Kaliningrad, xiv, 205, 206, 207, 209, 210
Karelia, 180
Kärnten (Carinthia), 154, 157, 175
Karpatendeutsche Bewegung, 139
Kazakhstan, 206
Kiev, 205
Király, Károly, 195
Klagenfurt, 155, 157, 161, 162
Klaus, Václav, 199
Kleindeutsch solution, 61, 76
Kleinstaaterei, 63, 64, 66, 67, 69, 79
Koblenz, 85
Kohl, Helmut, 239, 248, 249
Königsberg, 206, 209
Köpeczi, Bela, 195
Koralka, 131, 134, 136
Korfanty, Wojciech, 201, 223, 225
Kortrijk, 24
Kosovo: 17, Serbian attachment to, 3

Index

Kosovo Polje, 24
Krain, 156, 157, 162, 163
Kreisky, Bruno, 62
Kronlander, 117
Kuchelböhmisch, 125
Kulturkampf, 109, 218, 223
Kulturnation: 14, 59, 61, 116; discrepancy with German state, 62
Kun, Bela, 169
Kurpfalz, 89

Länder, 5, 42, 51, 56-7, 62, 66, 77, 79, 83, 84-9, 94, 97, 98, 251, 255, 256
Landesfrieden, 68
Landesherrschaft, 67-8, 70
Landeskirche, 69, 70
Landsmannschaften, 239
language, 15-16, 30, 115
Lauenburg, 51
Lausitz, 47, 119
League of Nations, 181, 225
Lebensraum, 226, 228
Lebenswelt, 7
legitimacy, political, 3
Lehnswesen, 67
Leitha, 169
Lemgo, 91
Liberal theories, 10
Liechtenstein, 50, 61
Lega Nord, 26
limes (boundaries), 32-4, 182
Linz Programme, 135
Lippe, 90-2
Lithuania, 202, 203, 210
Little German solution, *see Kleindeutsch* solution
Ljubljana, 149, 157, 159, 162, 164
localism, 3
Lombards, 34
Lombardy, 54, 111
Lorraine, 60, 82
Lothar (s. of Louis the Pious), 35, 44
Lothar II, 44
Lotharingia (Lorraine), xiv, 31, 44-5, 90
Louis the Pious, 35, 63
Louis XIV, 46

Lübeck, 51
Ludolfingians, 42
Ludwig of Württemberg, 102
Lusatians, 47
Luther, Martin, 69, 94, 104
Lutheranism, 221
Luxemburg, 45, 50
Luxemburgian emperors, 48
Lwów/L'viv, 200

Maastricht, 212, 256
Macedonia, 25
macroregions, xiii, 4, 56, 76
Magyar(s): 48, 49, 121, 130, 141, 149, 167, 168, 170, 176; national space, 138, 140, 146; peasants, 122
Magyarisation, 139
Mainz, 44, 85
Mannheim, 112
March revolution (1848), 75
Maria Saal, 155
Maria Theresa, Empress, 118, 123, 129
Markomanians, 47
Marxist theories, 10, 11
Masaryk, Tomás G., 189, 209
Masurians, 234
Mattias Corvinus, King, 156
Maximilian I, Emperor, 68, 156
Mazzini, Giuseppe, 28
Mecklenburg, 46, 51
Mecklenburg-Vorpommern, 95, 98
Meidlinger, George, 171
Meinecke, Friedrich, 59, 116
Meissen, 47
Merovingians, 34, 42
Mickiewicz, Adam, 203, 254
microregions: xiii, 56-9, 66, 69, 74, 89, 90, 92, 112-3; identity, 57-8, 73, 89
migrations, 15, 34, 94
Mikolajcyk, Stanislaw, 230
Milosz, Czeszlaw, 203
Ministerpräsident, 88
Mittelmark, 46
modernisation 13, 21-6, 115-17, 144, 160-1, 220, 243
Mohacs, battle of, 167

Moldavia, 189
Mommsen, Wolfgang, 62
Montabaur, 85
Monzambano, Severinus de (pseud. of S. Pufendorf), 70
Moravia-Silesia, 197-9
Moravia: xiv, 26, 48, 119, 120, 129, 130, 134, 146, 150, 169, 187, 188, 198, 199, 209, 210; Estates, 133; Germans in, 128; institutionalised space, 137; relationship with Bohemia, 117
Moravian National Party, 199
Moser, Johann Jacob, 70-1
Moson (Wieselburg), 166, 167
multilingualism, 127
Münsing, 102-3
mythomoteur, 22, 25

Napoleonic wars, 157
nation: 30, 122; early definition, 18
nation-building, 14, 30
nation-state: xii, 147-51, 176, 177, 182; Germany, 62, 80, 81; historiography, 147, 153; identity, 177; interwar period, 181
national: character, 7; identity, 224; minorities, 181, 187, 224, 225
nationalism, 116, 144, 147-51, 224, 254
nationality, 11-17
NATO, 89
Navarre, 35
Nazis, xi, 79, 80, 82, 84, 91, 95, 105, 109, 203, 227, 235
Neisse, river, 211
Netherlands, 44, 46, 56
Neumark, 46, 233
Neusiedler See, 169
Neustria, 35
Niedersachsen, 51, 68, 92, 98
Norddeutscher Bund (North German Confederation), 76, 77
Nordmark, 46
Noricum, 154, 155
North Frisia, 92
North Rhine-Westphalia: 51, 58, 69, 83, 85, 90, 91, 92, 176; construction of 'historical region', 153
Oberwart, 172
Obrigkeitsstaat, 108
Ödenburg, 172, 174
Oder-Neisse area/line: xiv, 47, 61, 211-57; 'peace frontier', 231, 237, 240, 246, 254, 255
Oderland, 249, 251
Oderraum, xv, 211-14, 248, 251, 257
Opole/Oppeln, 200, 201, 235
Organisation of the Hungarian People (MNSz). 192
Ortenburg, 157
Ost-Westfalen, 90-1
Ostmark, 48
Ostrogoths, 34
Otto I, Emperor, 31, 39, 42, 43, 49, 63, 154
Ottomans, 118, 122, 167, 188
Ottonian realm, xi

Palacky, Frantisek, 24, 131, 132, 136, 148
Palatinate, 73, 85
Papen, Franz von, 81
pan-Slavism, 162
particularism: xi, 82, 118, 123, 153; German, 75, 76, 80
Patry, Josef, 168
Peace of Lunéville, 71
Peace of Nijmegen, 46
Peace of Roskilde, 209
Peace of Westphalia, 44, 46, 64, 69-70
Pentecost Programme (1899), 135
perestroika, 209
Person, Hermann, 110
Pestalozzi, Johann Heinrich, 65
Pforzheim, 106
Pirenne, Henri, 7-8
plebiscites: *see* referendums
Plessner, H., 59
Poland: xv, 61, 185, 186, 200, 201, 203, 204, 207, 208, 211-57; change of frontiers, 184, 229-31; collectivisation, 242-3; division, 226; friendship treaty with Germany, 211; Generalgouvernment,

226-7; *kresy* and *pogranicze*, 188, 199, 209; national myths, 10; nationalism, 219, 223, 254; regional cooperation with GDR, 244-6; settlement of western areas, 234-7, 241-2; Soviet era, 187; Stolpe Plan, 248-50; treaty with GDR, 240
Poles: 61, 218, 220, 222, 223, 233, 254, 255, 257; deported, 226; in Germany, 225; in Lithuania, 203, 209, 210; in Silesia, 219; migrants to western areas, 184, 235-6; sense of community with Germans, 257
Polesia, 184
political organisation of space, 117
polycentrism, 89, 90, 111
Pomerania: 184, 199, 207, 208, 211, 217, 223, 233; Germans flee, 228
population transfers, xv
Posen/Poznan, 184, 219, 220, 223, 241
Potsdam Conference, 230
Pozsony (Pressburg/Bratislava), 150, 166, 167, 189
Pragmatic Sanction, 122
Prague: 119, 149, 150; Germans of, 125-6, 190; Spring, 198
Pressburg: 171; *see also* Poszony
primordialism, 8
principalities, 68, 74, 117
Pro-Europe-Viadrina, 211
Protestants, 69, 104, 107, 109, 112, 222
Prussia: 50-1, 61, 72-8, 81, 85, 91, 108, 200, 217, 220, 252; identity, 20
Prussian Poland, 218
Pustertal, 157

Rájk, Läszlo, 192
Ratzel, Friedrich, 151-2
Rau, Johannes, 88n.
Red Army, 230
referendums, post-war: 150-1, 152; Silesia, 200-1, 220, 224; western Hungary, 150-2, 169-71
Reformation, 104, 107, 129, 221
region(s): 3-7, 69; as structures, 180;

cf networks, 5; concept/definition xii-xiv, 54, 185, 178-83; continuity, 252; ethnicisation of, 190; functional, 152; historical, 8, 9, 31-2, 152, 153, 213, 255; in Middle Ages, 19; in Soviet era, 178-210; institutionalised, 115-16; isolated under Communism, 185-6, 207; revived, xv: significance of names, 179; transnational, 213-14, 257; West European model, 214-16: *see also* institutionalisation
regional consciousness, 6-7, 112
regional deep structures: xiv, 54, 56, 58, 59, 80, 88, 94, 97, 99; survival of, 63
regional identity: xiii, 11-13, 18, 20, 26-8, 54, 57, 58, 73, 97, 98, 99; challenge to the state, xii; Middle Ages, 19
regional rights, 20
regional symbolism, 118
regionalisation, 27, 53, 57-9, 64, 66, 79, 83, 97, 113
regionalism, 81, 83, 256
Regnum teutonicorum, 40
Reichsdeutsche, 61
Reichsgaue, 82
Reichskommisariat für die Festigung deutschen Volkstums (RKFDV), 227
Reichskreise, 68
Reichstatthalter, 82
Reitz, Edgar, 65
religion: 11-12; as ethnic marker, 16
religious: affiliation, 15; identity, 10-12
Renan, Ernest, 24
Renatus, Flavius Vegetius, 94
Renner, Karl, 171
Rhein-Neckar-Dreieck, 89
Rheinbund, 50, 71-2, 76
Rheinland, 73, 90, 91, 119; separatist activity, 79
Rheinland-Pfalz, 86, 89
Rhône-Alps, 111
Roman Empire, 32, 33, 39, 44, 49, 181, 182, 183

Romance languages, 36, 60
Romania, 144, 187, 189, 191, 208, 172, 227; Communist take-over, 192; Hungarian Autonomous Region, 192, 193; 'systemisation' of countryside, 196
Romanian-Transylvanian movement, 143-5
Romanians, 121, 122, 129, 130, 142-5
Romans, 32-6
Romanticism, 94
Ruhr, 85, 90-2, 243
Ruhrpolen, 219
Russia, 206
Russians, 203
Ruthenians, 204-5

Saar-Lor-Lux, 181
Saarland, 54, 61, 82, 86-8
Sachsen-Anhalt, 51
Sachsenspiegel, 67
Sajudis, 204
Salzburg, 155; Archbishop of, 155
Samis (Lapps), 15
Samo kingdom, 154
Savoy, 45
Saxe-Coburg, 50
Saxons (Hungary/Transylvania): 121-2, 129, 138-45, 168, 194, 208; cultural space, 140; Lutheran church, 129; wanted in Burgenland, 172
Saxons, 33, 34, 39, 41, 42, 49, 63, 73, 83, 213
Saxony, xiv, 31, 42, 50, 51, 54, 78, 90, 95, 96
Scandinavia: regional awareness, 54
Scania, 26, 209
Schleswig, 25, 51
Schleswig-Holstein, 23, 84, 92, 98
Schwanenberg, 127
Schwedt, 243
Scotland, 27, 225
Second World War, 254
self-determination, 30
Septimania, 35
Serbia, 25

Serbian Orthodox Church, 142
Serbo-Croatian, 15, 23
Serbs, 17, 188
Seton Watson, R.W., 149n.
sib (family clan), 63-4, 67, 80
Siebenbürgen, 121
Silesia: 47, 61, 119, 120, 134, 180, 184, 187, 198, 199, 200-2, 208, 209-10, 217, 219-24, 233, 240, 243, 253, 254; as bridge, 256; autochthons, 234-6: Germans flee, 228; partition, 200-1
Silingians, 47
Slavic cultural space, 136
Slavism, 134
Slavs, 33-4, 46-8, 49, 62, 69, 212, 218, 220, 255
Slonzaks, 200, 201
Slovak language, 24
Slovakia, 15-16, 184, 186, 189, 198, 204, 209, 227
Slovaks, 188
Slovenes, 148, 149, 150-1, 158, 159-61, 175; national awareness, 162-5, 176
Slupsk, 207
Smith, Anthony D., 21
Snellman, J.W., 24
Solidarity movement, 204
Sonderweg, 59, 80-1
Sopron (Ödenburg), 150-1, 166, 167, 174
Sorbs, 47, 83, 87-8, 96
South Tyrol, 61, 169
Soviet era: xv, 205; deregionalisation, 187
Soviet Union: 13, 83-4, 178, 181, 182, 184, 187, 204, 216, 225, 228, 229, 230, 231, 233, 238, 239, 240, 241, 242, 244; decline, 247; Pax Sovietica, 254-5
Sozialistiche Einheitspartei Deutschlands (SED), 233, 239-41
Spain: regional awareness, 53-4
Spanheims, 155, 156
Späth, Lothar, 111
spatial institutionalisation, 144

Index

Spitzzicken, 167
Spree-Neisse-Bober, 211
SS, 228
St Veit, 155, 157
Staatsbürger, 253
Staatsnation, 116
Stalin, J.V. 203, 226
state centralism, 82
state(s): xii, 14, 17; and identity, 12; competition, 2; nation-building, 13; origins of, 115; regionalised, decentralised and unitary, 56; *see also* nation-state
state-building, 22, 30
state-nation, 12, 13, 26
Staufers, 102, 107
Steed, H. Wickham, 149n.
Steiermark, 48
Steinacker, Edmund, 138-9
stem duchies, xiv, 31, 41-6, 48, 49, 51, 66-7
stems, 21, 37-9, 41, 63, 64, 67, 72-3, 76-8, 80, 83, 94, 102, 107
Stettin, 217
Stolpe, Manfred, 248;-Plan, 248-9
Stourzh, 127, 137
Stuttgart, 112
Styria, 154-6, 170, 173
sub-tribes (*Teilstämme*), 63
subsidiarity, 28, 182, 212, 216, 256
Süd-Baden, 85
Süd-Württemberg, 85
Sudeten Germans, 189, 190, 199
Sudetenland, 184, 197
Svebians, 43
Swabia, 43, 68, 73, 102, 106
Swabians: (Hungary/Transylvania), 128, 129, 138, 139, 140-2, 168, 208
Swabians, 21, 39, 63, 190
Sweden: 20, 26, 56, 107; administrative provinces, 4; nation-building, 13; regionalisation processes, 53
Switzerland: 46, 61, 75, 82, 106; canton model, 28-9; regional awareness, 53-4
Szekelian, 121-2, 143

Szczecin, 243

Tehran Conference, 229
territorial: affinity, 3; conflict, 1, 2; identity, xii; organisation, xii; principalities, xiv
territoriality, 1-4, 11, 26, 27; in early Central European history, 30-8
territory, 1, 2, 22; basis for distinction, 18; cf region, 4; more important than tribal community, 38
Teschen, 222, 224
Teutoburger Forest, 32
Third Reich, 81, 226-8
Thirty Years' War, 91, 107
Thoringi, 94
Thuringia, 42, 51, 94, 95
Thuringian Mark, 47
Thuringians, 33, 39, 63
Timisoara, 196, 197
Tito, J.B. 164, 165
Tökes, László, 196-7
topophilia, 18, 252, 254
Transylvania: xiv, 23, 130, 139, 142-5, 169, 177, 189, 190, 191, 207-8; cities Romanianised, 192; cultural identities, 140; institutionalised as region, 120-1; Military Border, 129, 142-3; integrated into Hungary, 137-8; regional privileges, 20; under Communism, 191-7
Treaty of Münsing, 103
Treaty of St-Germain, 151, 169, 170
Treitschke, Heinrich von, 81
Trianon, 177, 189
tribalism, 27, 60
tribes: 69; Germanic, 36-7, 62
Trier, 85
Troppau, 222
Tübingen, 111
Tübinger Vertrag, 104
Turkic peoples, 62, 128
Tyrol, 154

Uckermark, 46
Ukraine, 200, 203-5, 209
Ulm, 56, 57, 97, 111

Ulrich of Württemberg, 102, 104
Umgangssprache (language of daily use), 126, 137, 150, 160
Umsiedlung (resettlement) policy, 226, 228
Uniate Church, 129, 142
Union of Baltic Cities, 95
United Nations, 89
United States of Europe, xii
United States, 75, 247
universities, medieval, 18
urbanisation, 21

Vaclav Committee, 132
Vallakian liberties, 167
Vandals, 33-4, 47, 212
Varus, 32
Vas (Eisenburg), 166
Verona, 106
Versailles Conference/Treaty, 141, 146, 220-1
Viadrina, University of, 257
Vidal de la Blache, Paul, 7, 252, 253
Villach, 155
Vilna/Vilnius, 184, 190, 203-4, 209, 210
Visegrád, 189
Visigoths, 33, 34
Vogelweide, Walther von der, 59
Volga Germans, 61
Völkermarkt, 155
Völkerwanderungen, see Age of Migrations
Volksdeutsche, 61, 226, 229
Volksgeist, 15
Volynia, 184
Vorarlberg, 54

Wajda, Andrej, 203
Wales, 181, 225
Wallachia, 189
Wallonia, 54, 27, 188
Walloons, 8, 221
War of the Austrian Succession, 120, 221
Warsaw Pact, 182, 184
Wartburg, 94

Wasserpolacken, 200, 218, 235
'we-feeling', 92, 185
Weimar Republic, 50, 79, 91, 105, 109
Weimar, 94
Welfs, 42
Welphans, 48
Wends, 46
Wenzels Committee, 131
West Frankish/French empire, 60
West Franks, 43, 49
West Frisia, 92
West Hungary: 166-73, 176-7; Austrification, 170-2
West Prussia, 233
Western Europe: 178, 212, 215, 253, 256; ideal, 257
Westphalia, 71, 73
Wettins, 96, 98
White Russia, 203, 204
Wilhelm I, 77
Wilson, President Woodrow, 149
Windisch theory, 158-9
Winds, 158, 163, 176
Wirtenberg, 102
Wittelsbachs, 44, 48, 50, 96
Wohleb, Leo, 87, 99
Worms, 68
Wörthersee, 161
Wroclaw: 221, 236, 243, 245: *see also* Breslau
Württemberg, 50, 56, 71-3, 78, 101-11
Württemberg-Baden, 85, 99
Württemberg-Hohenzollern, 99

Yalta Conference, 230
Yugoslavia: 3, 9, 13, 150, 164, 165, 170, 187, 188, 227; SHS state, 150

Zagreb, 150
Zähringers, 106
Zakarpatska, *see* Carpatho-Ruthenia
ZIM (*Zukunftstinitiative Montanregion*), 83
Zollfeld, 157, 158, 175
Zollverein (Customs Union), 75